architecture —

the subject is matter

Architects are caught in a vicious circle; in order to defend their idea of architecture they often adopt practices, forms and materials already identified with the work of architects. Traditionally, architectural matter is understood to be the physical substance of buildings, and architects employ a limited palette of materials such as steel, glass, brick and concrete.

The aim of *Architecture – the Subject is Matter* is to expand the subject and matter of architecture, and to explore their interdependence. There are now many architectures. This book acknowledges architecture far beyond the familiar boundaries of the discipline and reassesses the object at its centre: the building. Architectural matter is not always physical or building fabric. It is whatever architecture is made of, whether words, bricks, blood cells, sounds or pixels. The fifteen chapters are divided into three sections – on buildings, spaces and bodies – which each deal with a particular understanding of architecture and architectural matter.

The richness and diversity of subjects and materials discussed in *Architecture – the Subject is Matter* locates architecture firmly in the world as a whole not just the domain of architects. In stating that architecture is far more than the work of architects, this book aims not to deny the importance of architects in the production of architecture but to see their role in more balanced terms and to acknowledge other architectural producers. Architecture can, for example, be found in the incisions of a surgeon, the instructions of a choreographer or the movements of a user. Architecture can be made of anything and by anyone.

Jonathan Hill is Senior Lecturer at the Bartlett School of Architecture, UCL, where he is Director of the MPhil/PhD Architectural Design Programme.

architecture–

the subject is matter

Edited by

Jonathan Hill

London and New York

First published 2001

by Routledge

11 New Fetter Lane, London EC4P 4EE

Simultaneously published in the USA and Canada

by Routledge

29 West 35th Street, New York, NY 10001

Routledge is an imprint of the Taylor & Francis Group

© 2001 Jonathan Hill, selection and editorial matter;

individual chapters, the contributors

Typeset in News Gothic by Wearset, Boldon, Tyne and Wear

Printed and bound in Great Britain by St Edmundsbury Press, Bury St Edmunds, Suffolk

British Library Cataloguing in Publication Data

A catalogue record for this book is available from the British Library

Library of Congress Cataloging in Publication Data

Architecture : the subject is matter / edited by Jonathan Hill.

    p. cm.

Includes bibliographical references and index.

ISBN 0-415-23546-4 (hbk) – ISBN 0-415-23545-6 (pbk)

1. Communication in architectural design. 2. Space (Architecture) 3. Architecture and
society. I. Hill, Jonathan, 1958–

NA2750 .A6816 2001

724'.6–dc21

2001019113

CONTENTS

Contributors   vii

Acknowledgements   xii

Introduction: Subject/Matter   1
Jonathan Hill

Section 1: Building Matter

CHAPTER 1
The Future is Hairy   11
Jeremy Till and Sarah Wigglesworth

CHAPTER 2
Two Architectural Projects about Purity   29
Katherine Shonfield

CHAPTER 3
Bloom   45
Niall McLaughlin and Martin Richman

CHAPTER 4
**Weather Architecture (Berlin 1929–30,
Barcelona 1986–, Barcelona 1999–)**   57
Jonathan Hill

CHAPTER 5
What's the Matter with Architecture?   73
David J. Gunkel

Section 2: Spatial Matter

CHAPTER 6
Notopia: Leaky Products/Urban Interfaces   91
Dunne + Raby

CHAPTER 7
Comfort, Anxiety and Space   **107**
David Sibley

CHAPTER 8
**Stairway Architecture: Transformative Cycles in the
Golden Lane**   **119**
Iain Borden

CHAPTER 9
The Place of Prepositions: A Space Inhabited by Angels **131**
Jane Rendell and Pamela Wells

Section 3: Body Matter

CHAPTER 10
**Bauhaus Dream-house: Forming the Imaginary Body
of the Ungendered Architect**   **161**
Katerina Rüedi Ray

CHAPTER 11
Black Matter(s): Such as? Does it?   **175**
Lesley Naa Norle Lokko

CHAPTER 12
Surplus Matter: of Scars, Scrolls, Skulls and Stealth   **193**
Mark Dorrian

CHAPTER 13
Animal Architecture   **207**
Peg Rawes

CHAPTER 14
Nanotechnology – the Liberation of Architecture   **223**
Neil Spiller

CHAPTER 15
Biological (or 'Wet') Architecture   **239**
Rachel Armstrong

Index   **249**

CONTRIBUTORS

Rachel Armstrong is a multimedia producer and medical doctor specialising in the evolution of humankind through 'unnatural interventions'. She teaches at the Bartlett School of Architecture, UCL, and is author of *A Gray's Anatomy*. Rachel is editor of *Sci/Fi Aesthetics*, an issue of *Art and Design*, and *Space Architecture*, an issue of *Architectural Design*.

Iain Borden is Director of Architectural History and Theory at the Bartlett, UCL, where he is Reader in Architecture and Urban Culture. He is co-editor of *The City Cultures Reader, Architecture and the Sites of History, Strangely Familiar: Narratives of Architecture and the City, Gender Space Architecture: An Interdisciplinary Introduction, The Unknown City: Contesting Architecture and Social Space*, and *Intersections: Architectural Histories and Critical Theories*. Iain is author of *Skateboarding, Architecture and the City* and co-author of *The Dissertation*.

Mark Dorrian studied at Edinburgh College of Art, University of Kansas, Istituto Universitario di Architettura di Venezia and at the Architectural Association. He graduated from Edinburgh College of Art with a first class degree in architecture and received a doctorate from the Architectural Association. He has taught in various schools including the Architectural Association and the Department of Architecture, University of Edinburgh where he runs the final-year design programme and teaches theory and historiography of architecture. He is currently working on two book projects: *A Critical Dictionary for Architecture* and a collection of essays on the Grotesque. He is Director of the Edinburgh Research Programme at the Department of Architecture, University of Edinburgh and is a partner in Metis with Adrian Hawker.

Anthony Dunne studied at the National College of Art and Design, Dublin, and has an MDes in Industrial Design and PhD in Computer Related Design from the Royal College of Art, London. He lived in Tokyo for two and a half years working in the Sony Design Centre on conceptual designs for TVs, radios, Walkmans and props for a film by Wim Wenders, and later as a freelance designer on projects for NEC, Daiko Lighting, Kei'ichi Irie Architects and Toyo Ito Architects. On returning to London, Anthony taught part-time at the Royal College of Art, Architectural Association and the Bartlett. He then set up a partnership with architect Fiona Raby, collaborating on the design of interactive terminals for Toyo Ito's 'Dreams Room' at the Victoria and Albert Museum, an interactive exhibitory for the Science Museum, London, and 'Fields and Thresholds' for the Netherlands Design Institute in Amsterdam. His work has been exhibited in

'Leading Edge' at the Axis Centre in Tokyo, NTT's 'Museum Inside the Telephone Network', 'Image and Object' at the Pompidou Centre, Paris, and at the 1996 Milan Triennale. Anthony is Senior Research Fellow in the Department of Computer Related Design at the Royal College of Art, investigating the critical and aesthetic potential of electronic products as post-optimal objects.

David J. Gunkel is Assistant Professor of Communication at Northern Illinois University. He received his PhD in Philosophy from De Paul University in Chicago, Illinois. His critical investigations of computer mediated communication and cyberculture can be found in *Critical Studies in Mass Communication*, *The Journal of Mass Media Ethics*, *Soundings* and *Configurations*.

Jonathan Hill is Senior Lecturer, and Director of the MPhil/PhD Architectural Design Programme, at the Bartlett, UCL. An architect and graduate of the Architectural Association, he has an architectural history MSc and an architectural design PhD from the Bartlett. Extracts of his PhD thesis 'Creative Users, Illegal Architects' have been published in *Architectural Design*, *Architekt*, *The Architects' Journal*, *Building Design*, *Ideal Architecture*, *The Journal of Architecture*, *HDA–Dokumente zur Architektur*, *Offramp*, *Quaderns*, *Scroope* and *Urban Studies*. Jonathan has exhibited widely. For example, in solo exhibitions at the Haus der Architektur in Graz, Matthew Gallery at the University of Edinburgh and Architektur-Galerie Am Weissenhof in Stuttgart, and in group exhibitions at the Mies van der Rohe Haus in Berlin and SCI-Arc in Los Angeles. He is author of *The Illegal Architect* and editor of *Occupying Architecture: Between the Architect and the User*.

Lesley Naa Norle Lokko was born in Scotland of Ghanaian-Scots parentage. She completed her primary and secondary school education in Ghana and studied languages and sociology in the UK and the US, and architecture at the Bartlett, UCL. She has taught at the Bartlett, the University of Greenwich, Iowa State University and the University of Illinois at Chicago, and worked in practice in France, Namibia, South Africa, Ghana and with Elsie Owusu Architects, an all-black women's practice in London. She is editor of *White Papers, Black Marks*, an anthology which explores the relationship between race and architecture. Lesley is currently Senior Lecturer at Kingston University, focusing on issues of race and cultural identity in architecture.

Niall McLaughlin studied architecture at University College Dublin and teaches at the Bartlett, UCL. He opened his own practice in 1990. Recent work includes the conversion of a monastery in London, houses in Oxfordshire and London, and

Phototropic, an automated flower farm. In 1998 he won the national award for the UK Young Architect of the Year.

Muf work as a collaborative practice. They have established an architectural notation that swells to absorb subject matter traditionally censored out of architecture. The team have taught since the late 1980s at the Architectural Association, the University of North London and Chelsea School of Art and Design, developing a body of theoretical work, which alongside built projects, has been published and exhibited internationally.

Ben Nicholson is based in Chicago, where he teaches architecture at the Illinois Institute of Technology. He studied at the Architectural Association in London and Cranbrook in the US. The author of *Appliance House* and the CD-ROM *Thinking the Unthinkable House*, his work has been widely published and exhibited, including at the Aedes Gallery, Berlin, the Canadian Center of Architecture, Montreal and the Cartier Foundation, Paris.

Frank O'Sullivan combines teaching, architectural practice and work as a building contractor. He has taught architecture at South Bank University, Kingston University and the Bartlett, UCL.

Fiona Raby has an MA in Architecture and MPhil in Computer Related Design from the Royal College of Art, London. She worked in Tokyo for two and a half years with Kei'ichi Irie Architects on varied projects including conceptual studies and exhibitions fusing electronic technologies with architectural contexts. In 1994 Fiona began a partnership with industrial designer Anthony Dunne. Dunne + Raby was formed to explore inter-relationships between industrial design, architecture and electronic media through a combination of academic research and practical commissions. Anthony and Fiona collaborated on the design of interactive terminals for Toyo Ito's 'Dreams Room' at the Victoria and Albert Museum, an interactive exhibitory for the Science Museum, London, and 'Fields and Thresholds' for the Netherlands Design Institute in Amsterdam. The latter project was exhibited at the British section of the Milan Triennale in Italy, 1996, and at 'Electra 96' in Oslo. Fiona is Senior Research Fellow in the Computer Related Design Department and studio tutor in the Architecture Department at the Royal College of Art.

Peg Rawes teaches at the Bartlett, UCL and Goldsmiths College, University of London. Having studied Art History at Leeds and Philosophy and Literature at Warwick she is currently taking a PhD in aesthetics at Goldsmiths.

Jane Rendell, BA(Hons), Dip Arch, MSc, PhD is Lecturer at the Bartlett School of Architecture, UCL. An architect and architectural historian, she is author of *The Pursuit of Pleasure* and editor of *A Place Between*, an issue of *Public Art Journal*. Jane is co-editor of *Strangely Familiar: Narratives of Architecture and the City*, *Gender Space Architecture: An Interdisciplinary Introduction*, *The Unknown City: Contesting Architecture and Social Space*, and *Intersections: Architectural Histories and Critical Theories*. Her research focuses on exploring relationships between different discourses: gender and space, critical theory and architecture history, spatial theories and spatial practices, art and architecture.

Martin Richman worked as a lighting designer for rock concerts before studying at St Martin's College of Art. His recent work includes the illuminated cladding of a power station in Birmingham and a freestanding light work at Broadgate in London.

Katerina Rüedi Ray is Professor, and Director of the School of Architecture, at the University of Illinois at Chicago. An architect and graduate of the Architectural Association, she obtained her MSc and PhD at the Bartlett, UCL. Katerina is co-editor of *Desiring Practices: Architecture, Gender and the Interdisciplinary*.

Katherine Shonfield lectures in the history and theory of architecture at South Bank University, and works in practice as Shonfield and Williams Architects and as a consultant with Muf. She is deputy editor of *The Journal of Architecture*, an Architectural Association Council member, a member of the Art for Architecture awards panel of the Royal Society of Arts, and a member of the Edge, a joint ginger group of civil engineers and architects. She writes a weekly column for *The Architects' Journal* and is author of *Walls Have Feelings: Architecture, Film and the City*.

David Sibley teaches social and cultural geography at the University of Hull. In theorising space, he is particularly concerned with the overlapping territories of human geography, social anthropology and psychoanalysis. This interest comes partly from a long period of involvement with English Gypsy families, where the contrast between 'Gypsy spaces' and the state's spatial prescriptions for Gypsies appeared acute. David is author of *Outsiders in Urban Societies* and *Geographies of Exclusion*.

Neil Spiller is an architect, artist and journalist. He is Senior Lecturer at the Bartlett School of Architecture, UCL. Neil is also a partner in Spiller Farmer Architects of London and Bratislava. His work has been published worldwide. Neil is author of *Digital Dreams* and *Maverick Deviations*. He is co-editor of *The Power of*

Contemporary Architecture and editor of the *Architects in Cyberspace*, *Integrating Architecture* and *Architects in Cyberspace 2* issues of *Architectural Design*.

Jeremy Till and Sarah Wigglesworth are architects, teachers and writers based in London. Among other awards, they are the only architects ever to be awarded the Fulbright Arts Fellowship. Sarah is co-editor of *Desiring Practices*, while both are editors of *The Everyday and Architecture* issue of *Architectural Design*. Their work, both individually and collectively, has been published worldwide. They are both Professors at Sheffield University; Jeremy is also Head of the School of Architecture. Their 'House of Straw' has received extensive international attention.

Pamela Wells is a visual artist exploring the boundaries between the ephemeral and the permanent, the virtual and the real. Interested in socially engaged practice, her work questions notions of authorship and the siting of art. She is currently undertaking a residency at the City Library and Arts Building in Sunderland where she is working on a project called 'Recipes for well-being' addressing the conceptual and physical flow of movement through this four-storey multi-functional building. She is engaging with staff and visitors to create a sculptural book.

ACKNOWLEDGEMENTS

This book developed alongside my work as a teacher and student at the Bartlett School of Architecture, UCL. I want especially to thank my teaching partners in Diploma Unit 12 – Ganit Mayslits, Francesca Hughes, Lesley Lokko and Elizabeth Dow – as well as the many students who have influenced the character of this book, notably graduates of the last few years, including Tick Wah Chew, Tony Davis, Simon Haycock, Martin Hopp, Toni Kauppila, Tina Lejon, Jonathan Manning, Duncan McLeod, Domi Oliver, Chris Roberts, Bradley Starkey, Wee Lian Tay, Yen Yen Teh and Sophie Ungerer.

Professor Philip Tabor has provided me with generous and thoughtful advice for many years, notably as my supervisor for the PhD by Architectural Design at the Bartlett. On the same programme, Nat Chard, Penelope Haralambidou, Yeoryia Manolopoulou and Victoria Watson have offered stimulating work and critical insight. Also at the Bartlett, Professor Peter Cook, Professor Adrian Forty and Professor Christine Hawley have been helpful.

Jean-Baptiste Joly, Director of Akademie Schloss Solitude in Stuttgart, where I had a studio in 1998, offered an environment in which I could develop ideas relevant to this book. In addition, for their comments and support, I wish to thank Xiaochun Ai, Paul Fineberg, Professor William Firebrace at the Staatliche Akademie der Bildenden Künste in Stuttgart, Catherine Harrington, Matthias Ludwig at Architektur-Galerie Am Weissenhof in Stuttgart, Neil Rawson, Roland Ritter at Vienna University of Technology, Ro Spankie, Tan Kay Ngee, Lesley Ann Staward at Wearset and Caroline Mallinder, Victoria Regan and Rebecca Casey at Routledge. Finally my thanks go to the contributors to this book.

Jonathan Hill

introduction

Subject/Matter

INTERDEPENDENCE

In many disciplines, ideas and things are often placed in a hierarchy that either states that one determines the other or allows each to be considered separately. But in *The Manhattan Transcripts* Bernard Tschumi states: 'In architecture, concepts can either precede or follow projects or buildings. In other words, a theoretical concept may be either applied to a project, or derived from it.' He continues: 'Quite often this distinction cannot be made so clearly, when, for example, a certain aspect of film theory may support an architectural intuition, and later, through the arduous development of a project, be transformed into an operative concept for architecture in general.'[1] A non-hierarchical relationship between subject, method and matter can be an explicit intention, whatever the discipline. For example, in *The Arcades Project*, Walter Benjamin's study of the nineteenth-century Parisian arcades, all are montage.[2]

The aim of *Architecture – the Subject is Matter* is to expand the subject and matter of architecture. Three understandings of 'Subject/Matter', the title of this introduction, are important. First, the interdependence of the subject and matter of architecture and the theories, methods and tools of design; second, matter as the subject of investigation; third, the relations between matter and the user, another understanding of the word subject.

OTHER MATTERS

To acquire social status and financial security architects need a defined area of knowledge, with precise contents and limits, in which they can prove expertise. Therefore, architects further the idea that they alone make buildings and spaces that deserve the title architecture.[3] Architects are caught in a vicious circle; in order to defend their idea of architecture they often adopt practices, forms and materials already identified with the work of architects, and thus learn little from other disciplines. Traditionally, architectural matter is understood to be the physical substance of buildings, and architects employ a limited palette of materials such as steel, glass, brick and concrete.

The practice of architects is yet to be influenced by ideas that have been so liberating in art, notably that an artwork can be made of anything and address any subject. This book argues that, although the building and city remain central to architecture, there are now many architectures, all related to the varied experience of the user and interdependent with an understanding of the building and city. In addition to buildings, drawings and texts have for many years been considered important

1 B. Tschumi, *The Manhattan Transcripts*, London, Academy, 1994, p. xix.

2 W. Benjamin, *The Arcades Project*, ed. R. Tiedemann, trans. H. Eiland and K. McLaughlin, Cambridge, Mass. and London, Belknap Press of Harvard University Press, 1999.

3 This is a claim architects make in many countries: in Britain, for example. Two bodies, the Architects Registration Board and the Royal Institute of British Architects, now define the architectural profession in Britain. In 1999 *Building Design* reported that 'The ARB wants new legislation to extend the scope of the 1997 Architects Act, which it feels is inadequate because it only protects the title "architect". The ARB wants the act to be extended to cover "architecture" and "architectural" – which are not protected at present.' David Rock, at that time RIBA President, supported the ARB's proposal. M. Fairs, 'ARB Seeks New Powers', *Building Design*, 15 January 1999, p. 3.

Jonathan Hill

architectural objects.[4] On to these one can add films, telecommunication networks, computer programs and bodies at the very least. Architectural matter is not always physical or building fabric. It is whatever architecture is made of, whether words, bricks, blood cells, sounds or pixels.

The richness and diversity of subjects and materials discussed in *Architecture – the Subject is Matter* locates architecture firmly in the world as a whole not just the domain of architects. In stating that architecture is far more than the work of architects, this book aims not to deny the importance of architects in the production of architecture but to see their role in more balanced terms and to acknowledge other architectural producers. Architecture can, for example, be found in the incisions of a surgeon, the instructions of a choreographer or the movements of a user. Anyone wanting to produce architecture should discard the preconceived boundaries of the discipline and learn from architecture wherever it is found, whatever it is made of, whoever it is made by. Architecture can be made of anything and by anyone.

THE FORM OF THE TEXT

The language used by architects and architectural historians has two obvious aims, to talk precisely about architecture and to exclude outsiders from the conversation. As one of the principles of this book is that architecture does not belong within the confines of the profession alone, it aims to present ideas in a seductive and accessible manner to ensure that a wide audience is involved in the discussion. It considers architectural matter in social, cultural, technological and experiential terms.

Architecture – the Subject is Matter acknowledges architectural matter far beyond the familiar boundaries of the discipline and reassesses the object at its traditional centre: the building. The fifteen chapters are divided into three sections – on buildings, spaces and bodies – which each deal with a particular understanding of architectural matter. Each chapter considers how a new, or newly acknowledged, matter transforms the subject of architecture, and vice versa. This book can be read in two ways: as three detailed discussions of specific categories of matter and as a field of overlapping connections between chapters in different sections.

Section 1 discusses building matter. Whether manufactured or natural, solid or ephemeral, the materials considered are often unfamiliar to architectural practice. The chapters, by Sarah Wigglesworth and Jeremy Till, Katherine Shonfield, Niall McLaughlin and Martin Richman, Jonathan Hill and David Gunkel, each discuss an architectural project. In the first four chapters the material of architecture is to differing degrees physical, in the fifth it is physical and virtual.

Jonathan Hill

In the opening chapter Till and Wigglesworth discuss the design and construction of their house in North London. Considering cultural and social resonance, as well as physical qualities, they combine conventional materials with others unfamiliar in a building, such as sandbags and strawbales. Till and Wigglesworth use an unexpected but everyday material and means of construction as an architectural Trojan Horse to question and expand conventional understandings of architectural technology and practice.

Inspired by Mary Douglas' work on pollution taboos, Shonfield discusses two architectural projects in London, one with Frank O'Sullivan, the other with Muf. The projects were sited in two quite different interiors: a public lavatory adjacent to Nicholas Hawksmoor's Baroque Christchurch, Spitalfields, and Alison and Peter Smithson's Brutalist building for *The Economist* magazine. To oppose the colour white's association in modernism with the eradication of polluting and corrupting elements, Shonfield and her collaborators inserted, respectively, nine tons of purified white goose feathers and a white, shiny, flexible, suspended ceiling system, bulging heavily with water.

McLaughlin and Richman discuss the project they produced together as part of an event in which artists and architects were asked to collaborate to transform spaces in the Royal Institute of British Architects headquarters in London. Their intervention was an equivocal response to the closed, faux-monumental quality of the building. Avoiding a detailed analysis or explanation of their project, McLaughlin and Richman propose that the poetic experience of space, light and form remains the subject of architecture even when, as in this instance, polycarbonate garden cloches and soap powder are used.

To affirm the status of the architect as an artist and architecture as an art, the experience of the building is sometimes equated with the contemplation of the artwork in a gallery. This argument is disturbed by the irreverent presence of the user but exemplified in the history of the Barcelona Pavilion. The exclusion of weather is a fundamental purpose of buildings. In Hill's chapter weather is an architectural material used, first, to disrupt the status of the Pavilion as an object of contemplation and, second, to affirm the creative role of the user in the formulation of architecture.

Gunkel's chapter, 'What's the Matter with Architecture?', discusses Ben Nicholson's architecture. Gunkel writes that Nicholson is not an insider or an outsider but a blasphemer, a knowing and heretical inhabitant of the very heart of architectural traditions. Nicholson's principal blasphemy occurs with regard to the matter of architecture, in that he questions the physical and the virtual. Architects are adept in the virtual because they have been engaged in it all along; their principal tool is the drawing, usually understood as a representation of an external reality, but just as much another reality. Gunkel argues that architects are caught between the physical and the virtual, exploring neither matter with intensity. But Nicholson's architecture is fully involved in both realities. It relishes, equally, the matter of bricks and bread tags, pixels and bits.

Section 2 focuses on space. Here architectural matter is formed from the dialectical engagement of the body, the physical environment and space. Spaces discussed include the domestic, urban and electromagnetic. The chapters are by Anthony Dunne and Fiona Raby, David Sibley, Iain Borden, and Jane Rendell and Pamela Wells.

Dunne + Raby touch on issues Gunkel discusses in the previous chapter, but their investigation of the physical and the virtual focuses on space. Criticising the familiar idea of cyberspace as a primarily visual information space, Dunne + Raby propose instead a fusion of the physical and the virtual that acknowledges the social, the cultural, and the sensual, fleshy body. Their chapter is divided into distinct sections, each considering a space and a tool; one section, for example, discusses Hertzian space and the broadband radio scanner. Instead of the contemporary fascination with the immaterial, they argue for a process of re-materialisation in which digital immateriality finds physical expression.

The home is supposedly the most secure and stable of environments. But it is also a response to fear of the excluded and unclassified. Comparing theories of space and child development, Sibley argues that although residential spaces may provide gratification they can also, simultaneously, create anxiety because the process of spatial purification, with which they are associated, can never be resolved. Sibley considers the advantages of weaker spatial boundaries and more heterogeneous spaces. But rather than favouring either strongly or weakly classified environments, Sibley argues for a dialectic engagement with both systems that considers residential spaces in combination with the spaces of neighbourhoods and cities.

In *Occupying Architecture* Borden gives skateboarding as an example of the positive appropriation of space through the everyday lived experience of the user. Borden identifies 'the principal contribution of skateboarding to architectural space . . . in the performative aspects of skateboarding.'[5] The skateboarder creates space by moving in reaction to the city and by projecting bodily movements on to the city. In his chapter in this book Borden extends a performative understanding of movement to an architectural interior that 'suggests an alternative to the commonplace notion of architecture being constituted purely from physical matter. Here, as we shall see, matter is produced out of a dialectical engagement between an architectural element (the staircase) and the human body and its various practices and senses.'

5 I. Borden, 'Body Architecture: Skateboarding and the Creation of Super-Architectural Space', in J. Hill (ed.), *Occupying Architecture: Between the Architect and the User*, London, Routledge, 1998, p. 201.

Jonathan Hill

Rendell and Wells suggest a definition of matter that incorporates the processes by which work is made. They argue that 'with work created through interaction and collaboration, the qualities of particular end-products become less important than the processes of making them'. Rendell and Wells support work that values 'the space of relationships made between people, over the building as an object-like thing'. Locating such work in feminist practice and theory, they distinguish a female, gift-giving economy from a male economy driven by profit.

In Section 3 the body is architectural matter. The first three chapters, by Katerina Rüedi Ray, Lesley Naa Norle Lokko and Mark Dorrian focus on social and cultural understandings of the body related to the discussions in Section 2. The final three, by Peg Rawes, Neil Spiller and Rachel Armstrong, suggest a fundamental re-reading of architecture's materials and sites, in which the impact of biological science and medical technology blurs the divisions between the body and architecture.

Rüedi Ray argues that the 'body and consciousness of the architect acts as matter or material for the process of architectural education'. Focussing on attitudes to gender in the Bauhaus curriculum, she identifies how, through the codes and practices of architectural education, the profession builds architects, reproduces itself and defines its difference to others.

Fusing personal observation with cultural, social and historical analysis, Lokko considers what it means to be black and what black means. In a collection of narratives set at different times and in different places, she discusses blackness in terms of body matter and building matter. Lokko contrasts what black means in Africa and America, and considers what architecture does to represent or deny 'Black Matter(s)'.

Dorrian suggests an early precedent for the fusing of the architectural and the bodily explored in the three subsequent chapters. Architecture is familiarly defined as healthy or unhealthy. Dorrian states that unhealthy architecture is associated, in particular, with errant matter. Drawing on historical and present-day examples, Dorrian argues that the categories of the monstrous and the grotesque are not simply excluded from western architecture but essential to it.

Rawes considers how concepts of form and matter in biological theories of evolution can influence architectural design. She contrasts the evolving matter and interdependence of form and matter in the biological sciences to the static objects and prioritisation of form over matter in architecture. Rawes states that the biological sciences suggest a model for architecture in which the designer and the user, and form and matter, are elements in a dynamic system.

Spiller states that the familiar palette of building materials is technologically, culturally and socially limited, and argues that the use of the term 'smart' to describe certain contemporary buildings and materials is highly misleading. Instead he

Jonathan Hill

considers the architectural possibilities of nanotechnology: self-replicating machines small enough to reformulate matter atom by atom. In nanotechnology, machines develop evolutionary intelligence and intervene in organic life, assuming similar patterns of growth. For Spiller, the consequence of nanotechnology is not just the creation of truly smart architectural matter but the liberation of individual architectural creativity and a diminished role for the 'aesthetic control police' of architects, designers and planners.

Armstrong discusses the potential new bodies developed at the interface of art, technology and medical science. She argues that the body is a site of architectural design and states that bodily matter is becoming more and more a fusion of the biological and technological. We accept the need to repair, refurbish and extend buildings, a principle Armstrong considers applicable to the design of bodies.

Jonathan Hill

SECTION 1

building

---

matter

Jeremy Till and Sarah Wigglesworth

1

the future is hairy

'GOD LIES IN THE DETAILS'

History is not sure that he said this but posterity has ascribed these words to Mies van der Rohe.[1] They have become a bead on the architectural rosary. Oft repeated, oft unthought, until they assume an inviolate status for the architectural supplicant. We need to believe the words were said by someone of his stature – otherwise we might playfully misread them as God telling lies: 'God fibs in the details.' But we cannot. They issue from Mies – fine, upstanding, well-dressed Mies – and as such transcend any mockery. The act of detailing has thus become a credo overseen by higher values. Architects claim this act as an integral part of their identity, a specific area of expertise, a demonstration of professional control that excludes the amateur. Detailing is one way in which architecture elevates itself above mere building ('architecture is not building' being another rosary bead). Builders simply do things as they know best through tried and tested methods, a kind of industrialised vernacular. Architects on the other hand use their expertise in detailing to refine complex conjunctions through the application of technical and aesthetic judgement. Detailing is difficult – an act of penitence that requires learning in order to reach the higher, spiritual plane of the discipline. Starting with the novice, levels of expertise are defined and initiated, each with increasing degrees of mastery.

This discipline of detailing sets architecture apart as a technocracy. Mies, and he really did say this, held 'that technology was a world unto itself'.[2] The architect/technocrat was divided from the world of the great unwashed – the surveyors, the public, the philistine. The architect's detailed designs are buildable only with specialised craftsmanship and expert labour. To be fully appreciated the final products of this process require a certain aesthetic and technical sensibility, an initiation into the faith. A world set apart, architecture becomes an autonomous discipline defined in part by an adherence to certain principles of detailing.

Is this an overstatement? We believe not. Mies has another aphorism: 'Architecture begins when two bricks are carefully put together.' As Beatriz Colomina pithily notes, this is 'just about the dumbest definition of architecture that I have heard'.[3] But it is another maxim passed down through architectural culture, a signal of our removal into a technically defined world. Specifications, legislation, contracts, performance standards and Agrément Certificates – the list goes on – provide institutional policing of the territory. Individual architects cannot expect to cover the whole territory, because the demands set by technical standards are challenging. They do indeed require application and devotion. Added to this, signs of progress must be demonstrated – architecture cannot be seen to stand still – and this demands technical development. Detailing thus becomes an unforgiving

1 Normally misquoted as 'God is in the details', the attachment to Mies is given through the assurances of Philip Johnson: P. Johnson, 'Architectural Details', *Architectural Record*, April 1964, pp. 137–47.

2 Mies van der Rohe, 'Architecture and Technology', *Arts and Architecture*, vol. 67, no. 10, 1950, p. 30.

3 B. Colomina, 'Mies Not', in D. Mertins (ed.), *The Presence of Mies*, Princeton, Princeton Architectural Press, 1994, p. 201. Colomina quotes Mies here, but also doubts the veracity of the statement.

Jeremy Till and Sarah Wigglesworth

treadmill of refinement and improvement, each conjunction judged in relation to its previous manifestation. Small wonder then that the territory is carved up and market niches are contested. Materials are classified (brick, glass, steel, concrete, wood, render) and methods of assembly are defined (hi-tech, eco-tech, lite-tech). Combine one or two from the first group with one of the latter and you have established an area of expertise. As in any language, only certain permutations are permissible, since transgression of categories affronts the rectitude and ordering of architecture.

TRANSGRESSION

The building was still rumbling, half-designed, around our heads when the call came. It was Interbuild, the largest trade show for building materials in the United Kingdom. They wanted us to build a section of our house on the main exhibition stand, in a display called 'Façades of the Future'. We were both flattered and gently amused at the idea of sneaking in a straw wall as an example of a pioneering future. A hairy Trojan horse. But we wavered. We had not even designed (or detailed) the wall yet, and the exhibition was to open in five weeks' time. What swayed us was the promise that our exhibit was to be placed next to a section of the Lords Media Centre by Future Systems, described to us as 7m long and shiny. The temptation of juxtaposing our hairy agricultural wall with the smoothness of their nautically inspired technology was too much to resist – the more so since each of us was somehow associated with the sustainable pie. Future Systems' ecological claim to a slice was based on the weird logic that aluminium (the building's principal material) was recyclable. Forget the oilfields of energy required to convert bauxite into aluminium, just be consoled by the fact that in order to fulfil this logic the Media Centre will one day be melted down into billions of Coke cans.

    Five weeks later we arrive, three amateurs (two of them women) in a self-drive van at a hall full of trucks and big, skilled men. We have three days to erect a wall using a method never previously used, a wall that will be seen by over 100,000 people. The lack of any technological precedent is scary (we have to research everything from scratch and improvise where necessary), but also consoling since there is nothing to judge it against, our method is neither right nor wrong, it is just there. But this does not stop endless big-bellied men coming over, curious and judgemental, waiting to see something they can shake their heads about in the time-honoured construction industry tradition ('you're doing it wrong, mate'), allied with conspiratorial winks to Jeremy ('lucky bastard, all those women around, mate') before turning away to reveal the sartorial cliché of the builder ('seen the crack in your arse, mate?'). Ours was the final laugh when three days later our wall went up on

Jeremy Till and Sarah Wigglesworth

time and according to plan, defeating their scepticism ('so who's sophisticated now, mate?'). Our only real disappointment is that when the promised 7m of the Lords Media Centre arrived it had shrunk to a sample 1m square. Something about a 'problem with production'. Well, we thought (borrowing from the automotive industry), 'Size matters'. [4]

The exhibit is consciously polemic, and through this becomes a signal for the forthcoming building. We have added a twist to our detailing. We suspect we have been called in as the token eco-people: straw = hairy = handholding = female = amateur = crude = non-rational. A convenient conflation to salve the collective conscience while others get on with the serious stuff. Our twist is to wrap the straw in a transparent polycarbonate screen sourced from an Italian DIY catalogue, so that the straw is exposed to view. It is a transgression of material and technical classifications. Slick meets hairy. The eco-people are offended by the polycarbonate (plastics are not wholesome). The technocrats are confused by the natural stuff. That is two targets in one wall.

4 In a UK television advertisement for a car, a woman sits seductively in the Barcelona Pavilion while images of a small (but very efficient) car flash by. The punchline is: 'Size matters'.

Jeremy Till and Sarah Wigglesworth

SERIOUS STUFF

The technocracy induced by the focus on the detail does not lead to the complete autonomy of architecture. Remember what initiated it: 'God lies in the details.' In the Miesian canon, detailing possessed a quasi-spiritual status; attached to it was an associated morality which equated honesty and transparency in visual expression (and in particular the detail) with truth and order in society. As Ignacio Solà Morales notes: 'The Miesian project in architecture is inscribed within a wider ethical project in which the architect's contribution to society is made precisely by means of the transparency, economy and obviousness of his architectonic proposal. This is the contribution of truth, of honesty. That is Mies' message.'[5] For Mies this was undoubtedly deeply felt; his philosophical and theological connections to such guides as the Catholic moralist Romano Guardini are well documented.[6]

Fifty years later the project to provide society's salvation through recourse to architectural honesty, truth, economy of means and precise tectonics appears deeply flawed and delusional. It might even seem funny if it were not, even now, revered with such intensity. But we are not allowed to laugh at the hopelessness of salvation through good detailing. This is serious stuff, a moral project that still holds certain sections of the architectural community in thrall. David Spaeth, a self-confessed disciple of Mies, states: 'Because Mies is so personally exacting, his work so uncompromising, he continues to be the architectural conscience of the age. This alone makes him worthy of our continued attention.'[7] The word conscience is telling. It is as if architects are in a state of potential truancy, in permanent danger of straying. In our secular age, we redeem our guilt through penitence to the rectitude of detail and tectonics. These days it is not so much God that lies in the details but Guilt. Residual guilt that the redemptive claims of modernism have never been fulfilled, that the sins of society cannot be solved by architecture alone. Not wishing to confront this failure head on, the profession retreats to the higher ground of truth and honesty in construction, one of the few challenges the architect can control. Disciplined making has become a security blanket against the realities, disruption and disorder of everyday life. But it is a blanket that can, with a little thought, be unpicked, taking apart the unsustainable interweaving of the weft of morality with the warp of technology.

5 I. Solà Morales, 'Mies van der Rohe and Minimalism', in Mertins, op. cit., p. 154.

6 See in particular F. Neumeyer, *The Artless World: Mies van der Rohe on the Building Art*, Cambridge, MA, MIT Press, 1999, ch. 6.

7 D. Spaeth, 'Ludwig Mies van der Rohe: A Biographical Essay', in D. Spaeth, *Mies Reconsidered*, New York, The Art Institute of Chicago, p. 33.

FUN

We are building a wall, the one next to the railway line, the one made out of sandbags. This technology has not been tested in London since the Blitz. We have been enthralled by

Jeremy Till and Sarah Wigglesworth

an image of the Kardomah Coffee house in 1941, its full length plate glass windows shielded from German bombs by a wall of sandbags, with refined Londoners attempting to maintain a semblance of coffee-morning normality behind a crude architecture. Sixty years later memories have faded and appropriate skills have been lost. We are now having trouble detailing the windows; framing them in zinc or standard pieces of timber feels too precious. Lying around the site (once a forge for the neighbouring railway) are some old pitch-pine sleepers. In a moment of vernacular inspiration Sarah realises they will make perfect window surrounds and, together with the builders, sorts out a way of making them work. In their making of the building, the builders have suspended their initial disbelief in the project, and have claimed the various unknown technologies as their own; construction pioneers.

Professor Gage visits us. He looks up at the sleepers. 'It looks like you are having fun here.' At first we are dismissive. Building one's own house is a notorious graveyard of relationships; it is hardly the definition of fun. Then we are slightly affronted. Residual guilt

Jeremy Till and Sarah Wigglesworth

about the seriousness and purity of architecture, perhaps. Finally, we are comforted by his words and are given the courage to laugh out loud when Steve the foreman labels the sleepers 'Flintstone architecture'.

BEAUTY

Mies again: 'Our real hope is architecture and technology grow together, that someday one will be the expression of the other: only then will we have an architecture worthy of its name, architecture as a true symbol of its time.'[8] Another of the moral imperatives for architects is to reflect the spirit of the age (whatever that means). One person's take on the spirit of the age may revolve around third-world debt, increasing social exclusion and global warming. Another person's may focus on increased consumer choice and better standards of living for the majority of western society. Architecture chooses technology as its *Zeitgeist* because we have made technology our signifier of progress. Technical development prefigures an aesthetic genealogy of progress – increasing simplicity, less and less material, leaner and leaner structures.

In this will to represent the age, architecture loses its basis in rationality and becomes simply an aesthetic. Bob Evans is wonderfully clear in this. 'We believe that Mies's buildings exhibit a sublime rationality because so many people have reported seeing it there. These sightings are only rumours . . . if Mies adhered to any logic it was the logic of appearance.'[9] We have always been confused by the publication of details of Miesian mullions as if they have some semblance of logic – why are skinny little I-beams, apparently glued and ending in mid-air, expressions of rational construction? Clearly they are not. They are to do with an apparition of rationality that is tied into an aesthetic will to beauty. Mies masterminds this illusion with greater skill than anyone else. He even seduces a critic such as Roger Scruton, who is hardly known for his defence of modernism. 'Some of the finest detailing of the modern movement was displayed by the immaculate lines and cruciform columns of the German pavilion'[10] – columns that are notorious for their structural sleight of hand.[11]

Mies' approach is indicative of another bead on the architectural rosary, namely that beauty can be achieved through the application of rational principles. Rational structure is *de facto* beautiful. Scruton again gives unwitting sanction to the modernists' white lie. 'It is through studying detail that the architect can learn to impart grace and humanity to the most unusual, troublesome and disorderly conglomeration.'[12] Morality, detailing and beauty are again conflated, but the winner in this heady mix is the aesthetic control over disorder. When push comes to shove, rationality will

8 Mies van der Rohe, op. cit., p. 30.

9 R. Evans, 'Mies van der Rohe's Paradoxical Symmetries, *Translations from Building to Drawing and Other Essays*, London, Architectural Association, 1997, p. 269.

10 R. Scruton, *The Aesthetics of Architecture*, London, Methuen, 1979, p. 213.

11 See Evans, op. cit., pp. 239–49 for a brilliant critique of Mies' disingenuous approach to structure.

12 Scruton, op. cit., p. 211.

Jeremy Till and Sarah Wigglesworth

be compromised in the pursuit of the higher goal of aesthetic perfection. No one really questions the lengths that Norman Foster goes to in constructing the image of structure to adorn the outside of the Hongkong and Shanghai Bank. We take it for granted that the shiny, muscular forms stand as an honest expression of the spirit of the age, because that is what modern architecture symbolises. But scratch beneath the skin and there is nothing particularly honest or rational here. Maybe, after all, God does lie, tell fibs, in the details.

BRUTE HONESTY

The plastic skin around the straw bales fulfilled a polemical purpose at Interbuild, but when it comes to building the house a number of contingent factors (legal, practical, economic, intellectual) push us towards another solution. This is to protect the straw bales with a cheap corrugated metal rainscreen. However, we have all enjoyed the transparency of the plastic with the bales visible behind. (In most strawbale construction the bales are plastered and thus disguised.) We decide therefore to have a large polycarbonate section set into the metal cladding. The question is how to do this. Should it be another window? Should it be

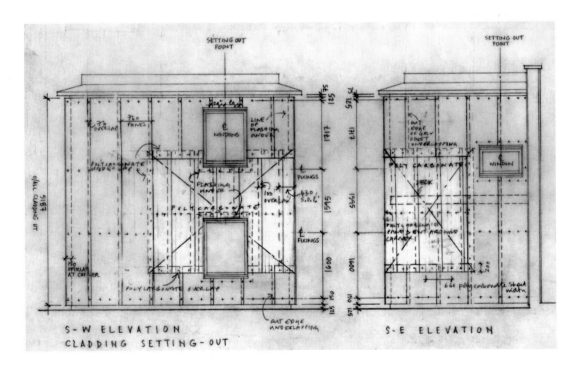

S-W ELEVATION
CLADDING SETTING-OUT

S-E ELEVATION

Jeremy Till and Sarah Wigglesworth

*symmetrical on the elevation? Should it be proportioned? Should it be framed? Finally,
Gillian takes the job into her own hands.*

*When it is built, Jeremy gulps. Privately, he is shocked. The polycarbonate window
randomly crosses windows, rounds a corner, cuts across elevations, lines up with nothing. In
this building full of aesthetic disruption, the polycarbonate section pricks a deep-seated sensibility. Is Jeremy simply looking wrongly or rather (because looking is always culturally
predicated), thinking wrongly? There is a brute honesty in the detail. Maybe in all its
gawkiness it is not a bad detail. It is like an exhibit in a science museum where layers are
cut back to reveal the underlying mechanism. It imparts to the wall a kind of vitality – the
secret life of the building. It also serves a useful purpose in allowing us to inspect whether
this life has an animal, vegetable or mineral involvement through invasion of rodent, rot or
condensation.*

GOOD DETAILS

Can there be any stranger front cover than that of the Austrian magazine *Detail*?
Where most architectural publications seduce the reader with pictures of smooth-
skinned buildings basking under the sun, *Detail* has just a stark, black-lined drawing to
entice the architect to look inside the covers of the magazine. A puritan ideal stripped
of any excess. A signal of the aesthetisation, and with it fetishisation, of the detail in
architectural culture.[13] Presumably only good details get on to the front cover.

A well-detailed building. A well-dressed man. Both sentiments of approval. It is no
coincidence that Mies insisted on handmade suits from the Viennese store Knize, the
same tailor that Adolf Loos used and for which he designed a shop.[14] Restrained.
Understated. Authoritative. Speaking through its details. Apparently simple ends
achieved through skilful execution. Miesian architecture and clothes – both aspire to
the same effects. But what does a 'well-detailed' building really imply? The phrase
signals an aesthetic judgement. So the good detail is the 'clean' detail, the 'crisp'
detail. In the profession's mythology, the architect has sole control over the mastery
of these effects, and only fellow architects can truly recognise the extent of that
mastery. The detail, coded and meticulously dimensioned, divorces design from
public recognition, securing the rarefied realm of the architect/technician.

The good architect also has to be the good detailer – and by corollary the good
detailer (who does nothing other than 'good' details) is judged a good architect. When
OMA first started building, the architectural establishment had no way of controlling
their affront (hardly surprising since Koolhaas hits so many of the sacred cows of
architecture at once). But rather than articulating this affront through a sustained

[13] For the fetishisation of the detail see S. Wigglesworth, 'A Fitting Fetish: Interiors of the Maison de Verre', in I. Borden and J. Rendell (eds), *InterSections: Architectural Histories and Critical Theories*, London, Routledge, 2000, pp. 91–108.

[14] This is noted by Beatriz Colomina, op. cit.

critique of the intellectual agenda behind the buildings, the disgust was concentrated on the details. OMA 'could not detail'.[15] Bad details ergo bad architecture. Of course such attacks missed the target completely. Koolhaas continually displaces the object of architectural attention from its normative concerns – including detailing. OMA's architecture is not badly detailed; it is made in a different way.

FAT WALLS

In a further mixing of classifications, we want to place the office element of the building on a domestic base. The aim is to evoke a set of cross walls 5.5m apart (the standard London terrace house dimension) as memories of the houses that might once have stood on the site; for this the walls should have the character of ruins, as if time has passed through them. At an early stage we chance upon the idea of using gabions, the wire cages full of rocks normally used in civil engineering as retaining walls.[16]

16 For detailing genealogists, this idea came prior to the publication of Herzog de Meuron's exquisite Napa winery, with its welded gabions and carefully considered cut stone.

The original idea was to fill the gabions with rubble salvaged from the buildings we were to demolish on the site, but our engineers (incredibly tolerant of most of our structural transgressions) put a stop to this. We therefore decided to use lumps of recycled concrete. With construction waste from both new build and demolition contributing to 30%[17] of all landfill in the United Kingdom, the use of recycled concrete in the gabions is an extremely minor, but quite visible, signal of an alternative to this prodigious waste. The plan is to use the gabions as load-bearing structures, something never done before. The structural logic has an elegant simplicity about it; the lumps of concrete are used for their compressive strength, and when they attempt to move outwards under load, they are held together by the tensional strength of the wire cage. Of course this solution does not meet normative criteria of economy and elegance (exemplified by lean, taut structures), but why should engineering always be about the minimal? Why not an economy of excess? Gabions, delivered as flat pack, filled with a surplus by-product by unskilled labour, and with a simple structural logic. So far so good.

17 The BRE puts the number at 17%, the Waste Council at 45%. We split the difference as an indication of the difficulty of quantifying sustainable issues.

The reality, as ever, is somewhat different. On the positive side, it is cheaper to bring a truck of recycled concrete to site than it is to take away a truck of rubble. With the introduction of a landfill tax in the United Kingdom in 1998, stockpiles of used aggregates have grown up around the fringes of cities. This is cowboy country, a marginal (and quite black) economy of trucks shifting around sand, cement and stone in various states of cohesion. We set out into this strange territory, clambering over small hills of crushed concrete, tape measure in hand, attempting to find lumps that will fit the gabion cage without spilling out. In one yard, Jeremy has a gun pulled on him as he leaves, carrier bag full of samples ('only joking, mate, you just looked a bit of a wanker'). In the end our effete

Jeremy Till and Sarah Wigglesworth

tracking system is fruitless, and we have to rely on the builders' bush telegraph (Steve's brother drives one of the trucks) to find a source.

More of a problem is the gabions' structural integrity. Theoretically their loadbearing capacity is massive, six times more than required for the job. The building inspector, however, will have nothing of it. In the case of fire the wires will melt, the rocks will spill and the office above settle down on to a ruined landscape. It might sound interesting, but it does not meet the Building Regulations or norms of convenience, and so we are required to cast sacrificial columns in the centre of the gabions as we erect them. We do this with some regret, inculcated as we still are with traces of architectural guilt concerning structural honesty.

This structural solution also changes the spirit of the constructional technique. We had enjoyed the idea of erecting industrial flat packs and randomly chucking in pieces of concrete. The job now becomes more complex, and as with much else on this site, the skill has

Jeremy Till and Sarah Wigglesworth

to be learnt from scratch. Martin, our project manager, here assumes as much a role in the design as we do. Between Martin, Steve and Pat (a carpenter by trade) and ourselves a method of construction is arrived upon, which is then adapted and refined by Pat when building work starts. They, and not us, assume aesthetic control over the process and far from randomly throwing in rocks, they hand place them. At the entrance, in a prominent position, is a piece of shiny granite. We have yet to ask Pat whether this placing is an accident.

When the gabions are finished they feel magnificent, like some standing stones an archaeologist has uncovered on site. At this stage, we are visited by a large group of Austrian architecture students, on a tour of London buildings. They are hot-foot from, and exhilarated by, the Lords Media Centre (we are haunted by this building). We can sense their unease in this muddy site with unfinished straw walls and rough, excessive gabions. And then one asks, smirking because he thinks he has found our architectural Achilles' heel: 'Those big walls, they are loadbearing?' With the answer, the admittance of the hidden column, one can see (tight mouths turned down) the whole group's unease transform into rank disapproval.

THE SIGNIFICANT DETAIL

18 M. Frascari, 'The Tell-Tale Detail', in K. Nesbitt (ed.), *Theorizing a New Agenda for Architecture, An Anthology of Architectural Theory 1965–1995*, Princeton, Princeton Architectural Press, 1996, pp. 500–14. When we were teaching in the USA in 1991, the article had samizdat status.

19 Ibid., p. 500.

20 Ibid., p. 507.

Against a tendency towards the aestheticisation and technisation of the detail, some writers and architects have upheld the signifying, significant role of the detail. In his influential article, 'The Tell-Tale Detail',[18] Marco Frascari optimistically interprets Mies' 'God lies in the details' in terms of ascribing meaning: 'The detail (here) expresses the process of signification, that is the attaching of meanings to man produced details.'[19] In Frascari's version of tectonics, the act of making is not a mere technical exercise but one that brings with it inherent meaning, so that the joint (as the most intense manifestation of detailing) is 'the place of the meeting of the mental construing and the actual construction'. Frascari holds up Carlo Scarpa as an exemplar, pointing to the way that Scarpa's approach to drawing overcomes the separation of design and construction that is evident in normal technical drawings. In Scarpa's drawings, with their multiple scales, projections and renderings, 'the marks on paper are analogues for the processes of construction and construing'.[20]

Architecture can speak through the joint, and in so doing the detail becomes a unit of signification in a language of construction. However, Frascari notes that this language is not read through a structuralist analysis of visual referents, but through a phenomenological engagement with architecture through the senses and an appeal to archetypal conditions. Thus Kenneth Frampton urges us to consider the 'ontological

Jeremy Till and Sarah Wigglesworth

consequences' of the differences between the frame structure and the mass wall, that is to say 'the way in which framework tends towards the aerial and the demateri-alisation of mass, whereas the mass form is telluric, embedding itself ever deeper into the earth'.[21] The argument is that through careful attention to the choice, disposi-tion and jointing of materials, matter is transformed from mere stuff into something that has significance. In this way detailing transcends the limitations imposed on it by the conventions of aesthetics or technics alone and becomes a means of summoning up deeper, more authentic, cultural resonances.

The argument for the significant detail is seductive, but it may in the end share the same myopia as an obsession with refinement. Frascari's identification of the detail as the basic unit of architectural signification is at one level a truism, but the resulting implication that architecture resides in the detail leads us up a dangerous atomistic path in which the detail is treated as an isolated artefact divorced from its wider spatial context. Frampton's 'call to order' is initiated in opposition to the sceno-graphic excesses of post-modern architecture. He has a suspicion of avant-garde exercises in spatial production, where progress is announced through new formal paradigms. Against such spatial (by which he means formal) distractions, Frampton argues that a return to the material base of architecture is necessary to overcome the 'cultural degeneration' of the process-driven, commodified, globalised society at the end of the twentieth century. His almost touching faith in the power of archi-tecture to re-establish a counter position is misplaced in its reliance on the agency of the detail (as artefact). With this small-scale focus, Frampton myopically avoids a con-frontation with the wider social and political context in which architecture is situated, and to which it must react. In this light, his claim for tectonics as a point of resistance 'against the commodification of culture'[22] looks fragile.

The warning signs may be found in the citing by both Frampton and Frascari of Scarpa as a master of significant tectonics, pointing in particular to the Brion Ceme-tery as an exemplar. As architects we all love this stuff and make pilgrimages across the hot Veneto plain to join other architects clambering over this intensely private place. Death. That's the most poignant moment of all for an architect to address and it brings out in Scarpa the most elaborate set of encrustations of his career. Lots of meaning. Lots of detail. But it wasn't the excess that bothered us – the place is still extraordinary – it was the desperate American architecture students (Frascari in back pocket) who ignored all clear signs (*privato* – that's clear in any language) to climb over gates into the inner sanctuary just to get a frontal view and all-important photo-graph of THAT detail. The silly one – we've said it now, that's us excluded from the high table – the gate-opening mechanism with wires contortedly looping their way around pulleys. The students' faces nod up and down as they trace their way through

21 K. Frampton, 'Rappel a l'ordre, The Case for the Tectonic', in Nesbitt, op. cit., p. 522. His term 'call to order' is indicative of an approach that sees the detail as an essential element in establishing visual coherence – and with it a more general order.

22 Ibid., p. 527.

Jeremy Till and Sarah Wigglesworth

these lines following the path of the mechanism. In a cemetery, that most primal of places, architects lose their heads, and humanity, in the complicated technics of a detail.

This is where one should sense danger: in the ability of even a 'significant' joint to distract. It is the same at the Barcelona Pavilion; even if Mies' overload of visual effect and Scarpa's intensely worked materiality are clearly different in their means, the end is the same. The Barcelona Pavilion, as Bob Evans notes, 'distracts . . . it is the architecture of forgetting'.[23] But this is not the gerontic forgetting of the amnesiac, this is a conscious forgetting, a displacement from 'a confrontation with violence and politics'.[24] The detail becomes a place to get lost in, a turning away from the world beyond. The forgetting induced by a myopic attention to the detail is also a forgetting of the social and political implications of spatial production. Of course the making, detailing of buildings contributes to this production, but it is only part of an interlocking matrix of relationships. The true resistive strength of architecture lies in its engagement with the various sites of contemporary spatial–social production, and not in its rearguard retreat into the essences of tectonics.

23 Evans, op. cit., p. 269.

24 Ibid., p. 270.

DIRTY NAPPY

25 In the second paragraph of the first chapter, 'The Lamp of Sacrifice'.

Somewhere in the Seven Lamps,[25] *Ruskin says that a carriage on springs can never be considered in the same light as architecture. We did not set our office on springs just to spite him – they are there to damp the juddering from the passing trains – but we still like this stick in the eye to Ruskin's pious morality. The office balances as a thin wedge over the mass of the gabions. The springs give it a precarious feel that flies in the face of the corporate stability normally associated with offices. The office is usually seen as a place set apart from the home and architecturally assumes an identity of decorum and order. There is a gender thing going on here, in the separation of the wilful domestic from the ordered office, and the identification of the female with the former and male with the latter. In our project, and in our lives (the two are intertwined by now), such separation is both impossible and undesirable. In a confusion of categories we wrap our place of work in a soft quilt. We want it to feel like domestic upholstery, puckered and buttoned, deflating any corporate pretensions. There is a gender thing going on here as well.*

We have invented our own DIY method of achieving this effect, but are nervous about it and so consult experts who have worked with the knights and lords of British architecture. An architectural genealogy is beginning to establish itself in the late twentieth century use of fabric. Frei Otto–Hopkins–Horden–Rogers. It is clear from the expert's reaction that our proposed solution does not fit into this family tree. It will flap and tear, he

Jeremy Till and Sarah Wigglesworth

says. It will pucker irregularly, he says. It will not be absolutely tight, he says. We are convinced enough by his arguments (in our nervousness we overlook how he conflates technical and aesthetic criteria) that we get him to quote for a highly stretched skin that only they can erect. They will have to fake the upholstery buttons that we have specified as fixing positions.

*When it comes, their price is four times our budget. It is a Barcelona chair when we can only afford an Ikea Chesterfield. So it is back to the DIY. A small sailmaker on the South Coast (an unwitting nod to technology transfer – what delicious irony if our cladding were made next to the South Coast shipbuilders who made **that** building, the one that haunts us) makes up the lengths that are then wrapped like bandages round the office. This other technology brings with it associations beyond our control. The builders quickly nickname it 'the nappy' ('that should stop any architectural shit coming out from the office'). Both our fathers ask when we are going to put up the final cladding – the quilt is too soft*

Jeremy Till and Sarah Wigglesworth

and fragile for them to cope with. More worrying is when an affronted student asks at the end of a lecture why we are doing this. 'What's wrong?', we ask. 'It is going to look dirty in a few years' time,' is the reply. Dirt is clearly a threat to the sanctity of proper architecture, ergo our building is not proper.

It is lucky that we have not told her about our plans for the sandbags. We intend for them to get dirty, to get rough, but unpredictably. As the bags decay ('we regret the delay to the 10.05 Edinburgh train, hessian on the line') the sand–cement–lime mixture inside them will set hard. When the bags finally disintegrate (who knows when) their woven pattern will be left on the rippling wall, surface osmotically melding with solid. Most walls are detailed to shrug off the effects of time, but this is a wall that has been designed to allow time to pass through it, and thereby to modify it; an evolutionary architecture.[26]

26 See J. Till, 'Thick Time', in I. Borden and J. Rendell (eds), *InterSections: Architectural Histories and Critical Theories*, London, Routledge, 2000, pp. 283–95.

OTHER DETAILS

For a discipline that addresses such a broad range of cultural conditions, the range of building materials employed by architects is exceptionally restricted. Architecture controls its boundaries through the definition of 'appropriate' materials and their subsequent transfiguration during the act of detailing.[27] Materials not included in the canon do not carry with them the recognisable genealogy of expertise and refinement that accords the architect his (sic) status. The only permissible supplementation to the limited canon of materials is through technology transfer, a mechanism by which architects draw on the technologies and innovations in other industries and adapt them to the demands of building. This transfer both provides architects with a technical authority and also signals progress in their work. Boat-building, armaments, biotechnics, motor industries, electronics – a select band of 'progressive', 'advanced' or 'hi-tech' industries – are raided for inspiration. Rarely is there an interest in a technology transfer from 'lower' or commonplace techniques, representing as it would a dilution of the self-defined authority and status of the architect. Materials from the vernacular (mud, thatch), the do-it-yourself shop (plastic, pine), mass-produced industry (cheap cladding panels), the domestic (fabric, paper, card) are considered outsiders. These are the materials of the everyday, a category of life from which high architecture has always set itself apart. These materials are regarded with suspicion, and the buildings that result from them are considered a degraded form of architecture.

For too long architecture has erected a defensive wall around itself, technically refining matter and twiddling with form in the deluded belief that this alone is enough. It is time to cross over these self-defined walls and engage with wider cultural forces.

27 In addition, materials are increasingly excluded through the threat of litigation. Lists of approved materials and constructional systems are becoming commonplace – and in some cases being insisted upon – by anxious insurance companies. Under current legislation it is the responsibility of the designer to prove compliance with regulations when using materials and/or techniques that fall outside the legal framework.

Jeremy Till and Sarah Wigglesworth

It is time to break the hold of authority and mystification that the technocracy of architecture has induced. The materials of the everyday and their associated technologies present an opportunity for architecture to open up its gates. The everyday does not respect the limited classifications that architecture has founded itself on; it asks why architecture is disinterested in the normal; it encourages us to transgress. This is an expansive and empowering move that allows architecture to reconnect as process and product with the vicissitudes of life. But to do this requires a loosening of the definition of what constitutes architecture. Relax, boys. It is acceptable for architectural technologies to be claimed by others (women, amateurs, untrained eyes) and for architecture to claim other technologies. Not only acceptable, but necessary if architecture is not going to exhaust itself chasing the next technical advance or blind itself by squinting at close-ups of buildings banished of time and life.

Our own experience suggests that storming the bastion of architecture by throwing transgression at it is a fruitless exercise. As we write the building is still not complete but brickbats – neat, dumb, Miesian brickbats – are already being thrown. 'Too many ideas.' 'Too much going on.' 'Inconsistent.'[28] These are not meant as compliments. But we grab them gladly and, rather than waste our time throwing our own rougher bricks back at the bastion, walk out of its gates and into a wider, more welcoming world.

This would remain just rhetoric but for another force that compels words into action. The environmental crisis brings all notions of technical neutrality to a juddering halt. It imposes on us an imperative to make judgements that transcend the limitations of the aesthetic or the rational. Can the making of architecture ever be judged 'good' again if it is knowingly unsustainable?

Environmental considerations give rise to a new value system in which many of the iconic details of the twentieth century are suddenly recast in a different light. They are in fact bad details, lacking connection to values lying outside the tiny concerns of architecture. Distressingly the environmental movement is in danger of being hijacked. On the one hand by disingenuous technocrats who have quickly changed their spots and are now trying to solve a problem created by (their) technology by inventing yet more. They apply the rules of technical determinism to arrive at a moral high ground, software programmes at the ready to justify how 'green' their buildings are. On the other hand there are eco-fundamentalists who potentially force the movement into a regressive cul-de-sac, in which unquestioned spatial (and thus social) patterns are disguised under a thick, woolly coat of worthy greenness. For this camp, spatial invention is seen as a distraction from the central issue of sustainability.

Our own way forward – in progress and fluid – takes seriously the issues thrown up by the global environmental crisis, but not in a way that excludes other social and

28 As Adrian Forty pointed out to us, consistency is a cardinal rule of detailing, because it is the mark of the single, master architect who controls everything. By being inconsistent, we break this rule.

Jeremy Till and Sarah Wigglesworth

cultural forces. It is a future that is not fully controllable or measurable – this is not a sign of weakness but an inevitable condition of architecture. Compromises are necessary and important if one is to engage with forces outside the neat boundaries that architecture has erected. Judgements have to be made. It is a future that is hairy.

CONFESSION

We have shadow-gaps around the doors.
They look lovely.

ACKNOWLEDGEMENTS

The project discussed is 9 Stock Orchard Street, London. It would have been impossible without the collaboration of numerous people who made it what it is; we are indebted to them all. Two must be mentioned. Martin Hughes, the project manager, without whom it would never have been built, and Gillian Horn who worked with us on the project for three years. The structural engineers were Price and Myers, acoustic consultants: Paul Gillierion Associates, main contractors: Koya Construction, site agent: Steve Archbutt.

Jeremy Till and Sarah Wigglesworth

two architectural
projects about purity

Dirt is Matter out of Place – Katherine Shonfield and Frank O'Sullivan

A disused nineteenth-century subterranean public lavatory in Commercial Street, London, next to Christchurch, Spitalfields, by Nicholas Hawksmoor – covered with white goose feathers.

Purity and Tolerance – Muf Art and Architecture with Katherine Shonfield

The Architecture Foundation exhibition space at The Economist Building, London, by Alison and Peter Smithson – with a white, bulgy, shiny ceiling.

Figure 2.1 Dirt is Matter out of Place, *View of Feathered Interior*. Photograph, Frank O'Sullivan.

Figure 2.2 Dirt is Matter out of Place, *Close-up*. Photograph, Frank O'Sullivan.

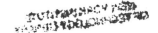

DIRT IS MATTER OUT OF PLACE – KATHERINE SHONFIELD AND FRANK O'SULLIVAN

The following text accompanied *Dirt is Matter out of Place* (Era No. 6). Published as a landscape format, A6 size, ring-bound guide.

1 The Pre-Lavatorial Era
The area of the site at this time was a mass of brown undifferentiated matter. It contained bits of building, earth, cobbles, bones, roots, worms and other crawling animals, all of them Dirty.

Figure 2.3 *Mudd Mask.*

Figure 2.4 *Vanish.*

Katherine Shonfield

2 The Evangelical Era

The evangelists of sanitation drove their message in the form of white, vitreous pipes through the sticky brown mass all the way from the West-End of London. An underground room was carved into the site, 500 cubic metres. All the carved edges were then sealed with cooked earth finished with an almost continuous and seamless white shiny germ unfriendly face of glazed brickwork.

3 The Era of Regulation and the Division of Labour

Regulating mechanisms for ordering the whole process of going to the lavatory, i.e. the production of Dirt through urination and defecation, were introduced in the form of:

a) Separate apparatus: slab urinal for urinating, w.c. stalls for defecating.

b) Communal partitioning for urinating.

c) Individual partitioning for defecating.

d) A centralised room allowing for constant supervision by a resident attendant.

4 The Era of Inversion

It became apparent that the ordering of the architectural elements both signified and permitted the development of disorder in the spaces in between these elements. The almost incessant effort involved in the excavation and the sealing of the space, demarcation of places for different acts of pollution, and constant washing down, was a sign not for victory in the War against Dirt, but for the impossibility of success. In particular, the implied choreography of public urination under the eye of an ever-present attendant allowed the possibility of open scrutiny and enjoyment of others' genitals. The delineation of private space for defecation made a place for subculture/germculture to flourish, in the warm and out of sight.

Figure 2.5 *WHITENS SOFTENS ALL IN ONE.*

Katherine Shonfield

Figure 2.6 *SQEZY SQEZY*.

5 The Era of Disuse

Understanding the futility of trying to control disordering Dirt, an attempt was made to dismantle the regulating mechanisms established in the third Era. The doors to all the w.c. stalls were taken away, three partition walls and three w.c. stalls were removed. The rest of the white vitreous place remained, but was closed off. Rather than admit defeat in the unwinnable War, the battle shifted ground. With Domestosticity, the activity of going to the lavatory was shooed away to the privacy of people's own homes – take your dirt with you.

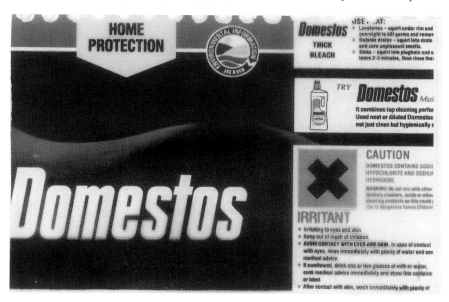

Figure 2.7 *Domestos.*

Katherine Shonfield

6 The Era of De-regulation through Feathering

Dirt was surreptitiously re-introduced in to the site in the form of white feathers. Vitreous sealed interior and apparatus were both spread with a homogenous cover of down, masking the crisp edge of the regularising geometry, and so disordering its individual character and function. At detail level the feathers confounded the ability of the dirt denying brick to repel its corrupting germ enemy.

7 The Era of Petrification through Conservation

The disused lavatory became a monument to a stale-mate in the war against Dirt. This was unacceptable to the new mission from the West End, now in the guise of the Heritage advance guard; they found another, more subtle way of effecting cleanliness. Instead of the trail-blazing bleach that formed the underground space in Era No. 2, the disused lavatory was now petrified, polished and perfected with conserving pickling formalin. The exterior railings were taken away to be pieced together, mended and preserved to be represented as a sign not for repression, but for something cosy, marketable and comfortably situated in the past. A reading of quaintness allowed the maintenance of the vitreous interior simultaneously with a purging of its history – by renaming it 'wine bar'.

Figure 2.8 *FAIRY SNOW.*

Katherine Shonfield

PURITY AND TOLERANCE – MUF ARCHITECTS AND KATHERINE SHONFIELD

The following text was repeated on the street level windows of the Architecture Foundation.

Figure 2.9 Purity and Tolerance, *Stretchy, Shiny Ceiling Filled with Water.* Photograph, Jason Lowe.

Until very recently most towels had straight edges. There was something a bit token about them; in addition to being rectangular and having no overlap, they were made of one material. If that failed and you leaked any blood at all it inevitably flowed over the edge of the straight cut, and on into the outside world. Of late, wings and layers of different materials have been introduced. They distort the purity of the towel's edge, and they overlap.

It's odd that it's taken a century to accept that a less purist towel makes for a lot less accidents. You could say the new towels are a lot more TOLERANT. A peculiar parallel exists in architecture. Panelled modern buildings – such as the one you're looking at – glory in their straight edges, and purity – only one material at a time as per the old style towel. Until quite recently some buildings weren't too bothered about how the panels joined up. If there was a lot of water around, they just leaked. Like the Emperor's New Sanitary Towels ordinary people seemed too cowed by the experts to mention this for a while.

Katherine Shonfield

FORM

It doesn't 'do' to explain architecture or art, anymore than it's OK to explain the purport of a joke, and still expect a laugh. You are expected to 'get' all three without explanation, and are met, in the case of architecture and art, with a cold superiority if you don't understand all the nuances. But all these precious nuances are, though, is a common set of cultural references. This chapter ruins the joke – and hence, like all such explanations, inevitably may seem a bit laboured. In it I attempt to unravel the two architectural projects described above by explaining these references.

The projects have a number of similarities. Both were temporary installations. So unlike conventional architecture they were both constructed in acknowledgement of their imminent demise. Both projects explore the extent to which architecture, in the sense of the manipulation of space, can and cannot carry *meaning*. And both projects were consciously conceived from the outset as explorations and extrapolations of a theory through the practice of architecture.

The theoretical inspiration, Mary Douglas' anthropological study of pollution taboos, *Purity and Danger*,[1] provides the titles of both projects: *Dirt is Matter out of Place* and *Purity and Tolerance*. They work as a take on a number of aspects of Douglas' theory that indicate architectural analogies. What is of particular interest here is that in her book Douglas tries to explain why certain things are considered dirty and unacceptable. In her thesis, matter is classified in terms of identifiable and clearly delineated *form*, in order to establish what is polluted and taboo – the *formless*. What happens is that 'Pollution dangers strike when *form* (my emphasis) has been attacked';[2] social well-being (purity) is identified quite literally in the form, or the edge of form, defined in opposition to a 'sea of formlessness'. The first point of interest then, to both projects, is the extent to which the clean and the unpolluted is identified in architecture with elements that can have an unequivocal, clear line drawn around them.

The 'sea of formlessness' is made of everything unclassifiable and unclear, against which form must defend itself. Douglas' famous example is the list of forbidden – i.e. polluted – foods in the Old Testament book *Leviticus*. Her argument is that the forbidden creatures – for example snakes and sea creatures without fins and scales – are perceived as dirty because they straddle two or more *distinct classes*. Snakes crawl along the land but have no feet; crustaceans swim without fins. It is not any objective condition that makes them unacceptable, but their hybridity. So the second point of exploration in these two projects, is the extent to which architectural purity is defined by the unambiguous classification of the elements of architecture.

The theory provides a starting point for explorations in the manipulation of space. But as well as this, both projects are immersed in a contradiction from their very

1 M. Douglas, *Purity and Danger*, London, Routledge & Kegan Paul, 1966.

2 Ibid., p. 104.

Katherine Shonfield

outset. They seek to create spaces with sufficient sensual power to bypass the intellect, to make a theoretical reading unnecessary for enjoyment and comprehension. In this way, they are aligned with a Baroque as opposed to a Classical tradition in architecture. But this apparently anti-theoretical position itself is theoretical – it opposes itself to an architecture – like Classicism – conceived as the sum of its clearly distinguished parts. The projects try to obscure rather than express the lines between the parts of architecture, whether it be the Brutalist construction of the Economist Building, or simply the distinction between walls, floor and ceiling in the Spitalfields lavatory. So more accurately, the underlying assumption of the projects might hope that theoretical understanding is imminent, and that it reaches you in unexpected and unpredictable ways, through conscious as well as unconscious means. The methodology and processes of these two projects about purity – some aspects of which are outlined below – reflect this ambiguous approach.

TEXT

This ambiguity is most apparent in the use of the text. Bearing in mind David Greene's aphorism – if you want your building to say something, then use words – each project has an accompanying text, reproduced above.

In the case of *Purity and Tolerance* we attempted to incorporate the text into the installation. It was inscribed on the street-level windows in the white, joined-up writing of a text to be copied down in an old-fashioned school (Figure 2.10). The text draws an analogy between the cladding panels of the Economist Building and contemporary sanitary towels. The inscription took several days, and provoked a number of intriguing encounters in this most respectable part of town. Passers-by looked on with approval at the laborious and accomplished act of handwriting the whole, only to be disgusted and surprised on reading its contents. The window text acted to semi-obscure the view of the interior installation from the outside. At night, the powerful street lamps served to project the writing deep into the interior, enlarging it and inscribing it over the exhibit. It was also written on a postcard for visitors to take away. The analogy between the evolution of sanitary towel and panel construction was suggested by the work of Katrin Dzenus and Tracy Chapman:[3] the refusal of both to acknowledge in the rigours of their form the presence of the liquid, i.e. the form-*lessness* of both blood and water, was illuminated by Douglas' *Purity and Danger*.

Within the interior of the building parallel films by Katherine Clarke were shown on monitors embedded within two white stub columns. The camera used its continuity to subvert the staccato rhythms of an architecture of parts. It roved over sanitary towels, revealing them as edgeless and snowy landscapes.

[3] K. Dzenus and T. Chapman, 'Extended Essay on the History of Sanitary Protection', completed as the theory submission of the Postgraduate Diploma in Architecture, South Bank University, 1993.

Katherine Shonfield

Figure 2.10 Purity and
Tolerance, *Text on Street Level
Windows*. Photograph, Jason
Lowe.

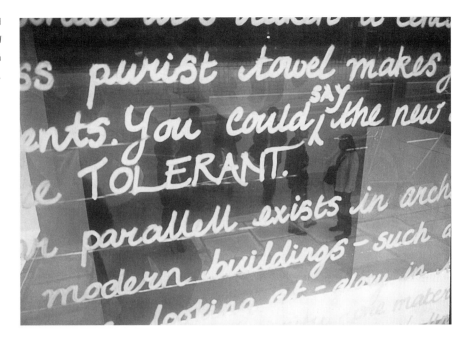

Figure 2.10 Purity and Tolerance, *Text on Street Level Windows*. Photograph, Jason Lowe.

In the case of *Dirt is Matter Out of Place*, we were commissioned by Siraj Izhar to do an installation as an act of faith on his part, before we had any idea what we were going to do. The immersion of this interior in feathers required an awesome effort by many people, and was a gut, not a rational, reaction to the space. The text arose out of the fact that we ourselves needed to know *why* we were doing it. As such it is separate from the installation: it accompanied it in the manner of a guide, a small A6 size ring-bound publication with a plain shiny white cover.

We wanted to acknowledge that the site had a history, and that our own installation was a stage, and obviously not the final one, within that history. Douglas provoked a fictional writing of the history of the site and its urban context in terms of a war against dirt, and our installation as a stage within that battle. The text provided a way to draw parallels between the lavatory as a controlling mechanism in the production of dirt – urination and defecation – and the understanding of dirt at a larger urban scale. The contextual maps in the A6 publication show the area just to the north of the lavatory, known in the second half of the nineteenth century as the Jago. In 1872 the Jago was a notorious no-go area, a labyrinth of streets which made a maze of safety for all the unofficial, unsanctioned activities of the city, including robbery, murder and prostitution. The area was subjected to wholesale demolition and appears as a white, clean blank in the Ordnance Survey map of 1893, and then as a classic

Katherine Shonfield

piece of urban renewal reminiscent of a panopticon, with streets radiating, star-like, into the surrounding neighbourhoods from a centre point. Each plan in the guide is twinned by an equivalent mapping of the site of the lavatory itself; as an unordered dirty site, as a site cleared preparatory to the imposition of architectural order, as an equivalent panoptic plan of the lavatory, showing the attendant's room strategically positioned on axis, to view all activity within. *The Era of Inversion* focuses on how the paradox of obsessive ordering allowed its opposite: the flowering of illicit, sexual activity within the lavatory itself: 'the possibility of open scrutiny and enjoyment of others' genitals' – to this day, the unspoken and unspeakable rationale behind the mass closure of public toilets in London. *The Era of Disuse* swiftly follows. Closure of the lavatory goes hand in hand with an equivalent erasure of public space at urban scale, illustrated in the reduction of the site plan to a figure ground of solid, largely impenetrable blocks. The installation (Era No. 6) is slipped in as a last ditch battle of dirt in disguise – white feathers – between the period of disuse, and No. 7, *the Era of Petrification through Conservation* – currently underway.

Adverts for cleaning products separate each fictional era – words and signs – Vanish, Fairy Snow and Domestos – uniting the operations of the private and the public war against dirt.

CONTEXT

In another twist on the relationship of architecture to theory, both installations try to embody a kind of commentary on their immediate architectural context. The nineteenth-century lavatory is buried in the street directly outside Nicholas Hawksmoor's Christchurch, a masterpiece of the English Baroque. It looks like a massive lump of stone, carved as a unified piece. It inspired the original understanding of the site as carved out, and the attempt to unify the space with the homogeneity of a single surface of feathers.

The Economist Building is the masterwork of the Brutalist architects Alison and Peter Smithson, and is also of iconic status. *Purity and Tolerance* was situated in the Architecture Foundation within the building's lower ground floor. The Brutalist context was used to generate an oppositional architecture of the hybrid, the fuzzy and the seamless.

SOLIDITY

Both projects present a challenge to architecture defined as 'solid state'. We understand the solid through its opposite. It confronts its opposite at its edges. In *Dirt is*

Katherine Shonfield

Matter out of Place, we covered every single edge we found with feathers, but for the sake of comprehension through its opposite, we left a quarter of the space untouched – solid. Figure 2.11 shows the lavatory before and after feathering.

Wading through feathers, touching feathers, looking at the sky through feathers, the aim was to dematerialise the solidity of the space. In Douglas' terms, you could

Figure 2.11 Dirt is Matter out of Place, *View of Lavatory Before and After Feathering*. Photograph, Frank O'Sullivan.

Figure 2.12 Dirt is Matter out of Place, *Close-up of Feathered Edge*. Photograph, Frank O'Sullivan.

Katherine Shonfield

no longer draw a line around the edges of the space. We had made it too fuzzy and too messy.

In *Purity and Tolerance* the premise was that the Economist Building in its guise as Brutalist icon understands solidity by virtue of the clarity of the edges between elements. Brutalism is defined here, in line with my later writing,[4] as an architectural expression of such a purity project, hence a preoccupation with the unobscured, classifiable origins – concrete (or in the case of the Economist Building, Portland stone) in its uncovered, original state, and with the clear delineation between architectural parts, especially at constructional junctions. In part the installation worked as an extrapolation of my own essay in *AA Files* also entitled 'Purity and Tolerance'.[5] The essay and the installation both questioned the compatibility of the very idea of tolerances in building construction – the acceptance of inaccuracies of lines, junctions and human fallibility – and the exigencies of an architecture entirely dependent on the assembly of rigidly defined parts.

Lurking behind the idea of building tolerances is the thing to be tolerated: *Purity and Tolerance* highlighted the confrontation of the rigidity of *form* in building construction and sanitary protection with the *formlessness* of the liquid it purports to exclude, whether water or blood. So a 'tolerant' building construction and sanitary protection needs to relax its rigour, the signs of its purity, and ends up with unclear edges and overlaps between otherwise distinct elements of construction.

The ceiling of the installation was a kind of physical expression of such tolerance *in extremis*. It was covered with a seamless, patented suspended ceiling, white and exceptionally shiny, and then filled to bulging point with water (Figure 2.9) in a pointed reference to the relative permeability of entirely inflexible, rigidly delineated forms of building construction. Here dematerialisation of the solid paradoxically revealed the liquid as a palpably solid form, a tangible drop in the ceiling, heavy with water. The first act of the adventurous on entering the exhibition was to go over to poke at it.

SURFACE

The ceiling had both moved and dropped to just above head height. In the spirit of the Baroque, *Purity and Tolerance* distorted conventional surface, to the extent that it challenged the notion of 'ceiling' as a distinct element in the first place. The wobbling, moving, highly reflective material worked as a distorted mirror to the entire space, holding and engaging the eye in an unfamiliar manner in watching its workings, like a topsy-turvy, undulating surface of water.

In *Dirt is Matter out of Place*, we used the feathering to challenge the separate-

4 See Katherine Shonfield, *Walls Have Feelings*, London, Routledge, 2000, Chapter 1.

5 Katherine Shonfield, 'Purity and Tolerance: How Pollution Taboos Affect Building Construction', *AA Files*, Autumn 1994, no. 28, pp. 34–40.

Katherine Shonfield

ness of the architectural elements: floor, distinct from wall, distinct from ceiling, distinct from interior fittings. The singularity of the feathered covering – in both the sense of 'peculiar' and 'single' – unified the space. This attempt was made in direct imitation of the way the Baroque fuses the myriad elements of Classicism – column, entablature, capital – into one spatial whole. The Baroque is an appropriate model for us, as it too uses architecture to convey a conscious message over and beyond itself – that is, that religious redemption is beyond the reach of rationality. The Baroque attacks the *form* of rationality, expressed by Classicism, whereas Classicism reduces architecture to a set of known parts, where the whole is the sum of these parts.

WHITENESS

White is a quasi-universal signifier of purity. *Purity and Tolerance* made use of white's unifying possibilities to obscure the distinction between the three parts of the installation – bulgy ceiling, films and text written on the windows.

In *Dirt is Matter out of Place*, the feathers were an attempt to use an unclean white, a white from an animal source which would, and did, decay and putrefy. The feathers were themselves acquired from a place of purification, the London Feather Company. A single-storey red-brick box successfully hides a triple height interior crammed with giant transparent tubes in which millions of feathers dance and twirl their way to purification. The underlying smell of suppressed animal, like shit partially masked by lavatory cleaner, pervades.

We grossly underestimated the number of feathers needed – thirty or more immense bags were dragged into the underground toilet, each to be painstakingly picked over. All but the purest white were rejected. The lavatory was scrubbed down and dried. We tried several glues. The thickest white wallpaper paste worked, the feathers were embedded within it forming a newly homogeneous skin over the entire surface of the interior space.

POST-THEORETICAL READINGS: PROJECTS SPEAKING BACK

Robin Evans once said that there was no point in doing a drawing if you already knew at the outset how it was going to turn out.

In *Dirt is Matter Out of Place*, only afterwards did it occur that the wallpaper paste was like a white tar. In Northern Ireland, perceived transgressors, especially women, have until quite recently been stripped, covered with tar and then rolled in feathers, and paraded in this symbolically transgressive state, neither human nor

Katherine Shonfield

animal, through the streets. In the name of architecture, we were tarring and feathering the lavatory beyond recognisability, beyond any functional use, beyond familiar spatial understanding. The difference was that we used white on white. Amongst the other categories smeared was the distinction between skin, the original surface, the black tar and the final layer of feathers – the process of what we had actually done itself became unrecognisable. Some read the increasing stink of the feathers as an olefactory counterpoint to the normative operations of architecture, with its unstated assumptions of a human rationality and order superior to mere animal mortality.

Purity and Tolerance surprised by its marked similarity to a pregnant belly, heavy, amorphous, ever-changing and unmissably present. Visitors linked this explicitly with the project's discourse on sanitary towels and the containment of blood. For them, the installation explored quite particular aspects of architecture – that is, the experience of blood, and its containment or otherwise as part of the female's unique apprenticeship into the spatial oppositions of the solid, the liquid and the unavoidable reality of the amorphous.

Katherine Shonfield

bloom

The RIBA Architecture Centre organised an event called *Fused* which looked at collaborations between architects and artists. The curators arranged for us to meet on a blind date because we share an interest in light. We had a coffee and looked at slides of each other's work. One common element was a fascination with the way in which natural and artificial light could be brought into play with each other. We talked about the possibility of using light to create space.

Each collaborating partnership was asked to locate a new work within the RIBA headquarters. The building has the closed, casket-like monumentality of a professional institute. We were offered a large room with high ceilings on the first floor. It has tall windows overlooking Portland Place. This room is usually used as a gallery with the blinds closed, the walls lined with drawings and the floor crowded with plinths for models. A wooden floor surrounded by a marble frame reinforces the grand, static quality of the space.

Figure 3.1 Niall McLaughlin and Martin Richman, *Bloom*, 1997.

Figure 3.2 Niall McLaughlin and
Martin Richman, *Bloom*, 1997.

Niall McLaughlin and Martin Richman

Figure 3.3 Niall McLaughlin and
Martin Richman, *Bloom*, 1997.

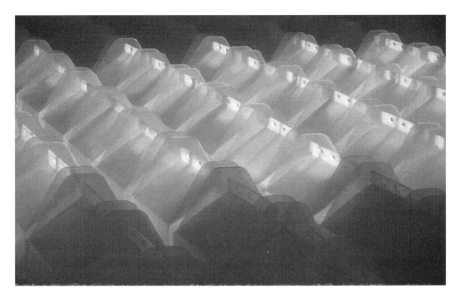

We experienced an early problem when we began to discuss the project. Both of us had a propensity to suggest fully-fledged ideas for interventions in the space. This stopped us from developing a single idea together. We decided to draw back from this by making separate lists of qualities that the space might have, but without making any proposals for how these would be achieved. The two lists displayed a remarkable consensus of ideas.

Figure 3.4 Niall McLaughlin and
Martin Richman, *Bloom*, 1997.

We emptied the room, pulled up the blinds and opened the windows. We found ourselves in a high, sunlit gallery open to the street. We talked about making a low field of light which would follow the form of the floor. This would have a relationship with the changing level of natural light outside. We wanted to make something within the room that would be manifest on the street.

Figure 3.5 Niall McLaughlin and Martin Richman, *Bloom*, 1997.

Niall McLaughlin and Martin Richman

1 C. Woodward, *The Buildings of Europe: Rome,* Manchester and New York, Manchester University Press, 1995.

2 Ibid., p. 78.

This would not shout out from the façade but might be subtly revealed. We remembered a passage from Christopher Woodward's *The Buildings of Europe: Rome* in which he describes the Pallazzo Farnese by Michelangelo.[1] The building is now the French Embassy and is closed to the public. Woodward suggests that visitors who want to see the fine ceilings should stand outside at dusk and watch the lights coming on.[2] We enjoyed the oblique nature of this experience. In our proposal, we imagined that angled mirrors on the ceiling of the space would reflect a field of light on the floor, making the installation visible to passers-by on the pavement below.

It was necessary for the piece to find a balance between abstraction and figuration. We needed a grain or a texture for the work. We searched for something that would have the qualities of both a field and a found object. We chanced upon a mail order catalogue for gardening accessories which had flat-pack 'cosy cloches' – small translucent polycarbonate structures for keeping frost off plants. When these simple forms were arrayed, complex geometries emerged.

Figure 3.6 Niall McLaughlin and Martin Richman, *Bloom,* 1997.

Niall McLaughlin and Martin Richman

We sent off for some cloches and began experimenting by lighting them internally, standing them in sunlight and creating groups. We tried out various light sources, gauging how they responded to daylight. Ultraviolet light provided an extraordinary range of conditions as the day changed. It was muted at midday and built up to a great violet haze at night. At dusk it shifted between mauve, pink and blue. In order to visually unify the cloches we arranged them in a grid format, setting them on to a bed of Daz detergent on the floor. The Daz fluoresced under the UV light, animating the space between the cloches.

Figure 3.7 Niall McLaughlin and Martin Richman, *Bloom*, 1997.

Niall McLaughlin and Martin Richman

Constructing the cloches and wiring the lamps took about a week. Many people came to help and we remember clusters of volunteers, like fishermen mending nets, sitting in a maze of cables and swathes of tinfoil on the floor. There was a picnic atmosphere in the room. In production line fashion, electrical tasks were divided into parties of screwers and strippers. There was a real concern throughout the week that the power circuits in the building could not support the number of lamps. We spent our time negotiating with safety men.

Figure 3.8 Niall McLaughlin and Martin Richman, *Bloom*, 1997.

Niall McLaughlin and Martin Richman

The Daz had to align perfectly with the edge of the marble surround and credit cards turned out to be the best way of achieving a neat line. Half way through the final day, we found out about the two kinds of Daz. Proctor & Gamble had decided to discontinue the old blue whitener in Daz and replace it with all white Daz. The bar codes and boxes for each kind were identical. All white Daz doesn't fluoresce, we could tell this because we had bought a hundred kilos of each type. With hours to go Niall, in his opening night suit, had to take a taxi to every Tesco Metro in central London and demand to inspect their Daz. Every box on every shelf was opened, paid for and removed only if it was the right type. Niall still fluoresces on opening nights.

Figure 3.9 Niall McLaughlin and Martin Richman, *Bloom*, 1997.

Niall McLaughlin and Martin Richman

Figure 3.10 Niall McLaughlin
and Martin Richman, *Bloom*,
1997.

Niall McLaughlin and Martin Richman

The sun moved over the cloches during the day, casting shadows of tall window mullions on to repeating white gables. In late afternoon, colours began to emerge from within the structures. At dusk there was a balance of internal and ambient light. Then the whole thing began to glow, flooding the street with violet light. *Bloom* was in place for a month and the perfume of detergent filled the building.

Figure 3.11 Niall McLaughlin and Martin Richman, *Bloom*, 1997.

Niall McLaughlin and Martin Richman

For us this was a sensory occupation of the space. It carried no explicit meaning. An elderly visitor to the opening demanded to know how it should be understood. He had a faintly glowing patch of Daz on the tip of his nose.

Figure 3.12 Niall McLaughlin and Martin Richman, *Bloom*, 1997.

weather architecture

(BERLIN 1929–30, BARCELONA 1986–, BARCELONA 1999–)

FATHER FIGURES

1 R. Banham, *Age of the Masters: A Personal View of Modern Architecture*, London, Architectural Press, 1975, p. 3. First published, without the introduction from which this and the following quotations derive, as *Guide to Modern Architecture*, London, Architectural Press, 1962.

Reyner Banham discusses his relationship with modernism and its architects in the introduction of *Age of the Masters*: 'I had the good luck to meet all of them – Le Corbusier, Frank Lloyd Wright, Walter Gropius, Richard Neutra, Mies van der Rohe – and for me, as for three generations of architects, they were father-figures who commanded awe and suspicion, affection, respect and the normal pains of the generation gap.'[1] The masters referred to in the book's title are the heroes of modernism and, in this quotation, their inferiors are other architects and architectural critics. Later on the same page Banham writes: 'Architecture must move with the times because it helps to create the times . . . It is more than a commentary on the human condition – along with war and peace and love and death and pestilence and birth, abundance, disaster and the air we breathe, it is the human condition.'[2] According to Banham, architecture is a heroic endeavour made by architects, guided by the masters:

2 Ibid., p. 3.

> *If, at the present time, many of us (including architects) begin to doubt if architecture has the resources to accomplish the tasks which its times demand, and to which the ambitions of the Masters committed it, one should note that architects seem to be the only people to notice that some of these tasks even exist, let alone might be accomplished. Their arrogance is appalling, but also encouraging. The demand of the Masters of the Modern Movement that architecture should respond unreservedly to the present time, however deep its roots were struck in past traditions, has forced their followers to accept moral responsibility for virtually the whole of the human environment.*[3]

3 Ibid., p. 4.

Banham recognises, however, that the moral authority of the architect, a tradition he associates in the twentieth century with modernism, has been under question since 1960: 'The gravest of all doubts was whether – or how – architects could continue to sustain their traditional role as form-givers, creators and controllers of human environments.'[4]

4 Ibid., p. 5.

THE DENIAL AND CONTROL OF THE USER

It is rare today to find a belief in the moral authority of the architect equivalent to that expressed in modernism and *Age of the Masters*, but the hierarchy of architect and user is evident in the discourse of architects even if it is expressed with less conviction. To acquire social status and financial security architects need a defined area of

Jonathan Hill

knowledge, with precise contents and limits, in which they can prove expertise. One of the aims of the architectural profession is to further the idea that only architects make buildings and spaces that deserve the title architecture, suggesting that the user is predictable and has no part in the creation of architecture.[5]

The user is an important consideration in the architect's design process. But the user is also a threat to the architect because the user's actions may undermine the architect's claim to be the sole author of architecture. Two related ideas maintain the hierarchy of the architect and the user. The first, the denial of the user, assumes that the building need not be occupied for it to be recognised as architecture, and the second, the control of the user, attributes to the user forms of behaviour acceptable to the architect. To imply that they can predict the use of a building, architects appropriate models of experience, such as functionalist theory and the contemplation of art, that suggest a manageable and passive user, unable to transform use, space and meaning.[6]

THE BARCELONA PAVILIONS

The denial and control of the user, and the assumption that a building is an artwork to be contemplated, are exemplified in the history of the Barcelona

5 This is a claim architects make in many countries: in Britain, for example. Two bodies, the Architects Registration Board and the Royal Institute of British Architects, now define the architectural profession in Britain. In 1999 *Building Design* reported that 'The ARB wants new legislation to extend the scope of the 1997 Architects Act, which it feels is inadequate because it only protects the title "architect". The ARB wants the act to be extended to cover "architecture" and "architectural" – which are not protected at present.' David Rock, at that time RIBA President, supported the ARB's proposal. M. Fairs, 'ARB Seeks New Powers', *Building Design*, 15 January 1999, p. 3.

6 In this chapter the experience of the building is a reference point to compare architecture to the experience of other objects and spaces. But the more an experience associated primarily with another discipline but part of the experience of buildings, such as contemplation, excludes other types of use, the less a building is architecture. An object or space not usually considered to be architecture, such as artwork, is architecture if the experience of it is similar to that usually expected of the building.

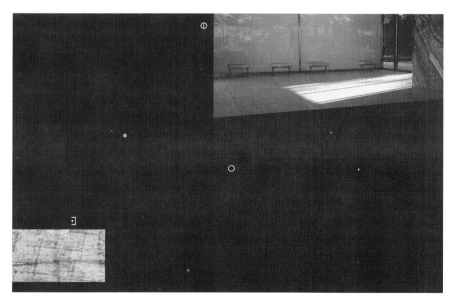

Figure 4.1 Jonathan Hill, *An Original Copy*, 1998. Berlin 3.06pm 12 December 1929 – Barcelona 3.06pm 12 December 1999. Travertine Wall: frost (Be); White Glass Wall: one-tenth cloud cover (Be), clear sky (Ba).

7 To distinguish one building from another, I use terms such as the 1929, or first, Pavilion, and the 1986, or second, Pavilion. The 1986 Pavilion is also referred to as the reconstruction. To refer to the project's complete history and various forms I use either Barcelona Pavilion or Pavilion.

8 W. Benjamin, 'Theses on the Philosophy of History', in W. Benjamin, *Illuminations: Essays and Reflections*, ed. H. Arendt, trans. H. Zohn, New York, Schocken Books, 1969, p. 255.

9 I. Solà Morales, C. Cirici and F. Ramos, *Mies van der Rohe: Barcelona Pavilion*, Barcelona, Editorial Gustavo Gili, 1993, p. 21.

Pavilion.[7] Histories are provisional and selective. The past is continuously remade to suit the present: 'For every image of the past that is not recognized by the present as one of its own concerns threatens to disappear irretrievably.'[8] Designed by Mies van der Rohe, the first Pavilion was built for an exhibition in 1929. Dismantled early in 1930, its various elements were dispersed or destroyed:

> The company that had supplied the marble, Köstner und Gottschalk, took charge of it for possible reuse. The chromed steel structures were also sent back to Berlin for a possible reutilization or resale, to help offset the deficit created by the Pavilion. The steel structure was sold off for scrap in Barcelona, and was almost certainly the only part of the structure to remain – but now unrecognizable – in the city. The unobtrusive foundations were covered over by a modest garden, planted with palm trees, which must have been laid out after the Civil War and remained that way for some fifty years. A small piece of the onyx did service as a table top in Dr Ruegenberg's home in Berlin; in Mies' apartment in Chicago, the metal structure from one of the ottoman stools supported a slab of marble to provide an occasional table. Philip C. Johnson, the first American admirer of the work of Mies van der Rohe, managed to acquire one of the armchairs to enrich his collection of 20th century art.[9]

Figure 4.2 Jonathan Hill, *An Original Copy*, 1998. Berlin 2.55pm 18 December 1929 – Barcelona 2.55pm 18 December 1999. Large Pool: calm (Ba), clear sky (Ba); Small Pool: snow (Be), clear sky (Ba); External Travertine Floor: fog (Be), clear sky (Ba).

Jonathan Hill

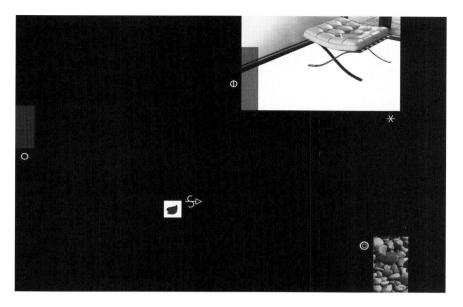

Figure 4.3 Jonathan Hill, *An Original Copy*, 1998. Berlin 11.09am 22 December 1929 – Barcelona 11.09am 22 December 1999. Large Pool: calm (Ba); Small Pool: clear sky (Ba); Internal Travertine Floor: snow (Be), one-tenth cloud cover (Be), storm (Be).

One expects an exhibition building to be demolished but this cool and melancholy inventory recalls the casual dissection of a body donated to a medical school or a family picking over the trivial possessions of a deceased relative. In a similar spirit Rem Koolhaas constructs an alternative history of the Pavilion in which, after a short period as a headquarters for the Anarchists, it is repatriated to Germany. The reunion with one father was, however, accompanied by the loss of another: 'It was now an architectural orphan: its creator had just left for the USA.'[10] In Berlin the dismembered components of the Pavilion were reused: 'Next the marble was incorporated in the construction of a ministry, where it became the floor of the service entrance.'[11] After the war the remaining elements of the Pavilion were unpacked: 'First the planners of the east side of the city suggested reassembling the entire pavilion as a gas station, for the time when each worker would own a car.'[12] Finally 'the fragments were exported in return for one medium-sized computer and a secret design for a new machine gun'.[13] In Koolhaas' fiction the final fate of the Pavilion is ambiguous. It is unclear whether the fragments were reassembled into a whole.

In 1986, Ignasi de Solà Morales, Christian Cirici and Fernando Ramos supervised the construction of a second Pavilion on the site of the first one. The materials of the 1929 Pavilion did not always follow Mies' design. For example, on the exterior side and rear walls, plastered brick painted green and yellow was used instead of green Alpine marble and travertine.[14] Solà Morales, Cirici and Ramos' intention was to recreate as faithfully as possible the 1929 Pavilion, but with improvements where

10 OMA, R. Koolhaas and B. Mau, 'Less is More', in OMA, R. Koolhaas and B. Mau, *S, M, L, XL*, ed. Jennifer Sigler, New York, Monacelli, 1995, p. 54.

11 Ibid., p. 56.

12 Ibid., p. 59.

13 Ibid., p. 61.

14 Solà Morales, Cirici and Ramos, op. cit., p. 14.

Jonathan Hill

15 Ibid., p. 29.

necessary in construction and in building those parts of the design either compromised by economic restrictions or never completed.[15]

Is the 1986 Pavilion a historical monument, a copy or a new building? A historical monument is representative of a particular time, and rarely allowed to change or age. A building may be restored a number of times and still be considered a historical monument but a copy is less likely to be given such a status. If the first Pavilion still existed it would be the historical monument. The reconstruction occupies the original

16 Ibid., pp. 38–9.

site and its architects wish it to be recognised as a historical monument even though they also describe it as a replica and reinterpretation of the 1929 Pavilion.[16]

THE BARCELONA PHOTOGRAPHS

The photographs that established the reputation of the Pavilion only record the parts of the 1929 building that followed Mies' design. Photographs of the other parts of the

17 Ibid., p. 15.

1929 Pavilion do not remain and may not have been taken.[17] The subject of the reconstruction is the design as it appears in the original photographs, as much as the building constructed in 1929. As in many respects the reconstruction is closer to the design than the first Pavilion, it is the truer monument to the architect's intentions.

The architectural photograph has a number of roles, two of which are contradictory: to present the architectural object as a higher form of cultural production so as to defend and promote architects and patrons, and to further the absorption of buildings and architects into consumer culture. Many architectural photographs have the same characteristics, such as blue skies and no people, because they mimic the perfect but sterile viewing conditions of the art gallery and product literature. The reputation of an architect is, in part, dependent on his or her ability to generate a good photograph. If an architect is successful the same image is published throughout the world, to be copied by other architects with little regard to cultural or social

18 J. P. Bonta, *Architecture and its Interpretation*, London, Lund and Humphries, 1979, p. 148.

differences.

Juan Pablo Bonta writes: 'The effect of the Barcelona Pavilion over the physical or social environment in the hills of Montjuich was negligible; its effect as an idea spread over the entire world by means of photographs and descriptions was enorm-

19 Solà Morales, Cirici and Ramos dispute Bonta's claim that the 1929 Pavilion did not receive favourable reports at the time of its construction. Solà Morales, Cirici and Ramos, op. cit., p. 12. Bonta, op. cit., p. 134.

ous.'[18] Between the demolition of the first Pavilion in 1930 and the construction of the second in 1986, the Pavilion became one of the most praised and copied architectural projects of the twentieth century.[19] The 1929 photographs, as much as the 1929 building, were copied. To realise the extent of the appropriation we just need to visualise the Pavilion with petrol pumps on its forecourt, a cashpoint machine in the wall or a barbecue by the pool. The extent of this copying is due not only to the quality of the design, and Mies' growing reputation, but also the Pavilion's status as an artwork.

THE CONTEMPLATION OF ART

In an attempt to maintain and reproduce the aura of art and the artist, which despite protestations to the contrary still maintains a hold over the familiar perception of art, the art institution requires precise codes of behaviour, particularly reverence.[20] Authority, value and the desired interpretation of an artwork are disseminated through publications, reviews and the codes of the space in which it is consumed. Protected against heat, light and decay, an artwork is usually seen at most a few times, but may have a second and equally powerful existence in memory. Although other experiences are possible, the artwork in the gallery is primarily experienced in contemplation: a form of visual awareness, of a single object by a single absorbed viewer, in which sound, smell and touch are as far as possible eradicated.[21] Contemplation reinforces the hierarchy of the senses that is the basis of western culture. Juhani Pallasmaa writes:

> Since the Greeks, philosophical writings of all times abound with ocular metaphors to the point that knowledge has become analogous with clear vision and light the metaphor for truth ... During the Renaissance the five senses were understood to form a hierarchical system from the highest sense of vision down to touch ... The invention of perspectival representation made the eye the centre of the perceptual world as well as of the concept of the self.[22]

Contemplation encourages an empathetic relationship between the viewer and the viewed. Walter Benjamin identifies concentration as a quality of contemplation: 'Art demands concentration from the spectator ... A man who concentrates before a work of art is absorbed by it. He enters into this work of art the way legend tells of the Chinese painter when he viewed his finished painting.'[23]

THE CONTEMPLATION OF ARCHITECTURE

If a building is of sufficient quality it is usually described as the work of a single archi-tect, most often the principal partner of an architectural firm, even though a number of architects will have been involved in its design. A building by a more commercial

20 W. Benjamin, 'The Work of Art in the Age of Mechanical Production', in Benjamin, op. cit., p. 221.

21 Ibid. p. 240.

22 J. Pallasmaa, *The Eyes of the Skin: Architecture and the Senses*, London, Academy Editions, 1996, pp. 6–7.

23 Benjamin, 'The Work of Art', in Benjamin, op. cit., p. 239.

Jonathan Hill

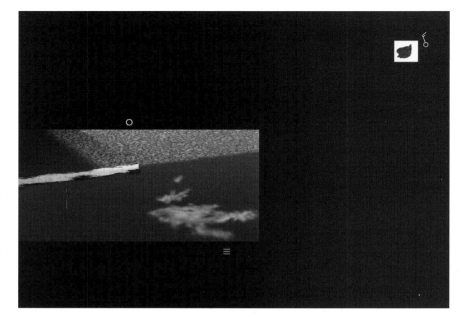

Figure 4.4 Jonathan Hill, *An Original Copy*, 1998. Berlin 10.32am 2 January 1930 – Barcelona 10.32am 2 January 2000. Large Pool: fog (Be), 13 knot east wind (Be), clear sky (Ba).

24 L. Lefaivre and A. Tzonis, 'The Question of Autonomy in Architecture', *The Harvard Architecture Review*, vol. 3, Winter 1984, p. 27.

25 R. Venturi, *Complexity and Contradiction in Architecture*, New York, Museum of Modern Art, 1966. C. Jencks, *The Language of Post-Modern Architecture*, London, Academy Editions, 1977. C. Rowe and F. Koetter, *Collage City*, Cambridge, Mass., MIT Press, 1979. W. Curtis, *Modern Architecture Since 1900*, London, Phaidon, 1982.

architectural firm is less likely to be identified with an individual architect. In practice the production of a building is a collaborative process involving a team of architects, structural engineers, contractors, quantity surveyors, the client and others in negotiation with various statutory bodies. However, the idea of sole authorship is important to architects because of the long-held, often false, assumption that art is the product of individual creativity. For architects, the classification of architecture as not just an art, but as an art similar to painting and sculpture, is desirable because of the high status accorded to gallery-based art and artists. To affirm the status of the architect, the experience of the building is equated with the contemplation of the artwork in a gallery, a condition disturbed by the irreverent presence of the user.

Sometimes architecture is described as an autonomous, self-referential practice.[24] Based on art history, architectural histories often discuss the building as an object of artistic contemplation and imply that this is the familiar experience of the building.[25] The photograph acts as the mediator between the writer and the reader, who is encouraged to assume that the experience of the photograph is the same as the experience of the building. The object of architectural discussion is often the photograph, not the building, because the former, not the latter, most closely fulfils

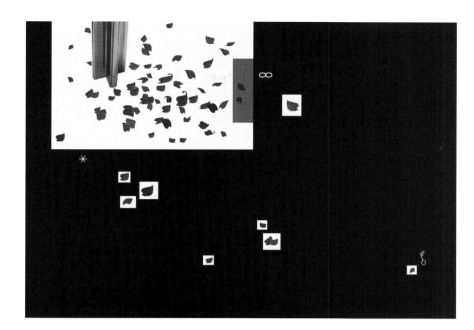

Figure 4.5 Jonathan Hill, *An Original Copy*, 1998. Berlin 10.03am 14 January 1930 – Barcelona 10.03am 14 January 2000. Internal Travertine Floor: snow (Be), 23 knot east wind (Be), haze (Be).

the desires and expectations of the architect and the architectural historian for an object of artistic contemplation.

Writing in 1974, Malcolm Quantrill states that the absence of people from the 1929 photographs, and the fact that this had not been noticed, indicates that 'A whole generation of architects and architectural photographers sought to abstract the art content from the life context.'[26] Of the six points Bonta identifies as characteristic of the canonical interpretation of the Pavilion, five refer to specific formal, spatial and aesthetic qualities. The sixth states that the Pavilion's status as a work of art and an architectural masterpiece are synonymous with each other.[27] Solà Morales, Cirici and Ramos state that the purpose of the reconstruction is to allow the building, rather than the photograph, to be experienced but the experience they describe is contemplation, in which the visitor is absorbed by the artwork: 'It is necessary to go there, to walk amidst and see the startling contrast between the building and its surroundings, to let your gaze be drawn into the calligraphy of the patterned marble and its kaleidoscopic figures, to feel yourself enmeshed in a system of planes in stone, glass and water that envelops and moves you through space, and contemplate the hard, emphatic play of Kolbe's bronze dancer over water.'[28]

26 M. Quantrill, *Ritual and Response in Architecture*, London, Lund Humphries, 1974, p. 105.

27 The six points are: flowing space; the free plan; the building as the object on exhibition; stylistic similarities to classicism, De Stijl, a Japanese sense of lightness, Wright, constructivism and cubism; the politics of Germany; the Pavilion as a work of art and architectural masterpiece. Bonta, op. cit., pp. 139–40.

28 Solà Morales, Cirici and Ramos, op. cit., p. 39.

Jonathan Hill

29 Bonta, op. cit., pp. 139–40. M. Tafuri, 'The Stage as "Virtual City": From Fuchs to the Totaltheater', in M. Tafuri, *The Sphere and the Labyrinth*, trans. P. d'Acierno and R. Connolly. Cambridge, Mass., MIT Press, 1987, p. 111.

30 J. Quetglas, 'Fear of Glass: The Barcelona Pavilion', trans. S. Allen, B. Colomina and M. Marratt, in B. Colomina (ed.) *Architectureproduction*, New York, Princeton Architectural Press, 1988, pp. 134–5.

31 Ibid., p. 134.

32 M. Tafuri and F. Dal Co, *Modern Architecture: Vol. 1*, trans. R. Wolf, London, Faber and Faber, 1986, p. 157, quoted in J. Wall, *Dan Graham's Kammerspiel*, Toronto, Art Metropole, 1991, p. 51.

33 R. Evans, 'Mies van der Rohe's Paradoxical Symmetries', in R. Evans, *Translations from Drawing to Building and Other Essays*, London, Architectural Association, 1997, p. 258.

34 Ibid., p. 251.

35 W. Blaser, *Mies van der Rohe: The Art of Structure*, New York, Whitney Library of Design, 1994, p. 26.

Bonta identifies flowing space and the free plan as two of the six points of the canonical interpretation of the Pavilion but more recent readings suggest that it prescribes movement.[29] The 1929 photographs are black-and-white; those in Solà Morales, Cirici and Ramos' book on the reconstruction are colour. However, the views they show are similar, in part no doubt due to Solà Morales, Cirici and Ramos' desire to show the similarity of the reconstruction and the 1929 photographs. However, another reason for the similarity of the two sets of photographs is that Mies' principal concern was vision rather than the other senses. Jose Quetglas writes: 'Mies's architecture is . . . formulated more by representations than by plastic realities.'[30] He adds that the Pavilion is intended 'to remain empty'.[31] Of another project by Mies, the 1935 design of the Hubbe House in Magdeburg, Tafuri and Francesco Dal Co write: 'The interpenetration between indoor and outdoors was treated as illusory: with no trouble at all, nature could be replaced by a photomontage . . . and become an object of contemplation.'[32] Recognising that the symmetry of the Pavilion is horizontal,[33] Robin Evans writes: 'Whether seascape, prairie, or desert, a vast and vacant scene tends to concentrate visual interest on the horizon. The same thing happens in the Barcelona Pavilion, as it does in many of Mies's buildings.'[34] However, unlike some other buildings by Mies, for example the Hubbe House, the Pavilion does not focus on the landscape. Werner Blaser lists the Pavilion under 'Court houses with steel columns' in *Mies van der Rohe: The Art of Structure*.[35] The horizon is within the Pavilion, and the gaze inward; the Pavilion is the object on view.

The Pavilion is an architectural icon, not only because it is seductive and much copied, but also because it has most often been perceived in conditions similar to that of the artwork. Between 1929 and 1930 it was an exhibition building to be viewed, between 1930 and 1986 it was known through photographs, and since 1986 the reconstruction's status as exhibit, gallery and historical monument discourages everyday use. The history of the Pavilion implies that contemplation is the experience most appropriate to buildings, affirming the authority of the architect and denying that of the user. It is possible to experience a building in circumstances similar to the contemplation of art, when visiting a famous building, for example, but contemplation is neither the familiar way to experience the building nor, on its own, a positive one.

WATER LILIES IN THE GERMAN PAVILION

As Solà Morales, Cirici and Ramos say they wish to be faithful to the 1929 Pavilion it is interesting to see what they ignored:

> As for the presence of floral elements, it is apparent that the large pool was planted with water lilies, which in due course covered its entire surface, even causing maintenance problems, while we know that the smaller pond did not contain any kind of vegetation. The more naturalistic treatment of the larger, more open and exposed pool, whose surface was continually ruffled by the breeze, was designed to contrast with the dark, sombre mineral severity of the enclosed area of the smaller pond, where the high walls controlled the access of daylight, creating hard, sharply defined geometries of light and shade far removed from any kind of natural vitalism.[36]

The water lilies are absent from the 1986 Pavilion. As Solà Morales, Cirici and Ramos attempted to resolve other technical problems, I assume that the water lilies were not planted because they would introduce life to the 1986 Pavilion, and an awareness of time, occupation and climate; all incompatible with the experience of a contemplative artwork.

Although now commonly known as the Barcelona Pavilion, it was commissioned by the Weimar Republic and built as the German Pavilion for the Barcelona International Exposition. Solà Morales, Cirici and Ramos state:

> On the day of the inauguration, in the speech Alfonso XIII gave in reply to that of the German commissioner, the king specifically alluded, almost ironically, to German industriousness and efficiency – qualities that had been demonstrated in completing in such an incredibly short time a building such as the one he was opening ... The speech by Dr Schnitzler, German general commissioner for the Barcelona International Exposition, was a wholehearted manifestation of the New Objectivity, taking the Pavilion's formal clarity and aesthetic rigour as a metaphor for the new German spirit.[37]

Although its relationship to Germany is a concern of critics and it is now commonly named after Barcelona, the Pavilion is more often associated with international modernism than a particular nation or city.[38] However, in denying the 'widely received idea, very much in line with the interpretation of Mies' architecture in the fifties, that saw the Barcelona Pavilion as a prototype',[39] Solà Morales, Cirici and Ramos argue that it has a precise relationship to its site and, by implication, to Barcelona.

36 Solà Morales, Cirici and Ramos, op. cit., p. 19.

37 Ibid., p. 20.

38 Quetglas, op. cit., p. 150. Evans, op. cit., pp. 236–8.

39 Solà Morales, Cirici and Ramos, op. cit., p. 28.

Jonathan Hill

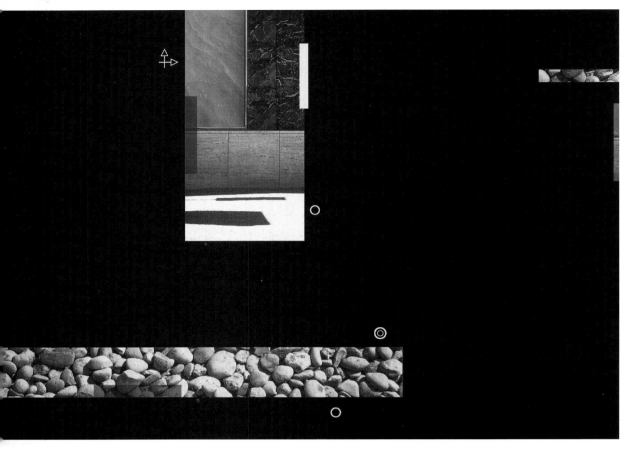

Figure 4.6 Jonathan Hill, *An Original Copy*, 1998. Berlin 3.39pm 20 January 1930 – Barcelona 3.39pm 20 January 2000. Large Pool: calm (Ba), clear sky (Ba); External Glass Wall: drifting snow (Be), clear sky (Ba).

It is possible that one of the purposes of the reconstruction is to emphasise the Pavilion's relationship to Barcelona and disregard its connections to Germany, Spain and internationalism. Two masts, 15.5m high, were placed symmetrically in front of the 1929 Pavilion. The German flag flew from one mast, the Spanish flag from the other. The size of the flags, each measuring 6m × 9m, gave them special prominence. The masts were rebuilt but the flags are absent in all the photographs of the 1986 Pavilion in the book by Solà Morales, Cirici and Ramos.

AN ORIGINAL COPY

Architects are caught in a vicious circle; in order to emphasise their idea of architecture they often adopt techniques, forms and materials already identified with the

Figure 4.7 Jonathan Hill, *An Original Copy*, 1998. Berlin 1.56pm 10 February 1930 – Barcelona 1.56pm 10 February 2000. Large Pool: calm (Ba), clear sky (Ba); Small Pool: ice (Be), calm (Ba), clear sky (Ba).

work of architects, and learn little from other disciplines. Instead, from art I take the principle that a space can be made of anything,[40] and from situationism the idea that architecture can consist of ephemeral conditions and appropriations. A defining role of the building is to provide shelter. In contrast to the unpredictable weather outside, the building provides a controlled climate inside. The exclusion of weather is a fundamental purpose of the building. But I use weather as an architectural material First, as a metaphor of the outside pouring into the discipline of architecture and, second, to introduce what is absent from the 1986 Pavilion: habitual occupation, Germany and the passage of time. My transformation of the 1986 Pavilion makes a copy original by mimicking the weather in Germany between the start of the construction of the first Pavilion in March 1929 and its demolition in February 1930. The source of the German weather is Berlin, the site of Mies' office in 1929. Its new location is the 1986 Pavilion. The weather on a specific day in Berlin between the construction and

[40] The critique of contemplation is another valuable development in art.

Jonathan Hill

demolition of the first Pavilion will be repeated within the reconstruction on the same day every year from 1999 onwards. For example, the weather in Berlin on 3 December 1929 will be repeated in Barcelona every 3 December.

Articles on the Pavilion mention its sensuality and cold purity, implying that these two terms are not mutually exclusive.[41] The weather conditions I insert into the 1986 Pavilion combine sensuality and coldness, such as frost, fog, snow and ice. All the transformations result in a temperature reduction but some are more visible than others. Snow on the travertine floor is seen immediately but the chilled surface of the red onyx wall, created by cooling elements concealed within it, is perceived more by touch than sight.

German weather is not inserted consistently throughout the reconstruction. The montage of different weather conditions and the 1986 Pavilion creates an ever-changing space that enlivens and disturbs the habitual nature of architectural experience. For example, like Mies' design, my transformation of the Pavilion, *An Original Copy*, emphasises the distinct qualities of the two pools.[42] On a day, such as 10 February, when the temperature in 1929–30 Berlin dropped below freezing but remains above freezing in present-day Barcelona, one pool freezes, but the other remains liquid. As it is difficult to clearly see from one pool to the other, the juxtaposition is not experienced immediately, making the gap between the pools appear larger than it is, both in time and distance.[43]

THE CREATIVE USER

The drawings of *An Original Copy* combine notation familiar in weather maps and architectural drawings.[44] A weather map records or predicts the weather; the status of the meteorologist is based on the accuracy of his or her prediction. The architectural drawing is both an instruction and a prediction. The ability of the architect to predict the form of a building is more accurate than that of the meteorologist to predict the weather, but the architect's ability to predict use is especially uncertain.

I wish, however, to make a number of predictions. First, the juxtaposition of the German weather of 1929–30, the 1986 Pavilion, and the weather in present-day Barcelona will disturb the current experience of the reconstruction as an object of contemplation. Second, the introduction of German weather into the 1986 Pavilion will make it decay, which is expected of the building but not the artwork. Third, the inhabitants of Barcelona will start to inhabit the 1986 Pavilion, and the weather within it, making the Pavilion less art and more architecture. The experience of a building

41 Tafuri, op. cit., pp. 111–12. Quetglas, op. cit., pp. 133–4. Evans, op. cit., pp. 255–7.

42 Solà Morales, Cirici and Ramos, op. cit., p. 19.

43 The montage of gaps structures the composition of the drawings of *An Original Copy* and the project they describe.

44 The drawings mimic photographs in architectural magazines but the disruptive presence of the German weather, and the gaps in the drawings, suggest a space of appropriation rather than contemplation.

depends on the way it is managed as well as designed. *An Original Copy* is intended to disturb the management of the 1986 Pavilion as well as the space itself.

An Original Copy refutes the assumption that contemplation is the most appropriate way to experience the building and questions function's role as a guiding principle of the design and use of buildings. Instead, it argues that the building that is most suggestive and open to appropriation is the one we do not immediately know how to occupy. Neither the building, nor its architect, suggests a use. Instead use is decided by the user. If constructed, *An Original Copy* would no doubt be used in ways I cannot imagine. It is located within another tradition of architectural practice which, in place of the passive user associated with functionalism and contemplation, recognises the creative user with a role as important in the formulation of architecture as that of the architect. To use a building is to alter it, either by physical transformation, occupying it in unexpected ways or conceiving it anew. A carpet of snow can be a bed or become a chair. Architecture is made by use and by design.

Jonathan Hill

David J. Gunkel

what's the matter with architecture?

The question, 'What's the matter with architecture?' may be understood on multiple registers. Taken colloquially, it asks about the current state of architectural practice and its product. Such query always denotes a worry or concern over something that has perhaps gone wrong, become a problem or deviated from accepted norms or anticipated outcomes. At the same time, however, the question may also be understood in a more literal and material sense. In this way, it inquires about the ontological status of architecture's matter, questioning both the subject matter of the discipline and the materiality of its product.

This complex question, which manifests itself in many places and in innumerable ways, is perhaps the query most appropriate to architecture at the beginning of the twenty-first century. It especially matters when, for example, the word 'architecture' has come to be expanded and contorted, applying as it now does to the rhizome structures of information networks, artificial virtual environments and cyberspaces of all kinds and stripes. The question, then, is perhaps most palpable at this moment when, as David Farrell Krell has suggested, architecture has entered into full crisis,[1] posing to itself critical and potentially disturbing questions like Paul Shepheard's 'what is architecture?'[2]

The following does not necessarily provide an answer to the multifaceted question 'what's the matter with architecture?' but endeavours to position the inquiry in such a way that its polysemia resonates and becomes material, as the jurist would say, for the subject matter of architecture. It does so by engaging the work of Ben Nicholson, studio professor of design and theory in the School of Architecture at the Illinois Institute of Technology. Nicholson's projects, which bear the unlikely titles of *Appliance House*, *Loaf House* and *B-52 Pickup*, provide sites where the multifaceted question 'what's the matter with architecture?' is lodged and takes up residence.

1 D. F. Krell, *Architecture: Ecstasies of Space, Time and the Human Body*, Albany, State University of New York Press, 1995, p. 2.

2 P. Shepheard, *What is Architecture?*, Cambridge, MIT Press, 1994.

BLASPHEMER!

3 D. Haraway, *Simians, Cyborgs, and Women: The Reinvention of Nature*, New York, Routledge, 1991, p. 149.

Perhaps more faithful as blasphemy is faithful, than as reverent worship and identification.[3]

It cannot be said that Ben Nicholson is an architect. In fact, stating such a thing is expressly prohibited by law. The prohibition became evident in the summer of 1996, during Nicholson's *Thinking the Unthinkable House* exhibit at the Renaissance Society Gallery on the campus of the University of Chicago. In a publicity essay written for the show, Nicholson was introduced with the following sentence: 'Architect Ben Nicholson has never shared the presumption that there is a truth in architecture.' The sentence

David J. Gunkel

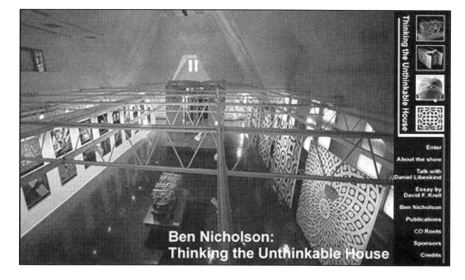

Figure 5.1 Ben Nicholson,
Thinking the Unthinkable House,
1996.[4]

4 B. Nicholson, *Thinking the
Unthinkable House* (CD-ROM),
Chicago, The Renaissance Society at
the University of Chicago, 1996.

caught the eye of an individual in the employ of a well-known architecture firm in Chicago who promptly filed an official complaint (docket #96-12900) with the Illinois Department of Professional Regulation. Nicholson's reply to the IDPR summarises the matter succinctly: 'I am fully aware that the law in Illinois forbids the use of the professional title "architect" to anyone who does not carry a license to practice architecture. I do not make any claim to be an architect, and do not make use of the word on my professional resume . . .'[5]

5 B. Nicholson, Letter to Illinois
Department of Professional
Regulation, 25 May 1996.

This unique episode, which Nicholson accentuates rather than avoids,[6] requires at least two comments. First, the architectural subject and the subject matter of architecture, at least in the United States, is a matter of statutory law. Architect and the practice of architecture have precise legal definitions stipulated by the State Legislature:

6 H. Walker, 'Many a House Hath Yet
to be Built', 1994, in Nicholson,
Thinking the Unthinkable House. M.
Sula, 'Virtual Reality: How to Build the
Unbuildable House', *Chicago Reader*,
6 March 1998, sec. 1, pp. 8–9.

> *305/5. Architect defined; Acts constituting practice. An architect is a person who is qualified by education, training, experience, and examination, and who is licensed under the laws of this State, to practice architecture. The meaning of architecture within the meaning and intent of this Act includes the offering or furnishing of professional services, such as consultation, environmental analysis, feasibility studies, programming, planning, aesthetic and structural design, construction documents consisting of drawings and specifications and other documents required in the construction process, administration of construction contracts, project representation, and construction management, in connection with the construction of any private or public building, building structure, building project, or addition to or alteration or restoration thereof.*

David J. Gunkel

7 Secretary of State, 'The Illinois Architecture Practice Act', in the *Laws of Illinois*, Springfield, Secretary of the State of Illinois, 1989.

8 S. Tigerman, '*(im)measurability: an (after)math*', in B. Nicholson, *Appliance House*, Cambridge, MIT Press, 1990, p. 87.

From the perspective of the official descriptions provided by 'The Illinois Architecture Practice Act of 1989',[7] Nicholson is clearly not an architect. Although his professional training is in architecture and his degrees bear the moniker 'architecture', he does not, properly speaking, create architecture. He has never constructed or provided services related to the construction of a private or public building. And even if one of Nicholson's projects, which according to Stanley Tigerman 'screams out to be built',[8] were actually erected, Nicholson would still not qualify. He does not have a licence, the modern mechanism by which one defines and regulates guild knowledge. What's the matter with Ben Nicholson is that he not only has never constructed anything that could be called a building but is also lacking the guild's official stamp of approval and sign of inclusion.

Second, although Nicholson is not, properly speaking, an architect, whatever he does somehow gets at the very matter of architecture. If Nicholson were merely impersonating an architect, like the fictional personae Art Van Der Leah (aka George Castanza) on the NBC television situation-comedy *Seinfeld*, it would be all too easy to dismiss him. But something Nicholson does or does not do matters profoundly for both architects and architecture. And whatever it is, it has the potential to disturb the entire architectural edifice. So much so, in fact, that licensed architects get pissed off – pissed off enough to write letters, file complaints and police the borders of the discipline. Nicholson's work, whatever it comes to be called, effectively 'terrorizes

9 Ibid., p. 16.

guild knowledge'.[9] Consequently, Nicholson cannot be simply excluded from architecture as a mere outsider or interloper who could be dismissed without a second thought. He occupies a position that is more complex and problematic. His is a unique position that is neither simply outside architecture nor comfortably housed within its hallowed halls.

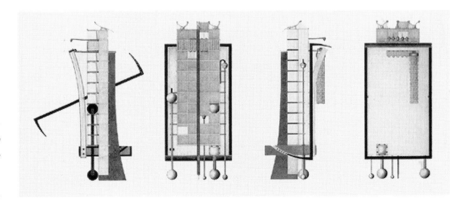

Figure 5.2 Ben Nicholson, *Elevations of the Telemon Cupboard*, 1990.[10]

10 Nicholson, *Appliance House*.

David J. Gunkel

Because of this curious situation that is simultaneously within and without architecture proper, Nicholson's work occupies a critical position that Haraway terms *blasphemy*.[11] Blasphemy, however, is neither mere impiety nor simple sacrilege. Instead, it consists of a kind of excessive faithfulness that 'requires taking things very seriously'.[12] Such extravagant earnestness, however, does not seek to reinforce and to identify with a specific tradition but endeavours to interrogate the traditionalism of the tradition from and within the functioning of its own system. Blasphemy, therefore, is otherwise than apostasy. It is not a mere departure from tradition in order to escape it or to strike against it from the outside. On the contrary, blasphemy is a form of precise and calculated intervention that requires perspicacious attention to the traditions in which and on which it operates. Whereas apostasy designates a mere renunciation and abandonment by which one comes to occupy a position that literally 'stands apart' or is separated from a specific tradition, blasphemy comprises a calculated response that understands, acknowledges and continually works on and over the tradition. Consequently, the blasphemer occupies a curious position that figures the outside in the inside and the inside outside of itself. As such, the blasphemer not only understands the intricacies of guild knowledge but does so to such an extent that s/he becomes capable of fixating upon the problematic but necessary lacunae of its system, exhibiting and employing them in excess of the system to which they initially and must continually belong.

Nicholson's activities and projects, whatever they come to be called, matter for architecture precisely because they blaspheme the very material and substance of architectural practice. The apostate or impostor is easy to detect, discredit and disavow as a mere outsider. The blasphemer, who occupies a position that is neither inside nor outside but somehow in-between, is much more threatening, elusive and dangerous. For this reason, the architectural heretic presents two possible and competing interpretations. From the perspective of architecture, a position that is stipulated and protected by law, such activity cannot but appear to be illegal, disruptive and transgressive. For what is at stake in the blasphemer's various infractions and apparent felonies, defined as such by the traditions of the guild, is the very matter of architecture. From another perspective, however, a perspective situated within the camp of blasphemers, heretics and guild terrorists, such operations are designed to liberate architecture, opening the practice to other possibilities and other matters.

11 Haraway, op. cit., p. 149.

12 Ibid.

David J. Gunkel

HACKING ARCHITECTURE TO BITS

13 B. Nicolson, quoted in D. F. Krell,

'Thinking Ben Nicholson's Collage

Thinking', in Nicholson, *Thinking the*

Unthinkable House, p. 7.

14 Tigerman, op. cit., p. 86.

Every artistic activity is one of making from bits – paper or no paper.[13]

Nicholson's blasphemy targets and intervenes in the subject matter of architecture, betraying the material limits of the discipline to itself. Or as Stanley Tigerman describes it in the postscript to *Appliance House*, Nicholson's work 'unmakes even as it unmasks architecture for what it is'.[14] But Nicholson is not a mere revolutionary. He neither plays by the rules espoused by the guild nor reacts against them through some kind of simple, knee-jerk negation. Both options are unacceptable in that they solidify, either by direct endorsement or through simple opposition, the hegemony of guild knowledge. On the contrary, Nicholson's interventions in the subject and matter of architecture exceed and deconstruct this either/or scenario, creating works that are no longer and, strictly speaking, never could have been comprehended by the epistemology of the guild. This thoroughly disruptive operation proceeds along two related and intersecting vectors.

Figure 5.3 Ben Nicholson, *Loaf House Viewed from the North-east*, 1996.[15]

15 Nicholson, *Thinking the Unthinkable House*.

David J. Gunkel

On the one hand, Nicholson's designs deliberately challenge the presumption of fabrication and materialism that have been definitive of architectural practice. His *Loaf House*, for example, comprises a design for a domestic dwelling that has, as the result of an almost unexpected and sudden change, slipped away from the traditional materials of architecture and become dissolved in the fluid matrix of cyberspace. 'The Loaf House,' Nicholson explains in an article for *Des-Res Architecture*, 'was originally planned for a site at 31st and Prairie Avenue in Chicago, where there had once been a turreted Victorian mini-mansion. Deflected by a technological squall, the house retrenched itself into the maybe world of cyberspace. Today it is entirely digital . . .'[16] *Loaf House* formally challenges the materiality of architecture. It both questions whether a house need be made of concrete, wood, steel and glass to qualify as a dwelling and suggests that one constructed of other bits, digital 0's and 1's specifically, might be just as much a house — an enclosure that permits one to occupy space, engage in various relationships and generally enjoy the view. For Nicholson, the challenge proposed by the nascent technologies and practices of clickable architecture in cyberspace is comparable to that presented by cubism: 'In 1911, when the world witnessed Picasso's Cubist paintings, it could not go back to what it used to know. Today, clickers present the same predicament, only this time the necessity of the builder's trowel, as the sole renderer of architectural space is being stared at in the eye — and someone's about to blink.'[17]

Loaf House gives the appearance of deliberately opposing the materiality and constructability of architecture, receding and dematerialising into the almost unreal complex of digital information. It would, however, be inaccurate to conclude that *Loaf House* causes this event. In other words, one cannot blame Nicholson or *Loaf House* for what the design demonstrates about the materiality of architecture. Instead, like the work of computer hackers, Nicholson's project merely demonstrates and exploits the necessary and unavoidable material flaws already built into and constitutive of the system in question. Consequently, the becoming virtual of *Loaf House* is not motivated by some deliberate and monstrous act of will. Rather, as Nicholson has pointed out, the project has found itself caught in a kind of global and atmospheric disturbance, over which he, unlike Prospero, has no effective control. Reading this general change in weather, Nicholson provides the following interpretation: 'It is no coincidence that today's information organizers unabashedly hand out business cards with the word Architect stated as their profession. For them the word "Architect" says it all, a way of thought that is truly accessible and pleasurable to do. They make and organize space that anyone can enter and get a buzz from. Theirs is a place where time forward, time backward, and time around are given value; they have the tools that make the profession of builders seem inadequate and pedantic.'[18]

16 B. Nicholson, 'Loaf House', *Des-Res Architecture*, January–February 1999, vol. 69, no. 1–2, p. 75.

17 B. Nicholson, 'Click It. Click It Good', *Transarchitectures*, 1998, vol. 3: no. 1–2, p. 1.

18 Ibid.

David J. Gunkel

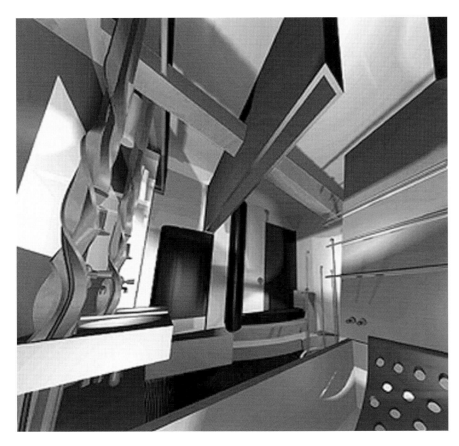

Figure 5.4 Ben Nicholson,
Bathroom of the Loaf House,
1996.[19]

19 Nicholson, *Thinking the
Unthinkable House.*

Loaf House does not, in any sense of the word, *cause* this wholesale alteration in the matter of architecture. It is merely a calculated and thoughtful response to an event that, although currently manifest in the design practices and products of 'virtual architecture', is part and parcel of what Michael Benedikt calls 'architecture's self-dematerialization'.[20] According to Benedikt's analysis, architecture, like all projects of western metaphysics, has been informed and directed by transcendental pretensions that aim at an ideal state of pure information that is uncontaminated by the imperfect substances of the physical world. Architecture's self-dematerialisation, therefore, is not some recent event caused by the introduction of digital media and effectively deforming a previously solidified subject matter. Rather, if Benedikt is right, demateri-alisation has been definitive of architecture's subject matter from the beginning. There are, of course, two possible responses to this original self-dematerialisation. Either one can deny it by reinforcing the already tenuous physical boundaries and

20 M. Benedikt, 'Introduction', in
M. Benedikt (ed.), *Cyberspace: First
Steps*, Cambridge, MIT Press, 1993,
p. 14.

positioning sandbags to try and resist the storm that has already broken out. Or one can surrender to it, becoming open to its new possibilities, operations and features. Nicholson selects or clicks-on the latter, deciding, in direct opposition to the conservative efforts of the guild, to go with the flow. Consequently, *Loaf House* comprises nothing more than a calculated response to an event, one might even say an inevitable occurrence, that has always already effected and infected the matter of architecture. *Loaf House* is offered as a kind of sign for architects, indicating that the material of architecture has always already been eroding and dissolving in ways that cannot simply be ignored, opposed or reversed.

On the other hand, Nicholson does not simply advocate an immaterial, virtual or even 'visionary architecture'.[21] He does not retreat into a conceptual space of ideas and idealism that shuns the heavy stuff of materialism, even if journalists and editors continually categorise and explain his work as 'conceptual architecture'.[22] He does not espouse the position of the 'virtual realists' who, following the precedent set by the protagonist of William Gibson's *Neuromancer*, advocate escape from the 'meat of the body'.[23] Nicholson knows all too well that such gestures inaugurate, in the words of Laura Gurak, 'the worst form of Cartesian thinking'.[24] His relationship to the material of architecture is, therefore, more complicated and interesting. In almost all his projects, Nicholson emphasises material in excess of what is considered proper to the matter of architecture. In other words, he deliberately pushes the materialism of architecture to and beyond its material limits.

The subject matter of architecture, whether defined by professional licensing boards, theoreticians of the discipline or in colloquial discourse, is unabashedly oriented toward material structures. 'What is architecture, after all,' asks Michael Benedikt, 'if not the creation of durable physical worlds . . . ?'[25] But architecture, if one were to be brutally honest, cannot bear the weight of its own materiality. The discipline cannot tolerate the gravity of a monstrous attention to the matter of material and materialism. A building, for example, requires concrete for the foundation, wood for framing and glass for windows. But what of this concrete, wood and glass? What of the stone in the quarry and its violent extraction from the earth? What of the years of growth experienced by the tree and its encounter with the saw blade? What of the silicon comprising the glass and the entire history of the art of glass making? To ask these questions is to exceed what is considered appropriate for building. In fact, posing these questions could make building difficult if not impossible. Nicholson not only entertains these questions but obsesses about them. In an interview with Alvin Boyarsky, Nicholson explains that one of his overarching interests in *Appliance House* was to think 'about lost moments that have slipped between the modern manufacturing process'.[26]

21 M. Novak, 'Liquid Architecture in Cyberspace', in Benedikt, op. cit., p. 244.

22 B. Nicholson, 'Urban Poises', *Critical Inquiry*, Summer 1990, no. 16, pp. 941–67. J. Woodard, 'Architect's Exhibit Focuses on the Conceptual', *Los Angeles Times*, 9 October 1997. Sula, op. cit.

23 W. Gibson, *Neuromancer*, New York, Ace Books, 1984, p. 6.

24 L. J. Gurak, 'Utopian Visions of Cyberspace', *Computer Mediated Communications*, May 1997, no. 1–2, pp. 1–2. Available on the internet at http://www.december.com/cmc/mag/1997/may/last.html

25 Benedikt, op. cit., p. 14.

26 B. Nicholson, 'The Appliance House: An Interview with Alvin Boyarsky', in R. Middleton (ed.), *The Idea of the City*, New York, Architectural Associations, 1996, p. 129.

David J. Gunkel

Figure 5.5 *The Material Remains of a B-52 Stratofortress.*[27]

27 Nicholson, *Thinking the Unthinkable House.*

28 Ibid.

29 Nicholson, *Appliance House.*

This interest in the forgotten moments of materials and material production reaches fever pitch in *B-52 Pickup*, a recent project that examines the decommissioning, demolition and recycling of the B-52 Stratofortress bomber. This project is incessantly concerned with the origin and fate of materials. It worries about the very molecules of aluminium and copper that comprise the airframe and command and control systems of the bomber. Nicholson investigates where the materials came from, how they were milled and what happens to them in and after the heat of the furnace.[28] This obsession with material is more than the practice of architecture can bear. At some point, the building materials must be distinguished from both natural resources and detritus. Sometimes you simply have to take out the trash. Nicholson, however, sees no justification for making any of these distinctions. The plastic tags that close the neck of slightly oily, plastic bread bags, for example, are just as interesting, diverse and worthy of consideration as architectural antiquities.[29] The origin and fate of copper wiring that had once carried the command and control information of years of cold-war paranoia should be a matter of national concern and is at least deserving of some kind of memorial. In fact, Nicholson's initial design for *Loaf House* incorporated the copper in the structure's upper floor, effectively juxtaposing *Dr Strangelove* foreign policy with the quiet solitude of the suburban domestic sphere.[30] In all cases, Nicholson's perspicaciousness takes the matter of architecture to its material limit and demonstrates that, however much it insists on material and materiality, the matter of architecture has never been sufficiently materialistic.

In the end, what these two movements show is the general ambivalence and self-contradictions of the architectural practice as it is currently constituted. On one side, reactions to projects like *Loaf House* demonstrate that architecture adamantly opposes its self-dematerialisation by relying on an appeal to material and fabrication. On the other side, projects like *Appliance House* and *B-52 Pickup* indicate that this retreat into materiality is both half-hearted and never sufficiently materialistic. What's the matter with architecture, therefore, is that it both resists its self-dematerialisation into the digital bits of cyberspace and is, at the same time, unable to solidify its dedication to materiality in opposition to such dissolution.

DE-SIGNING ARCHITECTURE

> *The picture is a model of reality. To the objects correspond in the picture the elements of the picture. The elements of the picture stand, in the picture, for the objects.*[31]

In hacking things to bits, the architectural blasphemer creates various designs that no longer conform to what are considered to be appropriate signs of architecture. Nicholson's drawings, collages and computer simulations do not function according to the mirror logic of representation. They are not *pictures,* and their elements do not correspond to and stand in for some object. Instead they constitute thoroughly ambivalent constructions that deliberately destabilise and deconstruct the concept and system of the architectural sign. In doing so, Nicholson produces monstrous designs that not only function otherwise but challenge the established signs of architecture.

The practice of architecture, as it is currently delimited and legislated, employs a number of different images: sketches, drawings, blueprints, models and computer simulations. Despite the diversity of materials and formal elements, these various images occupy a similar structural position within the discipline of architecture. In general, they are all understood, employed and valued as *signs.* 'The sign,' writes Jacques Derrida, 'is usually said to be put in the place of the thing itself, the present thing, "thing" here standing equally for meaning or referent. The sign represents the present in its

30 Nicholson, *Thinking the Unthinkable House.*

31 L. Wittgenstein, *Tractatus Logico-Philosophicus*, trans. C. K. Ogden, New York, Routledge, 1995, p. 39.

David J. Gunkel

absence. It takes the place of the present. When we cannot grasp or show the thing, state the present, the being-present, when the present cannot be presented, we signify, we go through the detour of the sign.'[32] The architectural image, whether it be the traditional drawing or a computer-simulated model, is comprehended and employed as the delegate of something else. It takes place by taking the place of some other thing that is, for one reason or another, no longer or not yet fully present. This general logic of the sign, which does not belong to architecture exclusively but informs the traditions of western art, linguistics, philosophy and all forms of mediated communication, has a rather long history and venerable pedigree. It is at least as old as Plato and supported by the entire cultural institution that is called Platonism.

Although the hegemony of this metaphysical system has been challenged in abstract art, modern literature and electronic media of all kinds, it still holds fast in the tradition of architecture. In response to this obstinate Platonic puritanism, Nicholson's images are de-signed and function otherwise. His drawings, collages and computer models deliberately work against and resist the classically determined structure of the sign. 'The result of Nicholson's drawing,' observes John Whiteman, 'is not a representation. His drawings do not show things. Nor do they symbolize or express other things, things beyond the drawing itself. Thus Nicholson's drawings do not work as analogy, where the object portrayed symbolizes a deeper reality which is claimed to lie beyond the object of the work itself.'[33] Nicholson's images do not constitute representations of something else to which they refer and necessarily defer. They do not function as a transparent medium through which one looks to see some other object. Rather, they remain monstrously opaque surfaces into which one looks and no more. Like the rear window situated at the back of the Kleptoman Cell in *Appliance House*, Nicholson's pictures are 'composed of pieces that help the viewer to look into something, rather than to look through it'.[34]

Nicholson's challenge to the classically determined structure of the architectural sign commences by intervening in the practice and product of drawing, the conventional mode of architectural expression. Early in his career, Nicholson intentionally abandoned the practice of 'fine drawing' for another not altogether accepted or understood form, collage. The practice of collage, according to Nicholson's own reflections on the matter, comprises a thoroughly disruptive practice from which no one or thing is immune: 'Every professional academy, institution or organization is vulnerable to collage, as orders of logic are broken apart by the collagist. Access is gained to information which is then reordered so that it "sits right" into the collagist system of thinking, oblivious of the accepted status quo.'[35] For Nicholson, collage provides a general technique of guild terrorism that intervenes in or hacks the traditional logic and structure of the sign.

32 J. Derrida, *Margins of Philosophy*, trans. A. Bass, Chicago, University of Chicago Press, 1982, p. 9.

33 J. Whiteman, 'Drawing Towards Building', in Nicholson, *Appliance House*, p. 8.

34 Nicholson, *Appliance House*, p. 70.

35 Ibid., p. 16.

David J. Gunkel

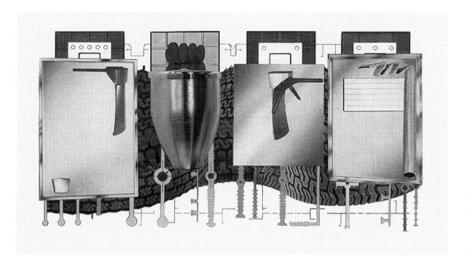

Figure 5.6 Ben Nicholson, *Face Name Collage*, 1990.[36]

36 Ibid.

First, the practice of collage undermines the intentions and activities of the designer, causing the material of the image to exceed his/her comprehension and control. 'Painting and drawing,' Nicholson explains, 'require every mark on the canvas to pass through the fingers of the artist. Collage making, on the other hand, cannot fully control what occurs in the juxtapositions because it uses readymade components. Unlike the pencil user, the collagist is introduced to a further set of ideas which simultaneously transcend the merely contemplative and go beyond traditional instruments of artistic expression.'[37] Through the process of collage, the designer necessarily and compulsively relinquishes authority over the image by surrendering to the exigencies of the material that is employed. With collage, therefore, shit happens that exceeds the intentions, understanding and will of the collagist. Like the monster hacked together by that 'great collagist Dr Frankenstein',[38] a collage has a life of its own that necessarily escapes the mastery of its creator. Cut lose from the dictatorship of intentionality, collage interrupts the process of artistic expression and challenges the dominant understanding of the image as a representation or communication of some ideal and purposeful content.

37 Ibid., p. 19.

38 Ibid., p. 20.

Second, the material of collage is comprised of readymade components culled from catalogues, magazines and other less than ideal sources. Nicholson's raw materials, for instance, are derived from sources as diverse as the recently discontinued Sears Catalogue which comprises a virtual encyclopedia of consumer products for modern living, the dilapidated components of derelict B-52 Stratofortresses recently removed from the lofty position of nuclear deterrence and now all but forgotten in the junk yards of Tucson, Arizona and the digital images and text files of the

David J. Gunkel

Figure 5.7 *Fragment of a Collage Comprised of Salvaged B-52 Wreckage.*[39]

39 Nicholson, *Thinking the Unthinkable House.*

40 Nicholson, *Appliance House,* p. 22.

41 Ibid., p. 23.

World Wide Web hacked together in the cut and paste medium of HTML. Consequently, the raw materials of collage are nothing less than a heap of ephemeral signs that have been, in one way or another, surgically extracted from their appropriate contexts and repositioned in the deranged system of collage. In the process of cutting, juxtaposing and layering, the materials of these signs become cut loose from their proper referent. They begin to lose contact with the object from which they were derived and to which they supposedly refer. 'When objects are snipped from magazines and reformed into an ephemera of collage,' Nicholson explains, 'they transcend their former pictorial candor. The identity of a frying pan might be lost but its associated smells still linger. The task of collage is to regurgitate the frying pan enough times so that the metal is worn away but its patina is left intact.'[40] In the process of collage, therefore, ephemeral signs no longer function as simple representations or delegates of something else. They come to be 'emptied of pictorial content' and, as a result, the complex junctions between fragments take on a thickness and opacity of their own that 'take precedence over the images depicted'.[41] In this way, collage is and remains a subversive activity that, through the deliberate use and reuse of signs, effectively suspends and undermines the significance and function of the sign as such.

Finally, Nicholson's collages, whether they be comprised of catalogue clippings, the twisted wreckage of B-52 bombers or digital information, do not confront the architectural sign as some external threat or impending catastrophe. Despite initial appearances, collage does not constitute a disturbance proceeding from the outside and afflicting a previously well established and perfectly functioning sign system. Instead, collage has always inhabited and determined the architectural sign as such. According to Nicholson, all artistic activity has been inextricably involved with and influenced by the practice of collage: 'Study sketches of painting can reveal that a figure might be a composite of different parts from different people and various fragments of sculpture drawn from antiquity. Conceptually, a collage is an aggregate of

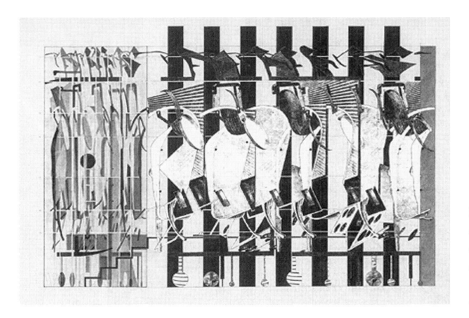

Figure 5.8 Ben Nicholson,
*Interior Elevation of the Flank
and Side Walls of Appliance
House.*[42]

42 Ibid.

various pieces which create an irresistible spectacle in the eye of the maker. Artists of the pre-printing age mentally transferred items from other sources through drawing . . . Similarly, the printed page has become the fertile ground for the collagist of the printing era where the source of pictorial and ephemeral views of the world, his picture plan, can be compared to the draftsman's glance at the world . . .'[43] Seen in this way, the images of art and architecture have never been mere representations of some object but are themselves composed of fragments, clippings and juxtapositions that use and reuse all kinds of ephemeral readymades. Nicholson's insistence on collage, therefore, is not the result of individual caprice or some devious act of barbarism. It is instead necessitated by a desire to remain faithful – exceedingly faithful – to the signs of architecture. Through collage, Nicholson merely demonstrates to the discipline of architecture that the architectural image has never actually functioned according to the traditionally determined structure of the sign but has always been involved in the seemingly monstrous and uncontrollable habit of collage making. For this reason, Nicholson can be neither credited nor blamed for what happens in and by collage. The blasphemer's designs are not the cause. They only constitute highly attentive and faithful responses to something that has always been operative within the signs of architecture.

43 Ibid., p. 18.

David J. Gunkel

CONCLUSION

44 M. Heidegger, *Being and Time*, trans. John Macquarrie and Edward Robinson, New York, Harper and Row, 1962, p. 24.

All inquiry about something is somehow a questioning of something.[44]

The question 'what's the matter with architecture?' is one of those annoying inquiries that resists conclusive answer. In fact, the answer to this question is actually immaterial. What matters are not the set of possible answers but the way in which such questions open the subject matter to questioning. 'What's the matter with architecture?' is a question that matters for architecture, precisely because it initiates a process of critical analysis and self-examination. It exposes architecture to an interrogation of its very subject matter. In the process, the discipline becomes open to the possibility of other subjects – practitioners who do not necessarily belong to the guild but nevertheless create things that matter for architecture. Through the material of this seemingly simple question, architecture is confronted with other matters that, technically speaking, exceed the material limits of what is usually considered to be architecture. And by entertaining this imaginative investigation, architecture imagines other kinds of designs, pictures that no longer and never could behave according to the simple logic of representation. Consequently, in asking the question 'what's the matter with architecture?' one does not necessarily look for a definitive response from architects and architecture but provokes the discipline to open itself to other subjects, other matters . . . an other architecture altogether.

David J. Gunkel

SECTION 2

spatial

---

matter

notopia: leaky products/urban interfaces

1 W. Gibson, *Neuromancer*, New York, Ace Books, New York, 1984.

DATE: 1984
LOCATION: WILLIAM GIBSON'S *NEUROMANCER*[1]
SYSTEM DESCRIPTION: CYBERSPACE
TOOLS REQUIRED: SILICON EMBEDDED INSERTS

TO ENTER CYBERSPACE THE BODY SURFACE IS VIOLATED; JACKING IN TO THE DIGITAL SYSTEM INVOLVES UNDER-THE-SKIN SILICON CONNECTIONS. ONCE PENETRATED, THE BODY IS LEFT BEHIND, IMMOBILE AND INACTIVE. THE IMAGINATION IS TAKEN ON A SENSORIAL JOURNEY INTO A FICTIONAL SPACE SO IMMERSIVE AND REAL THAT FICTION AND REALITY BLUR, THE FICTIONAL BECOMES MORE REAL AND DESIRABLE THAN THE PHYSICAL REALITY, THE EMPTY BODY IS LEFT ABANDONED, DISCARDED AND OBSOLETE.

Architects dream in cyberspace, escaping the constraints of matter and gravity. They dream of folds and dynamic form, of constant fluidity. A visual pornography of space denied, as yet, to biological material until it too can vaporise and contort. Our stable fleshy bodies remain on the outside looking on to windows filled with representations of forms and spaces we can never touch.

Attempts are constantly made to project our bodies into these spaces; entry is with special suits and small windows attached to our eyes. Alone, we move through poor representations of the world we have just left behind. Given poor tools for social interaction, we have awkward meetings with global strangers. Other windows made as large as possible are attached to buildings in public spaces with the hope of engulfing the viewer in some kind of collective social immersion, but we just stand at a safe distance and gawp. Whatever their scale they remain windows. The body is excluded. Cyberspace is a separated space, a visual experience, remaining untouched and bodily uninhabited. Although we cannot enter it, ironically it envelops us every day. Imperceptibly, through global networks conducting billions of daily transactions.

Today's perception of cyberspace is rather banal, an information space, useful, but devoid of sensory pleasure. Clearly defined boundaries separate virtual fiction and physical domain. The caress of the cursor is the only projected touch reaching into cyberspace and the window of the screen is our shared experience of this unfulfilling union.

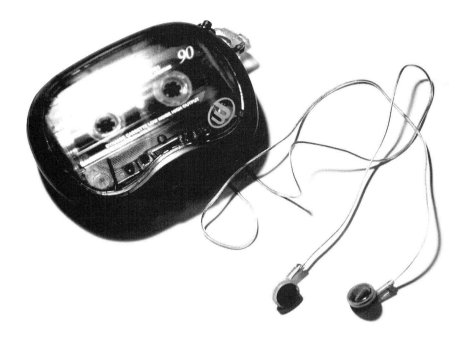

Figure 6.1 *Walkman, a personal urban sound track.*

DATE: 1989
LOCATION: LATE NIGHT EXPRESS TRAIN FROM TOKYO CENTRAL TO FUNABASHI
SYSTEM DESCRIPTION: SPEED, DARKNESS, NEON
TOOLS REQUIRED: WALKMAN

STARING OUT OF THE WINDOW WITHIN A WALKMAN 'BUBBLE', A TALKING HEADS SOUND TRACK JOINS THE ABSTRACTED FRAMES OF THE FILMIC NEON CITY.

Although the body remains still, material and visual matter, abstracted by speed and darkness, co-exist within the same space.

Dunne + Raby

Figure 6.2 *Noiseman, a proposal made to Sony Corporation in Tokyo. We made a mock-up device with recording Walkman and guitar effectors. However, the concept of a Noiseman was contrary to the Sony image of hi-fidelity.*

DATE: 1989
LOCATION: STEPPING OFF THE YAMANOTE TRAIN, SHIBUYA STATION
SYSTEM DESCRIPTION: TOKYO THE ACOUSTIC CITY
TOOLS REQUIRED: NOISEMAN

EVERY PHYSICAL SURFACE AND EVERY POSSIBLE AUDIBLE OPPORTUNITY IS SEIZED ON THE STREET TO CAPTURE ATTENTION.

The Walkman is a tool of separation, shutting out unwanted acoustic demands while creating an abstracted parallel domain, bodily engaged, but acoustically abducted. The Noiseman is an adapted Walkman, the tape removed and replaced by digital distortion filters. Competing street noise is transformed into smooth intricate sound textures. The source is live and spontaneous, generated by sonic city events, from the chatter of passing schoolgirls, pre-recorded religious megaphones and clattering pacinko halls to the greetings from shop girls and lift attendants. 'Irashamasai' they chant. Synthetic pleasure is created from the sonic texture of the city. A new territory is revealed, each journey through the city becomes a unique experience. A new land-scape is open for exploration. We do not enter cyberspace; the city is the medium. Or is cyberspace a modification of the city, a fusion of overlaying systems?

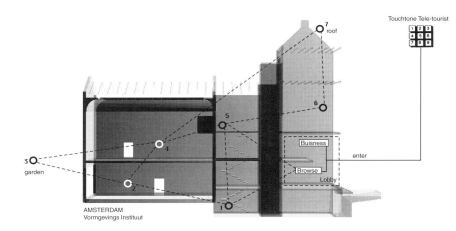

Figure 6.3 *Touch tone architectural interface, a proposal for the Netherlands Design Institute; rather than 'on hold' waiting, button pushing provides an acoustic exploration of the building. Privacy is retained using tele-proxemic filters.*

DATE: 1993

LOCATION: LONDON AND SAN FRANCISCO, SIMULTANEOUSLY

SYSTEM DESCRIPTION: TOUCH TONE TELEPHONE SYSTEM

TOOLS REQUIRED: ADAPTED TELEPHONES WITH TELE-PROXEMIC DIMEN-SIONS

'WELCOME TO THE DIGITAL CORPORATION, IF YOU HAVE SOFTWARE REQUIRE-MENTS PRESS ONE, HARDWARE REQUIREMENTS PRESS TWO, NETWORK REQUIRE-MENTS PRESS THREE, 3D MODELLING REQUIREMENTS PRESS FOUR, SOUND REQUIREMENTS PRESS FIVE, VIDEO REQUIREMENTS PRESS SIX, TECHNICAL SPECI-FICATION REQUIREMENTS PRESS SEVEN, GRAPHIC REQUIREMENTS PRESS EIGHT.' EIGHT IS PRESSED: 'WELCOME TO GRAPHIC REQUIREMENTS, IF YOU HAVE COLOUR REQUIREMENTS PRESS ONE, RESOLUTION REQUIREMENTS PRESS TWO, DRAWING PACKAGE REQUIREMENTS PRESS THREE . . .'

Concentrated breathing is transported through four more layers of the system on its virtual journey, ending in the capture and storage of a voice in a distant mail box. A strange pleasure comes from wandering around the system without purpose. Although fascinating, it's disappointing to travel so far for such a mean and efficient exchange. There is no sense of the other place occupied by the voice. Distance is not the only separating element. Regardless of the complexity of cultural difference, a simple time shift of eight hours creates a new juxtaposition of place. Here the day is slowing down, there it has just begun. Here it is cold and overcast, there the skies are blue and expansive. Rather than being locked in a digital cyberspace, separate and isolated, what would it be like to 'be' in a remote place, wandering around a distant building using a touch tone to move from room to room? Disembodied but extending a sense of presence into the other place.

Do the edges of cyberspace need to be so abrupt? Imagine a digital system where the edges are expanded, where virtual and physical elements interweave with each other occupying the same territory. Where sensors reach out from the digital domain to playfully engage with physical elements. Where new physical forms help to shape and reveal these new hybrid relationships. No longer are we 'on' or 'off', 'in' or 'out', spatial transitions become thresholds to systems.[2]

2 Dunne + Raby, 'Fields and Thresholds', in N. Spiller (ed.), *Architects in Cyberspace, Architectural Design,* vol. 65, no. 11/12, profile no. 118, London, Academy, 1995, pp. 60–5.

De-materialisation has always been central to the technological vision; ubiquity, seamlessness, all systems magically disappear, absorbed into the architecture. A wave of the hand initiates an action. A voice command accesses a database. LEDs and animated icons are the only acknowledgement that communication has taken place. So much attention is focused on total absorption of physical systems and technical parts that de-materialisation has overenthusiastically been extended into language and communications, while exactly the opposite is required: re-materiality. Digital immateriality needs to find material expression.

Human language and communications are not simply the articulation of sound and vision. Space, as a social medium, even almost subliminally, has an important part to play. A sensory envelope of kinaesthetic sensitivity, including thermal and olfactory signalling, which varies from person to person and culture to culture. Architecture and furniture design have always allowed this human sensitivity to the social use of space to find material and spatial expression.

At this junction between media, the spatial interface is primed for hybrid invention. New kinds of objects can escape a utilitarian personality and delight in a hybrid materiality of fiction and matter; the aesthetics is not to be found in form, but through the experience of use. Two objects from the Netherlands Design Institute sit on the edges of telephone space; they function as telephones, with adapted parts. They flicker between a space where the body partakes in the here and now and a space for the mind to imagine.

Figure 6.4 *Cabinet studies.*

Dunne + Raby

The cabinet offers the privilege of privacy. It is an object for keeping in touch, made of wood, a large volume with glass doors. The object is ambiguous, both cabinet and seat. However, with no shelves and an awkward sloping base, it is not for storing 'things', instead projected into it, and filling the cabinet is the colour of a distant sky. The time of day and the weather condition of the remote location are constantly part of the everyday activities within the space. The two remote places sit side by side and constantly offer comparative conditions. Holes cut in the glass doors allow a person to sit inside and open up a communication channel to the other place.

Figure 6.5 *Torso studies.*

A torso-like object located somewhere public, a large room or unused corridor. On entering its field, music escapes from the object, seducing the passer-by. The object can move freely and only by constant movement is the voice channel kept open, allowing conversations within the open system to be overheard. Illicit listening involves a continuous dance where the object is held close against the body. It has been designed to be used when nobody is looking, the risk of potential embarrassment is exchanged for the pleasure of eavesdropping. Rather than designing into the object what is and what is not socially acceptable, it is left to the people using it.

Re-materialisation involves the creation of hybrid situations that mix virtual and physical elements, the construction of spatial narratives, and the organisation of time-dependent media into spatial events and experiences. Is this the responsibility of architects and designers?

DATE: 1996

LOCATION: LONDON LATE AT NIGHT

SYSTEM DESCRIPTION: RADIO SPECTRUM

TOOLS REQUIRED: BROADBAND RADIO SCANNER

THE SCANNER SEARCHES FOR MOBILE TELE-PHONE FREQUENCIES, CAPTURING DISLO-CATED AMBIENT VOICES. THE CHATTER IS ORDINARY, A POCKET OF DAILY STABILITY IN THE GREAT URBAN METROPOLIS. NOTHING REALLY HAPPENS. UNLIKE THE PREFORMATTED DRAMA ON TV, WEST LONDON ENTERS THE BEDROOM LIVE AND UNCUT, BUT THE EVENTS ARE UNEVENTFUL, THE TONE AND CONVERSA-TIONS CLICHED, MIMICKING TV SOAPS. THE FASCINATION IS TO BE FOUND IN THE DETAIL. PERSONALITIES AND INTIMATE CHATTER FILL THE ROOM. LIVE SLICES OF LONDON LIFE, BEING LIVED IN CLOSE PROXIMITY, AS DREAM-ILY SLEEP TAKES OVER.

WAITING IN LINE FOR A PINT OF MILK AT THE CORNER SHOP THE NEXT MORNING . . . PEOPLE STAND SILENTLY AND SEPARATELY IN A QUEUE. THE ILLEGAL SCANNER MAKES A STRONGER CONNECTION WITH LOCAL PEOPLE AND THE IMMEDIATE NEIGHBOURHOOD THAN THE CORNER SHOP.

Figure 6.6 *Radio Scanner, £250 from Dixons.*

3 *The UK Scanning Directory*, Perth, Interproducts, 1994.

4 A. Dunne, *Hertzian Tales: Electronic Products, Aesthetic Experience and Critical Design*, London, RCACRD Research, 1999.

£250 from Dixons, the scanner is illegal to use with the *UK Scanning Directory*.[3] It lists over 20,000 different frequencies from 25MHz to 1.6GHz, from dog-catchers to milk floats, fast-food outlets to refuse collectors. A picture forms of a hidden land-scape. A radio space that unknowingly we already inhabit and within which we are totally immersed, but cannot yet see. A multitude of consumer electronics tune in and illuminate parts of this Hertzian space for us.[4] Two frequencies in particular attract attention: illegal bugging devices at 91.00MHz and Babycoms at 49.8200 to 49.9875MHz. Functionality similar, but socially opposed.

Dunne + Raby

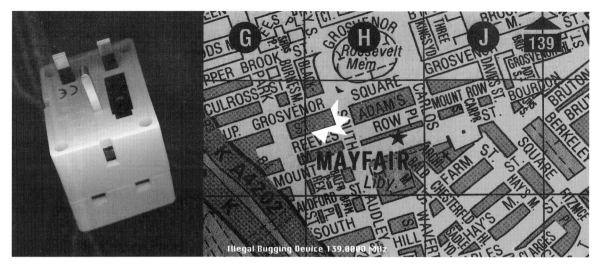

Figure 6.7 Plug Bug. We hired a car, tuned our scanner to an illegal bugging frequency and drove around the city in pursuit of leaky buildings, finding bugged spaces in predictable London locations. Reproduced by permission of Geographers' A–Z Map Co. Ltd. Licence No. B1167. This product includes mapping data licensed from Ordnance Survey ®. ©Crown Copyright 2001. Licence number 100017302.

Plug Bug 4000: 'It works as both plug and bug. It looks like an adapter plug. It works exactly as an adapter plug. But once plugged into a wall socket it also acts as a bug with a range of up to 1700 ft. It is as simple as that. So whether you have an office or a house in mind the Plug Bug 4000 offers clear and continual monitoring of

Figure 6.8 Babycom. We discovered whole streets in Chiswick where intimate bedroom sounds escaped on to public streets.

Dunne + Raby

5 *Science in the Service of Information*, London, Miracles of Science Ltd, undated.

6 Tomy Babycom, product literature taken from the box.

any room with extreme ease. Plugging one in now means surveillance on your target whenever the mood takes you.'[5]

Tomy Babycom: 'Extra special baby care. Combining plug-in simplicity with new technology the Tomy BABY LINK keeps you in touch with baby conveniently.'[6]

In this new radio landscape occupied by electronic things, walls dissolve and the contents of rooms, once safely contained within private boundaries, spill out into the streets. Private bedroom conversations become public bulletins. Embassies, legal districts and suburbs are already part of a tuneable city.

Figure 6.9 *Car radio for exploring the tuneable city; the driver can choose between legal or illegal listening.*

A realisation forms, a slow virtual infiltration has been imperceptibly growing and developing into a complex landscape that now envelops us. Not only are we immersed in it, it penetrates and passes through our bodies.

DATE: 1999
LOCATION: WEST LONDON
SYSTEM DESCRIPTION: ELECTROMAGNETIC
SPECTRUM
TOOLS REQUIRED: ADAPTED FURNITURE

'TECHNICIANS FROM THE NATIONAL RADIOLOGI-CAL PROTECTION BOARD (NRPB) HAVE FOUND A COLLECTION OF BIZARRE OBJECTS IN A HOUSE IN WEST LONDON. ALL OF THE OBJECTS ARE DESIGNED TO ALERT THE OWNER TO VARIOUS FORMS OF ELECTROMAGNETIC RADIATION AND SHIELD THE OCCUPANTS FROM ITS EFFECTS. THEY SEEM TO HAVE BEEN BUILT AS THE RESULT OF A MIS-READING OF A 1989 REPORT: "GUIDE-LINES AS TO RESTRICTIONS ON EXPOSURE TO TIME VARYING ELECTROMAGNETIC FIELDS". SPE-CIALISTS HAVE POINTED OUT THAT ALTHOUGH

Figure 6.10 *Dr Gauss, a device that measures electromagnetic fields.*

MOST OF THE DEVICES DO NOT PROVIDE PHYSICAL PROTECTION THEY ALMOST CERTAINLY DO OFFER PSYCHOLOGICAL PROTECTION AND MAY IN FACT POSTPONE THE ONSET OF ACUTE PARANOIA CURRENTLY AFFECTING SO MANY PEOPLE FOLLOWING CONTROVERSIAL ARTICLES IN THE PRESS.'

Furniture pieces are deployed within the room, watchful against straying transmissions. They demarcate a safe territory for the occupier to reach a desired state of oblivion, a temporary spot to luxuriate in, away from electromagnetic bombardment, free from invisible molestation. Alignment of the furniture is not determined by the physical edges of the room, but the edges of radio space.

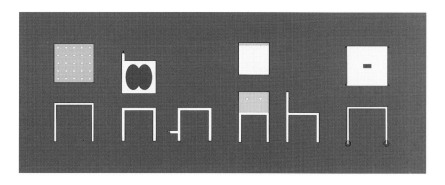

Figure 6.11 *Placebo Furniture, domestic objects that explore psychological wellbeing and the aesthetic of complicated pleasure.*

Dunne + Raby

The compass table, its needles carefully balanced, delicately twitches when air-borne signals brush against its surface. The chair faces a blank wall, its silicon nipples remain still but erect, when agitated like pointy fingers they push and gnaw between ribs and shoulder blades. The globally positioned table is pushed right up beneath the window, obsessively fixated on the sky, no coverings or plant growth obscure the immaculately cleaned panes. Its absolute position is displayed green and digital. It must retain an uninterrupted visual connection with the satellite. If disconnection occurs the table is lost. In the corner, opposite the bed, a stool with a highly polished stainless steel plate is plugged into the wall. The switch is on. The plug has only one pin. When naked flesh and cold steel join, excess electricity accumulated in the body during the day is drained away. Left on the floor are a pair of pyjamas made from metallicised rip stock fabric, altered to cover hands, feet and head. Although uncomfortable against the skin, they provide the sleeper with a different kind of comfort. A simple reading light with its long probing arm illuminates a page – the open book is kept at a safe distance. It sits half in and half out of the field, the stronger the leakage, the brighter the light. If the field dies away the light ceases to work.

Originally domestic space was simple, designed to provide shelter and comfort, a stable environment protected from climatic instability. However, electromagnetic weather, oblivious to damp proof membranes, effortlessly passes through, saturating everything. Its presence, disregarded by human inhabitants, becomes a luminary to a growing number of electronic devices that spring into life and chatter. No longer inanimate, their shifting personalities allow for misinterpretation. How do we inhabit this atmosphere? What kinds of objects furnish its spaces? Do we try to shut it out? Or do we play in its enchanted landscape?

DATE: 1999
LOCATION: HELSINKI STREETS, −7°C
SYSTEM DESCRIPTION: CELLULAR STRUCTURE
TOOLS REQUIRED: WAP ENABLED MOBILE TELE-PHONE

ELASTICITY DESCRIBES THE INVISIBLE STRUCTURE OF THE CELLULAR CITY. AS A PERSON MOVES FROM CELL TO CELL, THE CELL IS CAPTURED AND STRETCHES WITH THEM UNTIL THE SIGNAL STRENGTH IN THE NEXT CELL IS STRONG ENOUGH TO TAKE OVER. THE FIRST CELL IS THEN RELEASED AND SPRINGS BACK INTO SHAPE. TWO PEOPLE CAN PASS CLOSE TO EACH OTHER ON THE STREET AND OCCUPY DIFFERENT CELLS. WEATHER CAN ALSO CAUSE THE EDGES TO EXPAND AND CONTRACT. THE AMOEBIC CELLS ARE IN CONSTANT MOTION, ALMOST ALIVE, AS THEY CONNECT WITH THE TERRESTRIAL LANDSCAPE AND ITS FRENETIC INHABITANTS. IN ITS ATTEMPTS TO BE EFFICIENT, THE SHIFTING BOUNDARIES OF THE CELLUAR CITY UNINTENTIONALLY CREATE ZONES OF AMBIGUITY.[7] ACCIDENTLY, IT IS A STRUCTURE OF ECCENTRICITY.

Figure 6.12 *An adapted mobile phone, for use in a six week user trial in Helsinki exploring location based services.*

7 F. Raby, *Project #26765: FLIRT, Flexible Information and Recreation for Mobile Users*, London, RCACRD Research, 2000.

Figure 6.13 *Conceptual map: a tool to visualise the fusion of cellular network and down town Helsinki streets. Helsinki Telephone Company said it was not accurate but it was realistic.*

Dunne + Raby

Technologically the goal for mobile networks is to achieve precision, to define position; to fix people, buildings and things as points in a continuous isotropic plane; a process of de-materialisation that perpetuates the separation between digital space and city space. The cellular structure, however, with its clusters and groupings, when superimposed on urban territory reflects a sense of place and social space. It suggests location rather than position.

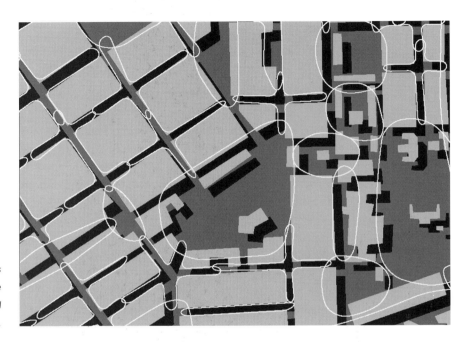

Figure 6.14 *Cell structures reflect locality and place. As the network develops, 'location' will be replaced with 'position'.*

Ambiguity is a strong constituent of re-materialisation. When used well it is a powerful instrument for tapping directly into the imagination without the need for silicon. Although it is not substance, it interferes with interpretation: it interferes with what you believe substance to be. In the Cellular City interpretation can be manipulated.

In the Cellular City locational proximity and data coincidence can create 'cellular nearness' between mobile phone users – a Pixel Kissing meeting. There is potential to generate and sustain an 'anonymous community', not like those of fiction, already played out on globally networked computer games, but communities inhabiting the same physical territories, sliding past each other with parallel but inscrutable lives.

A million people live in Helsinki. What proportion of them share the same birthday as you? One in 365? If you walked around the city and were alerted to all the people in

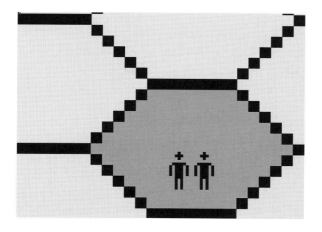

Figure 6.15 *Pixel Kissing, locational proximity and data coincidence create cellular nearness between members.*

the same locality as you who share your birthday, how many alerts would you get? What if we add year of birth and gender and a Pixel Kissing meeting occurs just as you board the tram. Instantly you might look at all the people immediately around you and start to imagine who you think that person is. In reality they are probably around the corner out of view, in a shop, moving in another tram, but they are there somewhere, nearby; they do exist, they are real.

Lovetectonics was conceived as a virtual service with a simple narrative – someone alone wants to find another someone alone. Unlike a dating agency which directly makes connections between potentially compatible people, Lovetectonics creates a living narrative where everyone is the central protagonist helping to sustain the collective fiction. Each participant can 'date' five people at a time. On joining they answer thirty questions about themselves. The answers are held in a database and released one a day. A month, being a good courting period, allows a picture of the person to form in the mind, providing raw material for Pixel Kissing meetings in the city. The rushed journey across the city, once a hostile immersion through intense turbulent space, becomes a rich texture of ever changing faces and backdrops. Usually shut out and ignored, in the Cellular City the place of non-place is brought back into focus, a fertile territory for parallel fictions.

Unlike a book or a film, which at any point is easy to step out of, within this situated daydream, in the back of the mind, is the thought that at any moment real life might break through.

'Love activity' is monitored and fed into the collective narrative. How many new lovers? How many virtual hankies and chocolates have been used for seduction? How many Pixel Kissing meetings? How many people have been dumped? How much 'love activity' has occurred that day? Who is the most popular? Who is the most predatory?

A new landscape evolves, a space that begins to blur fiction and reality. A space of daydreaming, a space of imagination played out in the city street. A space that uses the movements and activities of the participants as content, continuously feeding back into a fictional narrative, where fictional entities work themselves into peoples' everyday routines and start to infect real space. Information becomes communication. The screen is not the world, it's only a trigger.

The Cellular City overlaid on urban territory is the first extensive fusion of virtual and physical space, a fusion that does not exclude fleshy bodies and their sensual complexities. A fusion with two-way connectivity, in which the user is not only an observer but a participant in a complex social networked structure. Where ubiquity and de-materialisation of the technological system has been achieved extensively, but enough physical materiality remains to facilitate a sophisticated complex palette for spatial language and social communications. This is the beginning of a practical synthesis that will impact on everyday urban experience and architectural territory.

Figure 6.16 What kinds of new objects will inhabit the wireless landscape?

Ubiquity and wireless networks are developing at a phenomenal rate, expanding the landscape to include a new culture of active objects. With Bluetooth[8] technologies, objects will no longer remain isolated entities, they too will be connected, they will know where they are located and have communication capabilities. Location and context will play a large part in establishing the wireless landscape. How will we inhabit these new hybrid spaces and what will the architect's role be in this new wireless urbanism?

This essay is based on a paper presented in March 2000 at 'Hypologies', in Pergomeno, Tuscany, organised by Professor Nigel Coates of the Department of Architecture at the Royal College of Art, London.

8 Bluetooth wireless technology is a low cost, short-range radio link used to connect a variety of electronic objects (www.bluetooth.com).

Dunne + Raby

comfort, anxiety and

space

This essay is a reflection on homes and families but these homes and families have a particular placing in space and time that is quite difficult to specify. Thus, I begin with some qualifications. My comments allude to modernism but there are necessary exceptions which refer to geography, history, culture and class. I am not concerned, for example, with the kind of porous home spaces of Naples depicted by Walter Benjamin and Asja Lacis in the 1920s. They wrote, from a northern European perspective, about a characteristic of a Mediterranean culture that was then worth remarking on: 'So the house is far less the refuge into which people retreat than the inexhaustible reservoir from which they flood out . . . Just as the living room reappears on the street, with chairs, hearth and altar so, only much more loudly, the street migrates into the living room.'[1] Their observation suggests a lack of concern with the private/public boundary that may still be characteristic of southern European cities but which is evident only in the cases of some minorities in northern Europe, like Gypsies, for whom the improvised seating of a tyre or a milk crate outside the trailer may be as much a part of the furniture of the home as the benches inside.

Apart from some vaguely specified north–south split in Europe and the distinctive culture of nomads, the mingling of private and public is probably associated also with poverty. It is the poor who are less able to erect barriers to secure their home space from threats associated with the outside than the middle-class. It was poor districts in London in the 1950s, for example, that the photographer Roger Mayne used to demonstrate the vigour of London street life.[2] The porosity of home and street may be something that is lost in the most developed societies as families, architects and planners clarify distinctions between public and private. It is this process of clarification, and specifically distancing of the family from others who are assumed to inhabit public space, that I want to consider here, generalising, no doubt unduly, about middle-class families in rich countries.

PURIFIERS AND THEIR CRITICS

Homes have to be examined in wider contexts. Spatial practices that characterise the organisation of home space echo and feed into narratives of the city. Thus, throughout this essay I will focus on anxieties about social relationships that translate into concerns about spaces within and beyond the home. Generally, anxieties are expressed in the desire to erect and maintain spatial and temporal boundaries. Strong boundary consciousness can be interpreted as a desire to be in control and to exclude the unfamiliar because the unfamiliar is a source of unease rather than something to be celebrated. The kind of public/private mixing that Benjamin and Lacis

1 W. Benjamin and A. Lacis, 'Naples', in W. Benjamin, *One-Way Street*, London, Verso, 1979, p. 174. First published in 1925.

2 Z. Cheatle and M. Mack, *The Street Photographs of Roger Mayne*, London, Zelda Cheatle Press, 1993.

David Sibley

remarked on in Naples, conversely, suggests a relaxed attitude, an acceptance of others and of chance encounters although it is likely that interactions in poor Neapolitan neighbourhoods in the 1920s would primarily have involved familiars rather than strangers. The lines of belonging and not belonging might have been drawn elsewhere. In relation to spaces of the home and the city. However, a desire for strong boundaries and a distaste for mixing can be seen as characteristic of modernism, as is suggested by debates on urbanism for much of the twentieth century.

We might take Le Corbusier's writing as texts that dwell excessively on the purification of urban space. Although a canonical figure in modernist urban theory, he had particular problems with race, women and nature, themes that were closely related in his writing and which were central to his concern with separations and distancing. As Mabel Wilson has argued: 'Le Corbusier's skyscrapers, contemporary "white cathedrals" symbolise the restoration of Western culture that transcends and masters filth, the infiltration of "blackness", and the materiality of the body.'[3] Thus, he was disturbed by the transgressive potential of Black American culture and assertive American women. His Radiant City was, according to Wilson, designed 'to enforce and [guarantee] racial and patriarchal order'. This unease about race and gender relations found another expression in his concern about nature. Le Corbusier had a particular aversion to 'wild nature' which had to be kept in its place. In *Towards a New Architecture*, the antithesis of orderly construction was the disorder of nature: 'All around [the builder], the forest is in disorder with its creepers, its briars and the tree-trunks which impede him and paralyse his efforts.'[4] Again, in *The City of Tomorrow*, he maintains that: 'The house, the street, the town . . . should be ordered, otherwise they counteract the fundamental principles round which we revolve; if they are not ordered, they oppose themselves to us, they thwart us as the nature all around us thwarts us, though we have striven with it, and with it begin each day a new struggle.'[5] The need to order nature follows from the imperative of ordering all aspects of the city, with growth itself seemingly threatening. So, large-scale migration to cities in the nineteenth century is characterised as 'a sudden, chaotic and sweeping invasion, unforeseen and overwhelming'.[6] These comments betray a deep-seated anxiety about the unpredictable, the disordered and about cultural and social difference.

The bold assertions of Le Corbusier, together with city planning practices and many recorded instances of resistance to change and social mixing in western cities, have provided the material for critiques of spatial order. Some of these have pointed to the socially damaging consequences of spatial purification, particularly Richard Sennett, and others have emphasised the reduction in variety and diversity that are claimed to be essential qualities of urban living, notably Jane Jacobs and Christopher

3 M. Wilson, 'Dancing in the Dark: the Inscription of Blackness in Le Corbusier's Radiant City', in H. Nast and S. Pile (eds), *Places Through the Body*, London, Routledge, 1998, pp. 133–52.

4 Le Corbusier, *Towards a New Architecture*, London, Architectural Press, 1927, p. 71.

5 Le Corbusier, *The City of Tomorrow*, London, Architectural Press, 1929, p. 15.

6 Ibid., p. 25.

David Sibley

7 R. Sennett, *The Uses of Disorder*, Harmondsworth, Penguin, 1970. J. Jacobs, *The Death and Life of Great American Cities*, New York, Random House, 1961. C. Alexander, 'The city is not a tree', *Design*, no. 206, 1966, pp. 47–55.

8 E. Soja, *Postmetropolis*, Oxford, Basil Blackwell, 2000.

Alexander.[7] It might be claimed that these debates which featured in the planning literature in the 1960s and 1970s have lost their resonance as western cities have assumed a post-modern complexity, something that is reflected in more nuanced arguments about socio-spatial relations. Ed Soja, in particular, maintains that debates about the politics of space should have moved on from a concern with dialectics to 'trialectics', conceptions of space and social relations that capture the inbetween-ness and hybridity of urban culture.[8] While there is certainly some merit in this argument, I think that we still need to explain the persistence of strong boundaries, people's manifest need to hold on to the familiar which is defined partly in relation to disturbing perceptions of otherness. This is evident in current (summer 2000) debates about dangerous paedophiles in Britain. While parental anxieties about the safety of their children are entirely understandable, the focus on strangers who are responsible for from five to seven child murders a year might be seen as curious when more than eighty children are murdered annually within families. The familiar spaces of the home, however, do not generate the same anxieties as apparently less-regulated public space where some threatening 'other' often triggers moral panics. I will suggest that a socially and culturally situated account of body spaces (skin and residues) and the spaces of the home in western cultures can help in understanding why it is that distanciation is an important part of the production of socio-spatial relations and why the heterotopias imagined by critics of urban order are so rarely realised.

THE SKIN, THE PSYCHE AND THE OTHER

There are two questions that we might ask about the need for boundaries. The first is where does this need come from? The second is how do people feel this need, how is it manifest in anxieties and desires? The first question has been addressed by psychoanalysts concerned with object relations or the relations between self and others, where the primary focus has been on the relations between mother and child. There is general agreement among object relation theorists that fears and anxieties associated with the initial rupture of a state of oneness enveloping mother and infant are crucial to an emerging sense of self and a sense of social space. As Adam Phillips has argued, the fear of the loss of love associated with the realisation of not being at one with the mother 'instigates a project to secure something that, by definition, cannot be secured', that is, a project to achieve certainty and stability.[9] However, anxieties about uncertainty, about the precariousness of love and security, which follow from this initial sense of separation from the mother, can be *coped with*

9 A. Phillips, *Terrors and Experts*, London, Faber and Faber, 1995, p. 52.

David Sibley

through repetition: 'In this context, belief in repetition is a form of hope and children, of course, are passionate about repetition . . . repetition confirms our powers of recognition, our competence at distinguishing the familiar from the unfamiliar.'[10] This suggests that spatial and temporal routines are desired from early childhood because a lack of routine or predictability are associated with a loss of love. A sense of boundaries, of bounded time and bounded spaces, thus become important in the socialisation of the child.

10 Ibid.

One problem with Phillips' assertion, like many psychoanalytical arguments, is that it assumes no cultural variability. The separation of mother and infant may be more abrupt and final in societies equipped with crèches and day nurseries than in peasant societies, in rural Africa for example, where skin contact between mother and child is often prolonged. In other words, the anxieties of separation may not be universal but could be more pronounced in the most developed societies. It could be useful, therefore, to think about the bounding of the self and the anxieties and desires associated with the social production of the self in relation to peculiar sets of cultural practices and values. Different cultures bound themselves and establish internal order in different ways, as Mary Douglas has demonstrated, and dominant or hegemonic cultural practices in the west might be examined for their curiosity value as much as those of other cultures.[11] In this regard, Julia Kristeva's views on what constitutes the abject (and its other) seem particularly appropriate because they provide a means of connecting the spaces of the body, the home and localities as they are produced in 'the west'.

11 M. Douglas, *Purity and Danger*, London, Routledge and Kegan Paul, 1966.

PRODUCTION OF THE ABJECT

Julia Kristeva wrote about the abject as something *between* the self and the other.[12] It signals the impossibility of finally establishing a clear boundary between the self and that which is defiled or disordered. Thus, abjection is a process of trying to remove the threat posed by abject things or people. As Oliver recognised: 'Although every society is founded on the abject constructing boundaries and jettisoning the antisocial – every society may have its own abject. In all cases, the abject threatens the unity/identity of both society and the subject. It calls into question the boundaries upon which they are constructed.'[13] Every society generates a set of abject things or qualities but there is no unanimity about what constitutes the abject and this contestation is manifest in the identification of some people and groups as deviant and threatening. Thus, abjection can be seen to be fundamental to the process of marginalisation and exclusion.

12 J. Kristeva, *Powers of Horror*, New York, Columbia University Press, 1982.

13 K. Oliver, *Reading Kristeva*, Bloomington, Indiana University Press, 1993, p. 56.

David Sibley

Kristeva's writing on abjection is wide-ranging, including aspects of the relationship between mother and child and life and death. I want to focus more particularly on threats to the body which extend to abject qualities of the home and public space.

The skin constitutes one key boundary that is continually threatened, where socially constructed ideas of impurity result in products like sweat becoming a source of discomfort but so also do signs of ageing, like wrinkles. In a sense, the whole question of abjection is epidermalised, reduced to superficial signs of difference. Anxiety comes from the appreciation that bodily abject things cannot be eliminated whereas, socially, it is considered desirable to remove them. Comfort and security come from the thought that the deodorant is effective but anxiety comes from the knowledge that its effect will wear off. Signs of ageing are resisted and the elderly themselves become abject. It is clear that these sources of abjection are culturally specific. Gypsies, for example, try to maintain the purity of the inner body so the skin is not a surface that is threatened by transgressive residues to the extent that it is in the larger society (Gypsies are clearly not insulated from messages about cleansed and deodorised bodies but they tend to have a more relaxed attitude towards 'dirt' than many others in western societies).

The imperative of purifying the body and resisting bodily abjection is mirrored in consumer culture, particularly in relation to the organisation of space in the home. The abject qualities of dirt, infection and disorder relate to objects and spaces but also to social relationships. Aversion to 'dirt' and 'disorder' is conveyed by a recent Betterware catalogue which advertises a toilet brush and holder where 'the exclusively designed holder covers the brush when not in use and allows discreet corner storage', the brush's association with toilet bowls and excretion being carefully disguised. One social function of purification is indicated on Lever Brothers' Domestos Multi-Cleaner, a typical example of the agents available to maintain the purity of home space which is, according to the label on the bottle: 'A rich, thick liquid that cuts through grease and contains bleach for better cleaning and *germ kill,* giving *your family deep down home protection'* (my italics). Protecting the family is particularly important, involving both the ordering and purification of interior spaces and the maintenance of a strong boundary with the outside – the source of infection and undesirable others. During the twentieth century in industrialised societies, there was an understandable concern with the reduction of diseases which were, among other things, threatening the reproduction of the working class but this has shaded into a concern with the *elimination* of infection through zapping 'germs' and tackling 'dirt', contributing to a culture of purification (although there has been a recent realisation that the incidence of some childhood illnesses like asthma may have increased because the resistance of the body is reduced as a result of increased cleanliness of homes).

David Sibley

How can these anxieties about order and purity in home space be theorised? Kristeva followed Douglas in identifying disorder as abject or polluting (although the two terms are not synonymous). This means that things that are categorised as belonging elsewhere necessarily transgress. They disturb a sense of order and are, thus, a source of anxiety. This becomes important in families, for example, where there are children whose classification systems are different to those of adults so that the placing of children's things and the use of space by children become discrepant from an adult perspective. There may be an urge to impose order on children in an attempt to eliminate their abject qualities. Kristeva certainly provides some insights on this problem but a more systematic and, at times, explicitly spatial account of the enduring dialectic of order and disorder had been suggested earlier by Basil Bernstein, an educational sociologist whose ideas have not been widely acknowledged in architecture, design or the spatial sciences. I have written about the relevance of Bernstein's thinking to spatial theory elsewhere but I think that it is worth going back to his writing on curricula to demonstrate how sociological and psychoanalytical arguments can be connected in theorisations of home space.[14]

Bernstein's work on knowledge and pedagogy centred on power and the transmission of knowledge. He represented the problem simply in terms of dichotomies – open/closed, strongly classified/weakly classified – that characterised ways in which knowledge was represented and managed. Thus, a closed or strongly classified area of knowledge was one that could be contaminated by the presence of ideas that did not fit, belonging and not-belonging being determined by a classification process that emphasised homogeneity. The controllers of knowledge in a strongly classified system are concerned that ideas do not flow between different knowledge categories because this could lead to the dissolution of the very categories that they are concerned to control. Thus, they use their power to maintain strong boundaries and hierarchies within educational institutions. Power also penetrates discreet knowledge areas, with those in control at the top of the hierarchy determining the ways in which ideas are organised and transmitted – what Bernstein described as strong framing. Open and weakly classified systems, by definition, celebrate diversity and hybridised knowledge and a lack of concern with boundaries. Both the strongly classified and weakly classified systems are problematic but, initially, Bernstein evidently saw the more liberal forms of weakly classified knowledge as preferable to strong classification because the latter inhibited the generation of new ideas.

It is particularly interesting that Bernstein recognised that his schemata had spatial implications – these are indicated in several footnotes to his text on education.[15] He illustrates the connections between spatial order and anxiety through the rather eccentric example of lavatories. He wrote that: '[It is] the strength of the

[14] D. Sibley, *Outsiders in Urban Societies*, Oxford, Basil Blackwell, 1981. D. Sibley, *Geographies of Exclusion*, London, Routledge, 1995.

[15] B. Bernstein, *Class, Codes and Control, volume 3*, London, Routledge and Kegan Paul, 1975, pp. 142–5.

David Sibley

16 Ibid.

rules of exclusion which control the array of objects in space. Thus, the stronger the rules of exclusion, the more distinctive the array of objects in space; that is, the greater the difference between object arrays in different spaces.'[16] Bernstein then works through these propositions with reference to four lavatories, at one extreme one that is strongly classified with sharp boundaries distinguishing it from the rest of domestic space, where the user might feel constrained to defecate discreetly and with the minimum noise, and at the other extreme one 'where the rigour is *totally relaxed*'. In the latter case, the most weakly classified lavatory, 'we suggest that the door will normally be open; it may even be that the lock will not function. It would not be untoward for a conversation to develop or even to be continued either side of the door . . . Lavatory one is predicated on the rule "things must be kept apart" . . . Lava-

17 Ibid.

tory four is predicated on the rule that "things must be kept together".'[17] He continues: 'When the rule is "things must be put together", we have an *interruption* of a previous order, and what is of issue is the authority (power relationships) that underpin it. Therefore, the rule "things must be put together" celebrates the present over

18 Ibid.

the past, the subjective over the objective, the personal over the positional.'[18] Bernstein concluded this reflection by suggesting that it would be interesting to apply these ideas to an analysis of the design of housing estates and formal educational spaces.

These ideas provide the rudiments of a cultural geography, where style is reflected in attitudes to the organisation of space. Thus, details of domestic design, like the toilet brush cover in the Betterware catalogue, can be recognised as an instance of strong framing within an (implicitly) strongly classified space, an ordering that has an appeal for some people. Strong classification, however, is not just an expression of preferences in the ordering of interior space. It clearly affects social relationships both within what Michel Foucault referred to as 'micro-spaces', like the home and beyond the home. Whereas pure, uncluttered and clearly demarcated spaces provide aesthetic satisfaction and gratification, as they clearly did for Le Corbusier as well as Betterware devotees, they are also a source of tension. This is indicated by Bernstein through his emphasis on the need for boundaries and boundary maintenance in strongly classified regimes. There is always the threat of disruption or, in Douglas' terms, pollution and, therefore, a need to be ever attentive to boundaries.

At this point, Bernstein comes close to some psychoanalytic observations on the spaces of same and other. One manifestation of strong classification is the maintenance of defences to deter those transgressive others who inhabit the public realm but this anxiety about the outside could be similarly expressed in, say, the wish of a parent to keep a room free from children on the grounds that their presence might be

a threat to some desired level of order. The culture of consumption in western societies tries to satisfy such desires, for example, through the promotion of home security and spaces designed specifically for children, whether in the home or in
commercial play spaces. As Freud (1919) recognised in his essay on the uncanny
(*unheimlich*, unsettling or unhomely), this striving for the safe, the familiar or *heimlich*
fails to remove a sense of unease.[19] I would argue that it makes it worse. To quote
Martin Jay on Derrida's reflections on the *heimlich*: 'Noting that the seemingly positive
category of the *heimlich*, which implies a safe haven to be restored, is itself deeply
fraught in Freud's discussion of its implications, [Derrida] adds that Heidegger's
description of Dasein's relation to the world expresses *the same unfulfilled longing* for
an eerily familiar home that, however, was never really inhabited and therefore can
never be regained. *No interior can be made safe from the incursion of the alien other*'
(my italics).[20] Efforts to purify the spaces of the home or the locality will increase
anxieties about the *unheimlich* because the purification process heightens the visibility
of the threatening other, however this other may be embodied.

Although there are cultural forces encouraging the production and reproduction
of strongly bounded or strongly classified spaces, it is also argued by object relation
theorists that this desire for order and the security that is seen to be achievable
through the creation of an ordered environment, as opposed to heterogeneous
spaces which carry the danger of unpredictability, has its origin in the separation of
the infant from the mother (see Phillips' argument, p. 58). Kristeva, from a different
perspective, would support this view. For her, the first abject object is the mother and
the social and cultural forms assumed by the abject reflect this initial anxiety about
pain and transgression. The abject, like the *unheimlich*, is always there, defining the
boundaries of the self. Zygmunt Bauman, while not drawing specifically on psychoanalytical theory, also implies that there is something fundamental about strong boundaries and distancing from the other in his observations on the stranger: '[Strangers]
bring the outside in and, in so doing, they seem to disturb the resonance between
physical and psychical distance, the sought after co-ordination between moral and
topological closeness, the staying together of friends and the remoteness of
enemies.'[21] The market (supplying nice kitchens, toilet brush holders, gated
communities and so on) may be responding to a fundamental need, rooted in the
unconscious, but we have to recognise that abject things and social groups are culturally produced and enter the unconscious. The unconscious is also a part of culture
and cultures are complex and varied.

There seem to be a number of valid criticisms of strongly classified homes and
local environments. In particular, they involve the imposition of order which may
be oppressive, for children in relation to adults or for various discrepant others in

19 S. Freud, 'The "Uncanny" ',
Penguin Freud Library, no. 14,
London, Penguin, pp. 335–76. First
published in 1919.

20 M. Jay, 'The Uncanny Nineties',
Salmagundi, no. 108, 1975, p. 23.

21 Cited in K. Robins, *Into the Image*,
London, Routledge, 1996, p. 33.

David Sibley

relation to 'the community'. Recent comment on child development suggests that the common parental urge to eliminate risk through the maintenance of strongly bounded home spaces, including the creation of a 'germ-free' home environment and purified neighbourhoods, is detrimental to children, first, because we need 'germs' or 'dirt' in order to develop resistance to disease, and, second, because children cannot learn to manage risk if they are protected from it.[22] Minimising children's exposure to perceived risks involves maintaining a strong boundary between public and private space, moving through public space by car, which is an extension of private space, and thus minimising encounters with different kinds of people. The creation of a nested series of homogenised spaces from within the home to the wider public environment allows only predictable, adult-sanctioned interactions with others. The result is children who grow up with limited social skills, unchallenged prejudices, and a limited ability to cope with the dangers of the urban environment.

This negative view of strongly classified environments fails to take account of evidence from research in group therapy that children (and adults) need firm boundaries in order to develop a secure sense of self.[23] If members of a family 'live in each other's laps', in a boundary-less, weakly classified home, or they are 'enmeshed' as Salvador Minuchin put it, there is a danger that children, in particular, will not develop a sense of autonomy.[24] There is, therefore, a tension between strong and weakly structured collectivities and environments. The science fiction writer, Stanislaw Lem, saw order and disorder enfolded into each other. His own life, a privileged childhood in the Ukraine during the 1930s, was characterised by stability, predictability and orderliness but he recognised that the price he paid for this was social isolation. His life after the Second World War was marked by instability and unpredictability but 'it was open to the excitement of the streets and the dangers of chance'.[25] Subsequently, in his writing, Lem 'yearns to create a chaos that can defeat explanation; faced with chaos, he cannot resist entering into explanations'.[26] It is such a dialectical view that is necessary in attempting to understand the anxieties associated with the ordering of home environments.

THE HOME, THE NEIGHBOURHOOD AND EXCLUSION

Although the need for a dialectical and nuanced view of order/disorder and strong/weak classification is demonstrable, much of the literature on the rejection of the mentally ill or other 'imperfect people', to use Constance Perin's term, suggests that intolerance of difference is greatest in middle-class suburbs where a premium is put on order both within and without the home.[27] The desire for purity and homogene-

22 J. Heartfield, 'Is Fear Itself the Greatest Danger', *Living Marxism*, May 1998, pp. 24–30. K. Figes, 'Seen But Not Hurt', *The Guardian*, 14 August 2000, G2, p. 2.

23 D. Brown and L. Zinkin, *The Psyche and the Social World*, London, Routledge, 1994.

24 S. Minuchin, *Families and Family Therapy*, London, Tavistock, 1974.

25 K. Hayles, *Chaos Bound*, Ithaca, Cornell University Press, 1990, pp. 118–20.

26 Ibid.

27 C. Perin, *Belonging in America*, Madison, University of Wisconsin Press, 1988.

David Sibley

ity seems to generate fear of others. According to Sennett, there is in such places a collective denial of otherness in people's own lives, and anxieties about threats to the order realised in the home and the locality are projected on to discrepant groups or individuals.[28] The 'myth of the purified community' depends on the identification of a deviant other. Michael Dear's research on responses to the mentally ill in Canadian cities as well as Sennett's own historical research on North American cities provide some empirical support for this argument.[29] Certainly, people who have the power to buy order and security may feel that their material well-being is threatened by negatively constructed forms of difference but it is simplistic to suggest a necessary connection between pristine fitted kitchens, neat lawns, a lack of litter, on one hand, and hostility to outsiders on the other.

Some British experience suggests that it is in poor neighbourhoods, which have less power to maintain strong boundaries than do the residents in middle-class estates, that intolerance of difference is greatest. Campaigns to 'get rid of Gypsies' in the 1970s, for example, were primarily associated with poor districts in northern cities like Hull and Sheffield.[30] Similarly, demonstrations against suspected paedophiles on the Paulsgrove estate in Portsmouth in the summer of 2000, suggest that people with little control over their own lives or material conditions in their locality are in greatest need of a threatening other. Weberian closure theory, the argument that people who are themselves excluded from the material benefits of a society will attempt to deny a weaker minority access to the meagre resources they enjoy, provides one plausible explanation. However, a material culture that puts a high value on hygiene and spatial order and a political regime that signals anxieties about threats to national identity from refugees and asylum seekers cut across class and do not encourage the celebration of difference.

28 Sennett, op. cit.

29 M. Dear and J. Wolch, *Landscapes of Despair*, Cambridge, Polity Press, 1987. R. Sennett, 'Middle-Class Families and Urban Violence the Experience of a Chicago Community in the Nineteenth Century', in T. Haravan (ed.), *Anonymous Americans*, Englewood Cliffs, N.J., Prentice Hall, 1971, pp. 280–305. R. Sennett, 'Destructive Gemeinschaft', in N. Birnbaum (ed.), *Beyond the Crisis*, Oxford, Oxford University Press, 1977, pp. 171–200.

30 Sibley, *Outsiders in Urban Societies*.

CONCLUSION

I began this essay by suggesting that ideas about spatial and social order and the identification of the discrepant and abject are culturally specific. What at one time might have been recognised as North American and northern European material culture is now widely diffused, however, although reworked in different regional contexts. Thus, the assertions I make about anxieties and disgust and the ways in which they are played out in the spaces of the home and the neighbourhood may, if they are valid, have some generality. Although it is necessary to work with dichotomies like order and disorder, strong and weak classification, pure and defiled, in a dialectical sense, the immediate political problems that we have to confront – concerning the

David Sibley

identification of asylum seekers as 'bogus' or 'economic migrants', the rejection of the homeless and mentally ill within localities, moral panics about paedophiles, and so on – are concerned with abjection. What people feel to be abject, what makes them anxious and fearful and triggers attempts at distanciation, is a cultural problem. The cultural peculiarity of our feelings about bodily residues, for example, can be recognised if we consider attitudes to the body in other cultures, like Gypsies, for example. Unease about bodily residues is then mirrored in concerns about the pure and the defiled in the home. If dirt is matter out of place, then spatial order itself becomes a source of anxiety. Disorder is dirt. Importantly, what is abject can include bodily residues: scurf, faeces, saliva once it has left the mouth, and so on; qualities of things, such as sticky substances on coffee tables; and people. An aversion to certain others, represented in negative stereotypes, cannot be separated from these abject qualities of bodies, homes and localities. Many people, if they have enough money, are able to keep things in place, to maintain a distance from abject others, although this does not remove them as a source of anxiety. Others who lack this power, who feel overwhelmed, may take to the streets or may react violently.

David Sibley

stairway architecture

TRANSFORMATIVE CYCLES

IN THE GOLDEN LANE

The concrete interior staircase is a menace and *a source of noise from my next-door neighbours.*[1]

We don't think enough about staircases.
Nothing was more beautiful in old houses than the staircases.
Nothing is uglier, more hostile, meaner, in today's apartment buildings.
We should learn to live more on staircases. But how?[2]

[1] Private letter from Golden Lane resident of 30 years to the author, 9 July 1997.

[2] G. Perec, *Species of Spaces and Other Pieces*, London, Penguin, 1997, p. 38.

In the typical house typologies of England, the internal stairway is conventionally enclosed by walls, that is, the stair*way* is contained within a stair*case*. Hidden from view (except, of course, when one is actually ascending or descending the stairway and, even then, it is amazing how many people do not consciously look at the tricky construction they are negotiating), the stairway is treated as a distasteful device, like a dumb waiter for the moving of dishes, a country house backstairs for the circulation of servants or, worse still, a rubbish chute down which debris periodically tumbles. Within the staircase an even more forgotten space lurks, the under-stair cupboard, which, if one should be brave enough to peer inside, one finds to be stuffed with acrid-smelling cleaning fluids, musty rain-gear and, in the most rearward and inaccessible niches, god-knows-what-else. Both stairway and cupboard are boxes within the staircase, into which one ventures darkly and as infrequently as possible.

A stairway with which I am intimately acquainted assumes a quite different attitude,[3] and so suggests an alternative to the commonplace notion of architecture being constituted purely from physical matter. Here, as we shall see, matter is produced out of a dialectical engagement between an architectural element (the staircase) and the human body and its various practices and senses. In short, architecture is here interproduced as a simultaneous combination of space, bodily action and physical matter.

My home is a 1950s two-floor maisonette, part of a medium-sized estate constructed on a large bomb-site for London's City Corporation and now known as Golden Lane.[4] The intended residents, who still form the majority of the estate's inhabitants, were local single people and couples (not large families), many of whom worked nearby at Bart's hospital and Smithfield meat market. These residents would have been quite accustomed to the more constricted rooms and staircases of tenement flats, terraced rows and sub-divided urban villas. Despite this clientele, or perhaps because of it, the architects – Joe Chamberlin, Geoffry Powell and Christoph Bon – chose to celebrate the stairway, having it rise directly out of the living room. In order to open the space below the stairs, and in complete denial of traditional under-stair cupboard storage, there is no evident support within the room – no lower wall, no stringer between the treads, no supportive columns and no veiling screen. Instead, the treads are individually cantilevered out from the side wall, projecting outward in a heroic yet commonplace gesture. This is most apparent whenever the sun shines through the large south window at the base of the stairway, when tread shadows radiate out across the bare side wall and proclaim their fantastical existence free from the constraints of gravitational physics. Even the newel post (in fact a sweeping continuation of the handrail), which on first sight might appear to be providing some kind of ground-based support, passes clean through a neat circular hole in the lower-most tread. The startling simplicity of construction is underlined by the

3 An earlier version of this essay first appeared in J. Bell (ed.), *Transformable Architecture*, special issue of *Architectural Design*, London, Academy/John Wiley & Sons, 2000.

4 For the early history of the Golden Lane Estate, see 'Flats: City of London Chamberlin, Powell and Bon', *The Architectural Review*, vol. 115, no. 685, January 1954, pp. 51–4; 'Flats: City of London Chamberlin, Powell and Bon', *The Architectural Review*, vol. 119, no. 709, January 1956, pp. 34–8; *Architect and Building News*, vol. 209, 17 May 1956, pp. 526–7; *The Architects' Journal*, vol. 123, 7 June 1956, pp. 632–6; *AA Journal*, vol. 72, April 1957, pp. 214–23; 'Housing in Golden Lane Estate', *The Architects' Journal*, vol. 125, June 1957, pp. 415–26; J. M. Richards, 'Criticism', *The Architects' Journal*, vol. 125, 20 June 1957, pp. 911–15; Chamberlin, Powell and Bon, response to J. M. Richards, *The Architects' Journal*, vol. 125, 27 June 1957; *The Architectural Review*, vol. 121, June 1957, pp. 414–26; 'Criticism', *The Architects' Journal*, vol. 126, 11 July 1957, pp. 78–9; and *Bauen-Wohnen*, no. 4, April 1960, pp. 146–8.

Figure 8.1 Chamberlin, Powell
and Bon, *Stairway, Golden Lane
Estate, London.* Photograph, Iain
Borden.

Iain Borden

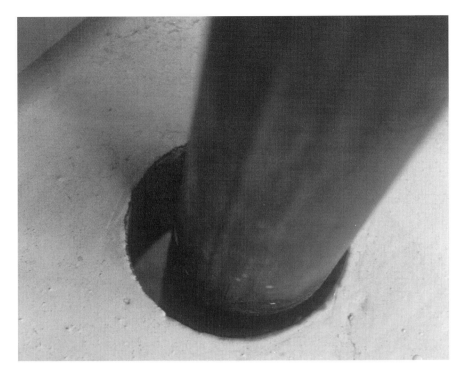

Figure 8.2 Chamberlin, Powell and Bon, *Stairway, Golden Lane Estate, London.* Photograph, Iain Borden.

balusters, or more precisely by their fixing nuts exposed beneath the treads, and whose crude nature boldly states that what you see is indeed what you get. This stairway has no deathly, shrouding coffin.

Architectural historians will be quick to note that this stairway arrangement may well have been adapted from Le Corbusier's Unité d'Habitation in Marseilles, whose construction finished the same year, 1952, that Chamberlin, Powell and Bon won the Golden Lane competition. Others will be equally quick to point out that another entry for the Golden Lane competition, the infamous street-deck scheme by the Smithsons, has been far more influential upon subsequent architectural developments. More prosaic, but equally important, is the notion that it is in the incredibly precise detailed design of such architectural elements as stairways that one finds clues as to the essential core of modernism. Consider, for example, the following introductory design guidelines for a precast terrazzo stairway (similar to that used at Golden Lane) in an in-house document produced by the large British modernist architectural firm of YRM in the early 1970s.

Here we find concerns with standardisation and construction, research and subcontracting, fabrication and specification, design variation and aesthetics all bound up within a dominant logic of rationalisation, efficiency and professional ethics. By such

Figure 8.3 Chamberlin, Powell and Bon, *Stairway, Golden Lane Estate, London.* Photograph, Iain Borden.

04

Detailing

04.4 Concrete: Precast Terrazzo

1. If stair is in multi-storey building keep design consistent to enable repeated use of formwork and ensure economy. Method of support as 'G' on Fig. 14, and details as Figs. 22 to 25.

2. Precast terrazzo treads, risers and wall strings manufactured, ground and polished at works. Check thicknesses (with specialist sub contractor at design stage – any approach to specialist firms for technical information should be limited to those who will be given the opportunity to quote for the work) in relation to selected stone aggregate grading and size of units.

3. Use fair faced concrete to soffits, exposed edges of flights and landings where this offers an acceptable standard. By projecting the ends of treads and risers as detailed, slight inaccuracies in the insitu concrete can be disguised.

4. Metal balustrade, fixed with balusters set into structural concrete through terrazzo treads, grouted in epoxy mortar. Running the mortice joint in molten lead is the traditional method, and can still be used.

    The termination of the raking handrail at the top landing is a matter of aesthetic preference, i.e. details A or B.

    Fixing of balustrades other than mild steel may be as Fig. 29 for marble staircases.[5]

5 YRM, 'Stairways' document, ca. 1972. Thanks to Victor Kite for this information.

Iain Borden

procedures, a small architectural element like a staircase becomes a condensation of architectural principles as a whole.

Yet it is not the placing of the Golden Lane stairway within the canon and design rigour of modernism that gives it architectural life. More important is the way in which each stairway is integrated into the flat as a whole, for as a contemporary architectural magazine noted the 'volume of the stair running through the two floors and the two-storey window associated with it become a visual part of the living room'.[6] How, then, does this staircase 'become' a 'visual part' of the living room? What is this process of becoming, what is this relation and in what way is it visual, and how is the architecture transformed as a result?

The answer to this kind of question lies not just in the constructional, visual or spatial analysis of the stairway, although such things do play their part; the stairway can, of course, be seen in plan, section, elevation, photograph, working drawing, direct experience and all the other ways of observing a piece of architecture. But such representations as plans and even sections do little to articulate the more dynamic aspects of architecture, particularly those involving verticality. As the German architectural theorist Paul Frankl wrote in 1914, '[t]o understand a secular building we must get to know it as a whole by walking through it'.[7]

This kind of concern with movement can be identified within much of British modernism at the time of construction of the Golden Lane Estate. For example, Tom Ellis, a partner in the firm of British modernist architects Lyons, Israel, Ellis, Gray and a contemporary of Chamberlin, Powell and Bon, thought movement important enough to publish his only articles on the subject. In 1960, just after the final completion of the Golden Lane Estate, an essay entitled 'The Discipline of the Route' appeared in *Architectural Design* wherein Ellis rails against the 'confusion and frustration' caused by illogically planned buildings disposed like 'rabbit warrens or tins of worms'.[8] By contrast, he argues, an adherence to the notion of the 'route' within a building – by which he means its plan sequence and, in particular, its stairways – produces a 'Unity of Intention' with no possible deviation from a pre-determined path. Although Ellis does allow for a certain poetic and sculptural quality in architecture, his analysis of buildings by Le Corbusier and Alvar Aalto discloses on over-riding concern with clarity of expression and a certainty of knowledge:

> *The route and destination within his [Aalto's] buildings, the way in and the way out, the changes in volume and daylighting, the awareness of the external conditions from within, the identity of your position anywhere within the building, the clarity of the segregation of the parts of his building, and the dramatic use of changes in level – all these illustrate once again the discipline of the route in great architecture.*[9]

6 'Flats: City of London Chamberlin, Powell and Bon', *The Architectural Review*, vol. 115, no. 685, January 1954, p. 52.

7 P. Frankl, *Principles of Architectural History: the Four Phases of Architectural Style, 1420–1900*, Cambridge, Mass., MIT, 1973, p. 78.

8 T. Ellis, 'The Discipline of the Route', *Architectural Design*, November 1960, pp. 481–2. A second article, also called 'The Discipline of the Route' and published in *Architectural Design* in 1966, deals with similar issues at site, masterplanning and urban scales. My thanks to Jonathan Hall for drawing Ellis' publications to my attention.

9 Ibid., p. 481.

lain Borden

Despite, then, an explicit interest in movement, and an implicit one in aesthetics as experience, this kind of modernist thinking gives little room for a more phenomenological concern with staircases and other elements of architectural route. We are therefore offered only limited clues here as to how the Golden Lane stairway might be such a central part of the flat as its construction suggests. The main limitation with Ellis' thinking on the subject is that, despite an ostensible concern with movement, this is movement as abstracted into spatial types, elements and paths, and hence is

Figures 8.4 & 8.5 Chamberlin, Powell and Bon, *Stairway, Golden Lane Estate, London.* Photograph, Iain Borden.

Iain Borden

far removed from the more visceral nature of actual bodily movement. By contrast, Frankl, in a continuation of the quote already given above, states that 'the entrance, the vestibule or passage leading to courtyard or stair, the connections between several courtyards, the stairs themselves and the corridors leading away from them at each level, like the veins of our bodies – these are the pulsating arteries of a building'.[10]

It is thus not only the Ellis/modernist concern with path and route but also the more bodily and everyday nature of its occupation intimated here by Frankl that helps us understand the Golden Lane stairway. At the Golden Lane it is when walking up and down, as one must repeatedly do during the course of daily routines, that one first encounters the unique phenomenological character of these stairs. Such a condition was recognised by the modernist British architect Berthold Lubetkin when he remarked that 'any staircase is a sort of machine to climb up or to descend, but in the best beaux arts interpretation it is a display, it is a dance'. Lubetkin continues, 'and it certainly enriches the conception of human surroundings and the body if architecture can bring in everyday experience a sort of ballet like quality – semi poetic choice – in what otherwise is a purely utilitarian conception'.[11] Such a stairway is more than a conveyor belt; it is also a social stage.

While the quotidian body may be transformed into that of a dancer through the device of the stairway, so too is another transformation effected upon the stairs themselves. When experienced by the motile and rhythmic body, the treads are revealed as individual planes, each forward step being met by a corresponding, independently supported platform on which to tread, and, simultaneously, as the steps continue, by a connected series of such planes; the stairs are at once unique and repeated, autonomous and integrated. Ascending and descending, combining bent knees, measured steps and a cautiously balancing hand (for the Golden Lane stairway is unusually steep, a fact brought into sharp relief by the absence of solid risers), one enunciates these stairs as a sentence, a chain of moments and movements each unique in itself yet inseparable from the others. Walking creates a unity of the stairs; hence it is the act of movement together with the physical architectural element, and, not this element by itself, that makes the stairway. These stairs are as pearls on a necklace, complete *qua* necklace only when placed against the body.

It is not, however, simply that the stairway is a production of bodily space and movement, for, as in Baroque stairs, it itself is also a focus of attention,[12] an intellectual as well as material endeavour. At Golden Lane, just as walking unites the stairway and the stairway unites walking, so too does the stairway give aesthetic expression to the possibility of movement – each cantilevered tread, ever visible to the eye, suggests that walking on these treads is not only possible but probable, and hence that

10 Frankl, op. cit., p. 78.

11 B. Lubetkin, quoted in J. Allan, *Berthold Lubetkin: Architecture and the Tradition of Progress*, London, RIBA Publications, 1992, p. 540.

12 A. Gibson, 'From the Landing to the Lobby: Stairways and Elevators, an Experiential History of Vertical Movement', Master's dissertation, The Bartlett, University College London, 1996, p. 31.

Iain Borden

Figure 8.6 Chamberlin, Powell and Bon, *Stairway, Golden Lane Estate, London.* Photograph, Iain Borden.

the floors of the flat are continually interrelated. In further reinforcement of this view, the vertical metal balusters are, although evenly spaced horizontally, given a 1:2:1 rhythm across the series of treads. Each tread is thus expressed separately yet as part of the series, with a dynamic composition subtly transferring the eye from one to another. Through such aesthetic operations, the stairway offers the continual

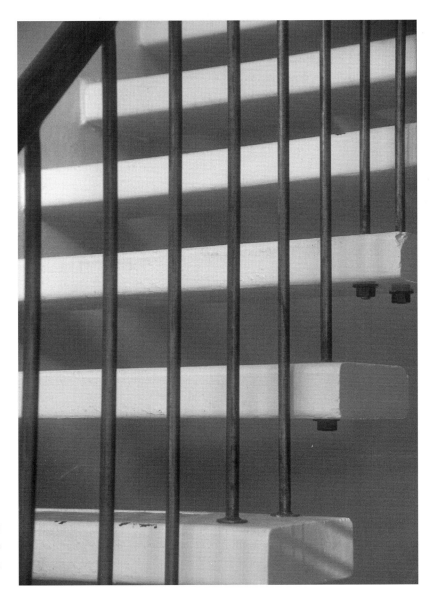

Figure 8.7 Chamberlin, Powell and Bon, *Stairway, Golden Lane Estate, London*. Photograph, Iain Borden.

reminder that there are other spaces within the maisonette, and that habitation conjoins them. The same could perhaps also be said of the double-height space that sits over the stairway, for this too gives volumetric connection between floors. Yet it is only the eye and not the body that travels in this space (indeed, I have physically entered it only once, in order to complete a precarious piece of DIY). The stairway, by contrast, is the more corporeal of elements by encouraging the resident to at once mentally and physically pursue the arch-modernist Sigfried Giedion's assertion that in order 'to grasp the true nature of space the observer must project himself through it'.[13] Whether located in the living room or the upper landing, the visibility and detail of the stairway both promotes movement and gives expression to the possibility of that movement. Indeed, this facet of the stairway is revealed in the very naming of its parts, where the *step*, *tread*, *going*, *flight* and *riser* are, along with the door *handle*, near unique in architecture in being not only the noun given to the element in order to identify it, but also the verb used to describe the bodily encounter with that element: we *step* and *tread* on a stairway, we *go* along, we *fly* and *rise* up, and we *handle* door furniture. This very nomenclature demands that an action, and an overtly bodily action at that, be performed against the element, such that its essence ultimately lies not within the material or form of the architecture but in its reproduction within the motile body and within the expressive means (language and architectural design) by which we represent that reproduction.

After living in this flat for a while, another connection also gradually makes its presence felt. The stairs are made from hard terrazzo (although in our home they have been partly covered with paint and tiles) and when trod upon, each creates a distinct sound, such that every descent and ascent provides a short, repetitive melody to the life of the flat – a keyboard of everyday movements, punctuating space with its peculiar form of music. (It is perhaps no coincidence that the hi-fi in our flat is placed beneath the stairway; unconsciously, this area has been made into the sound-hearth of the home.)

Nor is it just one's own flat that is enervated so. Although there are no public stairway social condensers in the Golden Lane Estate – those spaces beloved by the designers of social housing where residents are expected to unavoidably meet and thus forge new social relations – the internal stairways nonetheless act in their own small way within this social frame. Each cantilevered tread is balanced by its mirror-element on the other side of the party wall, creating exactly the same stairway for the flat next door. And so my paced sound-rhythms are transmitted with extraordinary efficiency through the terrazzo to my South African neighbours, just as their sounds are to me, creating a sonorous and social connection between our otherwise separate existences. After some years, I know when they sleep and when they arise, I know

13 S. Giedion, *Space, Time and Architecture: the Growth of a New Tradition*, Cambridge, Mass., Harvard University Press, fourth edition, 1963, p. 432.

Iain Borden

when they are in a hurry and when A. has put on high heels, just as they must know the same kinds of detail about us.

This, perhaps, is what is so intriguing about the stairway: its continual shifting from one condition to another. What goes up must come down, what is moving is also rendered as aesthetic form, what is given is always returned. The stairway may at first seem to be a linear arrangement, but in fact it is a transformative cycle, periodically rendering architecture and everyday life into a new and delightful composition.

Iain Borden

jane rendell and pamela wells

the place of prepositions: a space inhabited by angels

a conversation beyond us: from london to wolverhampton, between theory and practice

jane rendell: what do you think your work is about?

pamela wells: creating temporary architectures. of a sort.

making places for things to happen.

hallways, doors, stairwells, passages.

why do you make these places?

less about the mastery of technique,

they are more thresholds of discovery.

spaces that we can move through;

gathering and unravelling.

how do you position yourself in relation to your work? where are you in that space – conceptually and materially?

where am i? who am i? where am i going?

we need to make spaces to ask these questions,

pliable spaces to lose yourself . . .

giving yourself away in order to reconvene.

so how are others involved in making that space?

we help one another navigate.

space, as an architectural concept is nothing if not a relationship.

it's easier, for me, to orientate in a crowded room, bumping into others.

people help me – physically and conceptually – to create these places.

i find parts of myself that i didn't know about,

they find something of me

and they may take it with them.

we lose ourselves by connecting with others.

the architectures you create have a very particular materiality. why do you like working with plastic for example?

i work with ordinary materials that have their own narrative potential.

like plastic carrier bags.

an overlooked by-product, discarded after use.

(the woman in the kitchen after shopping.)

jane rendell and pamela wells

plastic protects, but things stored in plastic go off quickly.
a suffocating potential . . .
breathing, semi-permeable, like skin.
translucent and opaque,
it contains and yet has no fixed form.

what's the story with beads and stitching?
loose, we can't grasp them,
strung together they are precious.
on their own, they are unnecessary,
stitched on top of plastic they are transformative.
just like words.
words we don't usually pay attention to.
like prepositions.

jane rendell and pamela wells

intersubjectivity: between theory and practice

1 L. Irigaray, *Thinking the Difference*, London, The Athlone Press, 1994, pp. 48–9.

in general, women are much more interested in others. this can be seen, for example, in the use of transitive verbs with the person as the animate object – 'je le lave' [i wash him], m'aimes-tu?' [do you love me?] – or of prepositions expressing intersubjectivity; avec [with], entre [between, amongst], à [to], pour [for], etc.[. . .].[1]

there is something appealing in the challenge of creating 'spectacular' work without falling into the trap of the commodifiable spectacle. i have found interaction and collaborative making to be effective strategies for disrupting fetishistic, purely objective relationships (between maker and consumer, between thing and use, between monument and audience). i straddle the lines between social sculpture, community animation, personal vision and public art.

there appear to be parallels between two bodies of feminist work produced in the 1970s. on the one hand, there are the theoretical and philosophical enquiries of french feminists around feminine desire, morphology and space. the insights of luce irigaray and hélène cixous – notions of écriture féminine and économie feminine – suggest modes of writing, new forms of creativity.[2] they also suggest new ways of making relationships between one another, ones that differ from the masculine – differ from an economy of appropriation and the self-same, where more is better and the other is only regarded in relation to the self. for me, french feminist critical theory provides an emancipatory impulse, an opportunity for self-reflection and a chance to imagine new places between men and women.

2 See for example E. Marks and I. De Courtivron, *New French Feminisms: An Anthology*, London, Harvester Wheatsheaf, 1981. A. A. Jardine and A. M. Menke (eds), *Shifting Scenes, Interviews on Women, Writing and Politics in Post-68 France*, New York, Colombia Press, 1991.

on the other, we have the work of radical feminist artists in the US, such as judy chicago, cheri gaulke, miriam shapiro and others, exploring female sexuality, the body and desire.[3] these artists also developed an interest in techniques, materials and processes traditionally connected with women's work – such as sewing and inter-action. the US has also produced a wealth of overtly feminist artists who deal specifically with public space such as suzanne lacy and kim abeles, as well as critics attentive to issues of gender and place such as suzi gablik, dolores hayden, lucy lippard and arlene raven.[4] educated in los angeles, pamela wells comes out of this rich seam of work so relevant to today's more theoretical discussions of feminine topographies and figurations in architecture.

3 See for example Witney Chadwick's account of various feminist art projects in W. Chadwick, *Women, Art and Society*, London, Thames and Hudson, 1996, chapter 12.

4 See for example S. Gablik, *The Reenchantment of Art*, New York, Thames and Hudson, 1991. D. Hayden, *The Power of Place*, London, MIT Press, 1995. S. Lacy (ed.), *Mapping the Terrain: New Genre Public Art*, Seattle, Bay Press, 1995.

both influences have been treated with scepticism by many british feminists. in different ways they are too 'messy', too sexual and, for marxist feminists, they run the risk of essentialising and dehistoricising the difference between men and women. the resonance of french feminist theory in architectural discourse in the UK is only

jane rendell and pamela wells

just being felt, having found its way through feminist art history and geography, as well as through less squeamish feminist architectural critics in the US.[5] the legacy of the US based radical feminist art practice can be seen in the work of someone as unlikely as tracey emin. although emin does not overtly associate herself with feminist issues, her focus on personal life and her choice of techniques, such as stitching and quilting, connect her to the history of feminist practice.

this essay is written in between two places – between feminist critical theory and feminist critical art practice. pamela wells' art practice and jane rendell's theoretical writings have developed apart. here, these two subjects speak in between. but what allows a mediation of this space between two: between words and things, ideas and matter, makers and users, jane and pamela? what we aim to do here is jostle back and forth (in between) in order to negotiate the relation that theory has to practice. never an easy task. we are not interested in using examples of practice to illustrate theoretical positions, nor in applying theoretical insights to modes of practice, but rather to create another space where a new relationship between the two may come into being. remaining on the cusp, the threshold between the two, it is possible to be attentive to the concerns of both. what follows are sets of threes, one thing and then another, and then a negotiation between the two. these speaking subjects, speak in threes.

both/and: between one and one is three

deconstruction as a process is profoundly creative . . . deconstruction, then, is a process that can never stop or cease; it is profoundly resistant to closure. it works like a critical utopia . . . in particular it creates new conceptual exploratory space by resisting dualistic thought, thereby undermining the structure or system through which meaning is created.[6]

in contemporary critical theory there are at least two ways of dealing with twos. dialectics, the language of 'on the one hand . . . yet on the other', the art of clarifying ideas through the exchange of questions and answers. another way of understanding this relationship is through deconstruction, the language of 'both/and'. there has been a great deal of debate as to whether deconstruction expresses any kind of political possibility, especially for feminism, given the place of the 'feminine' in derrida's writings. but here i follow diane elan, in positing that deconstruction provides a place of radical undecideability and that this position is a politicised one.[7] lucy sargisson argues for a similarity between deconstruction and utopianism in that they both go further than reversing binary oppositions, but rather 'subverts and undermines the

5 See for example the work of Tamar Garb in art history and Gillian Rose in geography, as well as Jennifer Bloomer and Vanessa Chase in architecture. See T. Garb, 'Unpicking the Seams of her Disguise – Self-Representation in the Case of Marie Bashkirtseff', *Block*, August 1987–8, no. 13, pp. 79–85. G. Rose, *Feminism and Geography: The Limits of Geographical Knowledge*, Cambridge, Polity Press, 1993. J. Bloomer, *Architecture and the Text: the (S)crypts of Joyce and Piranesi*, New Haven, Yale University Press, 1993.

6 L. Sargisson, *Contemporary Feminist Utopianism*, London, Routledge, 1996, p. 105.

7 D. Elan, *Feminism and Deconstruction*, London, Routledge, 1994.

8 Sargisson, op. cit., p. 104.

system which constructs those hierarchical relations'.[8] the work of luce irigaray and hélène cixous can be understood within this context. in their writing one witnesses a glimpse of something new, the traits of a feminine economy – a willingness to take risks, to let go, to allow transformation . . .

prepositions: transformational messengers

9 M. Serres, *Angels: A Modern Myth*, Paris, Flammarion, 1995, pp. 140–7.

that's prepositions for you. they don't change in themselves, but they change everything around them: words, things and people . . . prepositions transform words and syntax, while pré-posés *transform men.*[9]

the figure of transformation is the angel. within angelology, an angel is 'a spirit or heavenly being who mediates between the human and divine realms', but the basic meaning of the term is messenger. the angel appears in philosophical texts as diverse as irigaray and walter benjamin, but it is within the work of michel serres that the angel takes central stage. serres' intellectual project is enormous and wide ranging. truly interdisciplinary, he travels across science, literature, philosophy and art, constantly interrogating, in the most poetic fashion, the nature of knowledge itself. in earlier texts serres' interest in angels was more implicit – through figures of the guide and the messenger. in the *hermes* texts the fascination is with information theory, transport and the multiplication of messages through diverse spaces of communication. later in *the troubadour of knowledge*, in a discussion of the passage between the exact sciences and sciences of man, serres refers to the importance of points of exchange and conditions of passage.[10]

10 M. Serres, *Hermes: Literature, Science, Philosophy*, Baltimore and London, The Johns Hopkins Press, 1982. M. Serres, *The Troubadour of Knowledge*, Ann Arbor, University of Michigan Press, 1997.

in a more recent publication *angels: a modern myth*, a narrative of sorts set at an airport, angels appear through the conversations of the two main characters both involved with travel. serres' work highlights the angelic condition as a temporal and spatial one. his emphasis is on communication, mediation and transformation as a result of exchange. serres suggests that there are certain places where messages from angels increase in number and intensity; he calls these 'passing places of angels' – they are places of transition and passage, spaces of interchange, such as airports, places of mass transit, new technologies.[11] serres emphasises the unstable nature of angels, they are 'wandering with no fixed habitat',[12] and their dual role as verbal messengers and elemental fluxes: 'intermediary. angel. messenger. hyphen'.[13] but perhaps the most interesting thing serres has to say about angels is that they are the personification of prepositions.

11 Serres, *Angels: A Modern Myth*.

12 Ibid.

13 Ibid.

jane rendell and pamela wells

here we use the angelic properties of prepositions as a means of making connections between two, between people and places, between theory and practice. some prepositions emphasise position, the relation of an object or a subject to place, such as **on**, **in**, **between**, **through**. others focus on relationships between subjects and objects, for example, **among** and **with**, and the directional nature of these connections, like, **for** or **to**. yet others contain elements of time, as in **beyond**. we also suggest that art objects and processes can function like prepositions: they change everything around them. here we look at 9 sets of 3's: prepositions, and the theories/practices, concepts/objects they hyphenate. 9 is the number of change.

it is the fluidity of **between**
where i lose my **on**,
the in of **to**.
then, seeking **with**,
the **among** *of* **for**,
we slip **through**
and reach **beyond**.

jane rendell and pamela wells

with: where have you been?

a double walled room-like structure filled with objects.
objects shrouded by skin-coloured, translucent plastic.
objects dealing with personal histories in the outside wall,
including a lobster carcass, dead bird, used tea bags, snail shells and hatpins.
beans. a staple food, a beginning, filling the inside wall:
questions imbedded in the structure.
an evocative mysteriousness.

with: 'écriture de la femme'

writing is working: being worked; questioning (in) the between (letting oneself be questioned) of same and of other without which nothing lives; undoing death's work by willing the togetherness of one-another, infinitely charged with a ceaseless exchange of one with another – not knowing one another and beginning again only from what is most distant, from self, from other, from the other within. a course that multiplies transformations by the thousands.[14]

14 H. Cixous, 'Sorties', in S. Sellers (ed.), *The Hélène Cixous Reader*, London, Routledge, 1994, p. 43.

with: a space of encounter with the other

'écriture de la femme' – a writing to free women from a language governed by the presence of the phallus. a symbolic language in which a feminine presence can make itself known. a language not based on a syntax of has/has not. not merely the reversal of the hierarchy of male and female but a challenge to the opposition itself, showing that the feminine and female sexuality exceed the complementary role that they have been assigned in the opposition male/female. a writing shot through with

jane rendell and pamela wells

figure 9.1 pamela wells, *where have you been?*, 1993.

differences displays a different relation to 'the other', puts the isolated autonomous self at risk, to question and be questioned.

in *where have you been?* the artist presents herself through traces. these traces make a place to enter. this place, created by an abundance of objects, suggests more than the history of one person. this place invites one to consider a myriad of histories – those of the objects, the artist and the occupiers. recognising potentiality produces a density of possibilities. this rhetoric of excess refuses to measure against a standard, against scarcity, against certainty. to enter this place is to be with another, to encounter all the questions this entails.

jane rendell and pamela wells

in

in: lair

white chocolate, melted and formed into walls,
into windows. coloured orange, green, light blue.
a pink, leg-like pedestal topped with fake grass.
there are no divisions in the space inside.
it bulges slightly.
it lasts longer than you might expect.
a miniature chandelier glows, hanging from the pitched roof,
illuminating the singular space.

in: the question of place

15 Irigaray, *Thinking the Difference,*
op. cit., p. 49.

women are more attentive to the question of place: they are close to things, to others
(autres, which is related to one of the indo-european roots of the verb être [to be]).[15]

in: a critical dwelling space

recent work in feminism, cultural studies and human geography, has increasingly
focused on issues of identity, difference and subjectivity. the language of these texts
is highly spatialised, with words such as 'mapping', 'locating', 'situating', 'positioning'
and 'boundaries' appearing frequently. academics might 'explain' this new emphasis
on space as typical of post-modern discourse. (post-modernism in this context refer-
ing to a questioning of truth, history and the all-knowing modern subject and instead
describing a series of discourses exploring new epistemologies and ontologies.)

these searches for new ways of knowing and being are being framed in spatial
terms. for those concerned with issues of identity – race, gender, sexuality and ethnicity – spatial metaphors constitute powerful political devices that can be employed as
critical tools for examining the relationship between the construction of identities and
the politics of location. in such on-going theoretical disputes as the essentialism/con-
structionism debate, positionality provides a way of understanding knowledge and

jane rendell and pamela wells

figure 9.2 pamela wells, *lair*, 1998.

essence as contingent and strategic – *where* i am makes a difference to what i can know and who i can be.

the dwelling places for woman defined by men are problematic. in patriarchy, through ownership and appropriation, men have 'placed' women within male symbolic systems and constructed dwellings for themselves within their bodies. women are confined within walls which are closed, fixed and permanent – prisons. women do not own their own space but provide place for men – wombs. *lair* is a sickly sweet smelling house made of pastel coloured chocolate sitting on a table topped with astro turf.

the viewing condition is made uncomfortable when you realise that the height of the turf corresponds to the height of the artist's pubic hair. inviting yet claustrophobic, a hiding place but also a trap, *lair* creates a critical space for the mind to wander in. the house occupies a space corresponding to the cavity in the artist's body containing her guts and womb. the viewer finds that she is peering into herself.

jane rendell and pamela wells

on

on: pretty

a body bag fashioned from patchworked plastic,
head detachable with hooks and eyes.
pink and purple and red.
dimensions variable (approximately 5'7").
patterned from my own form.
with beads, sequins and buttons sewn on
and gold threads dangling.
she waits on a coat hook until called upon.

on: mimicry

16 L. Irigaray, *An Ethics of Sexual Difference*, London, The Athlone Press, 1993, p. 11.

woman must be nude because she is not situated, does not situate herself in her place. her clothes, her makeup, and her jewels are the things with which she tries to create her container(s), her envelope(s). she cannot make use of the envelope that she is, and must create artificial ones.[16]

on: a space of surface

acts of looking – voyeurism, narcissism, gazing and fetishisation – and being looked at – exhibitionism, spectacle, masquerade and display – are circuits of complex visual exchanges. traditional models of psychoanalysis that describe the construction of the gaze in relation to various stages of childhood development, provide a simplistic model: the active male gazer and the passive female spectacle. in visual art practice, the objectifying function of the male gaze has been reinforced by positioning women as the focus of the look within the space of the image. even at a time when we are keen to reject notions of intentionality, the ways in which we interpret what we see depend often on what is known of the gender politics of the artist. in *pretty* we are given a surface with no inside. does the artist want us to believe that she is colluding, fetishising the female body by displaying its outside? or that she is problematising the fetishising gaze?

jane rendell and pamela wells

figure 9.3 pamela wells, *pretty*, 1996.

pretty invites you to look at her, and also to inhabit her. between looking at her and imagining being within her skin, a gap is created. a gap between the surface and what it is to lie beneath. for some, woman *is* surface, femininity is masquerade. but irigaray's theory of mimicry suggests a conscious strategy for destabilising masquerade. mimicry is a subversive act that seeks to expose the limitations of the thinking of the feminine as a flat surface. through imitation, a gap appears between the female subject and the feminine sexed identity she is imitating. *pretty* is that gap. she is that surface skin made manifest. a lair, a trap, a prison, a womb, a condom, a sheath, a dress, a house, a skin. *pretty* is a full body suit made of plastic. *pretty* is not just any space for the imagination to enter, she is a moulting, a second skin.

made to measure, she is a strange sort of protection. she begs a fitting. try her on.

jane rendell and pamela wells

to

to: tea for 2000

sewn tea bags – light muslin stuffed with raspberry leaf and mint.
hung from ceiling panels with golden thread.
scent is overwhelming, fading slowly.
an invitation to take one, putting something else in its place.
(a banana peel, a train-ticket, a photo of her grandson).
hot water, hand-made tea bowls, tables and chairs.
an invitation to share a cup of tea.

to: relationships between people

i love to you *means i maintain a relation of indirection to you . . . the 'to' is the sign of non-immediacy, of mediation between us . . . the 'to' is the guarantor of two intentionalities: mine and yours . . . thus: how am i to speak to you? and: how am i to listen to you?*[17]

17 L. Irigaray, *I Love to You*, London, Routledge, 1996, pp. 109–13.

to: a space of exchange

the making and receiving of art work is an economy – a series of relationships of exchange between people. art is not produced just by artists – it is the product of viewers, users, subjects and makers of all kinds. for irigaray the potential of the 'to' in 'i love to you' suggests a new social order of relations between two different sexes. this might also suggest a new order to relationships between maker and user, between theorist and practitioner. with work created through interaction and collaboration, the qualities of particular end-products become less important than the processes of making them. working methods that necessitate engaged and committed contact with others present opportunities for questioning one's own ways of thinking and making. real space for critical dialogue is transformative.

jane rendell and pamela wells

figure 9.4 pamela wells, *tea for 2000*, long beach, california, 1993 and 1995.

the management of inter-personal skills is not considered the domain of the 'intuitive' individual artist; but it is precisely in these areas that some of the most creative work in public art is currently being produced. the ways in which relationships between makers and users are constructed can constitute a major part of the conceptualisation and realisation of a project, effecting aesthetic and formal decisions. this may tend towards the choreographic, where the work manifests less as an object and more as an event, a series of exchanges people make with one another. in *tea for 2000*, a simple act of inter-action encouraged people to engage with one another. through the exchange of objects, *tea for 2000* offered a space of conversation where the actions of the audience created a place.

jane rendell and pamela wells

for

for: nonconsumables

a performative collaboration with hermione allsopp:
a translucent plastic wall. (8' × 24').
erected in a busy london marketplace,
glowing in the dim light.
pockets filled with small, mostly food-based but inedible things.
typed text on red and green plastic
(from guy debord's society of the spectacle).
given away over three days at the peak of holiday shopping.

for: 'women on the market'

18 L. Irigaray, 'Women on the Market', *This Sex Which is not One*, Ithaca, Cornell University Press, 1985, pp. 170–91, p. 172

the economy – in both the narrow and the broad sense – that is in place in our socie-ties thus requires women to lend themselves to alienation in consumption, and to exchanges in which they do not participate, that men be exempt from being used and circulated like commodities.[18]

for: a space of gift giving

19 Irigaray, 'Women on the Market', op. cit., pp. 170–91.

luce irigaray's seminal essay 'women on the market' is a key reference point here.[19] iri-garay reworks the marxist analysis of commodities as the elementary form of capital-ist wealth to show the ways in which women are commodities in patriarchal exchange – the objects of physical and metaphorical exchange among men. the female commod-ity has two irreconcilable categories – use value and exchange value. in irigaray's sym-bolic order, women have three positions, the mother who represents pure use value, the virgin who represents pure exchange value, and the prostitute who represents both use and exchange value. implicit in irigaray's work on the three representations of the female commodity – mother, virgin, prostitute – is the importance of space and prop-erty. in patriarchy, men distinguish themselves from women through their relationship to space. men own space and women as property; women are confined by men as and in space. as the only property owners, only men can perform acts of exchange.

jane rendell and pamela wells

figure 9.5 pamela wells and hermoine allsopp, *nonconsumables*, spitalfields market, london, december 1997.

this suggests that women exchanging goods pose a threat to patriarchy. instead irigaray asks: 'how, within this society, can women initiate certain rites that allow them to live and become women in all dimensions? how are systems of exchange to be set up *among women*? . . . where are the traces of a *currency* among women?'[20] it could be argued for example, that maternal gifts — love and milk — escape the logic of the commodity economy both in terms of competition and appropriation.

but what role do things play in a relationship between people? despite a healthy scepticism concerning the 'turd in the plaza' i suggest that we should not reject things outright. things are not always dumb, they have an important role to play beyond their object-like qualities. things are not only commodities defined by their exchange value. things may be non-exchangeable or 'of no value', both of which open up new uses. in processes of production (making) and reproduction (using), things occupy a place between people. animate objects tell stories, bridge the private worlds of separate individuals, mediate between real and imaginary and suggest new forms of action. things suggest a number of different narratives about their histories and their potential future uses. considered as props they play an important role as mediators. as toys they encourage play and speculation, as gifts they challenge capitalist notions of profit and ownership.

nonconsumables was an experiment testing our relationship with objects in the public realm. giving things away in such a social context questions the role of art as commodity. we are led to believe that public art is a sort of communal property, whereas object-making falls into the realm of private enterprise. by situating ourselves in a place of commerce, we were able to juxtapose these conflicting impressions and modify the terms of exchange by focusing on the interaction with the artists.

20 L. Irigaray, 'Women, the Sacred, Money', *Sexes and Genealogies*, New York, Columbia University Press, 1987, p. 80.

jane rendell and pamela wells

among

among: finders keepers

19 altered books:
burned and cut.
painted in, scribbled on and pasted over.
hollowed out for keys and stones and bumblebees,
carved drawings on pressed ceramic pages.
placed in grippa bags and left, anonymously.
on a bus, in a field, under a bridge, in an alley, on a bench, outside a closed shop.

among: économie feminine

21 H. Cixous, 'Sorties', in Marks and De Courtivron, op. cit., pp. 90–8, pp. 96–7.

there is no reason to exclude the possibility of radical transformations of behaviour, mentalities, roles, and political economy ... then 'femininity', 'masculinity', would inscribe their effects of difference, their economy, their relationships to expenditure, to deficit, to giving, quite differently.[21]

among: a space of generosity

cixous rejects the masculine libidinal economy and gestures towards a female libidinous economy – a gift economy based on generosity and not lack – endless and without closure. from woman's ability to have a child within her body and yet allow its existence, comes an image of positive giving, an ability to embrace difference and the other, not to dominate and to incorporate. the ability to sustain this diversity contradicts the phallic desire for unity and appropriation and stems from a woman's closer links to the imaginary, where the difference between mother and child has not yet been established. the mother's love or breast cannot be understood in terms of an economy based on the exchange of commodities – quantifiable exchange values or the law of return. the mother is willing to give without reserve or expectation of return.[22]

22 A. D. Schrift (ed.), *The Logic of the Gift: Toward an Ethic of Generosity*, London, Routledge, 1997, pp. 12–14.

jane rendell and pamela wells

figure 9.6 pamela wells, *finders keepers,* 19 sites around london and the west midlands, 1994.

the feminine economy could be described as a theoretical construct or poetic utopia that can inform practice. masculine economies make exchanges to accumulate profit, feminine economies operate differently, deferring profit in order to continue the exchange of giving. giving is not a means of exchange transacted in order to demand something in return. giving is an affirmation of generosity.

in gift giving, the economy of exchange is deferred. there is no knowing if and when a gift will be returned. there is also no knowing how a gift will be received. an economy where the artist relinquishes all control over the mediation of the work, instead giving directly to the user, can be described in terms of cixous' notion of a gift economy or a politics of generosity. some interventions choose to subvert the existing hierarchical relationship between maker and audience re-positioning the user in such a way that they are able to take an active role in the production of art. when artists give work away in public places or leave it to be found by accident, chance determines the form of the network of relationships and hence the end product or social sculpture.

by removing myself as the authored and known producer, the interaction was obscured, allowing the exchange to become more intimate – a series of private discoveries. this potential was mapped as a concealed social sculpture, a slowly moving architecture crawling under the skin of recognisable urban form.

the anonymous component of the work was also – maybe ultimately – a gift to myself, a temporary freedom from the constraints of a prying profession's obsession with the cult of personality. the fact that even my documentation focused on the books' covers and not their content released me to write/create in a way that i would never have allowed myself had the results been trackable.

jane rendell and pamela wells

149

through

through: feeding each other

a time-based interaction.
emerging from a call and response.
beginning with a poem,
asking 'how do you fill up if you give it all away?'
i made and painted bowls based on responses.
arranged in shrine-like configurations.
9 days i fast and listen whilst participants attend their shrines.
barriers slowly evaporate;
participants begin to engage with one another.
breaking with a feast,
participants disperse taking bowls with them,
to give away.

through: fluidity

23 L. Irigaray, *Elemental Passions*, London, The Athlone Press, 1992, pp. 65–6.

my lips are not opposed to generation. they keep the passage open.
[...] The wall between them is porous. It allows passage of fluids.[23]

through: a space of undecideability

irigaray's most common metaphor to rethink, to represent and construct the spatiality of the female subject are the 'two lips'. two lips suggest space and time together, suggest a different syntax of meaning, a symbolism that auto-erotically challenges the unity of the phallus. the 'one' of the male subject becomes 'two' constantly in touch with each other. the 'two' are not separated by negation but interact and merge. they are not unitary but diffuse, diversified, multiple, decentred. they are a threat to masculine discourse because of their fluidity and double role as inside and threshold. two lips allow openness as well as closed-ness.

jane rendell and pamela wells

figure 9.7 pamela wells and participants, *feeding each other*, 1993.

irigaray's talk of mucus is essential to exchange and communication between the sexes. at the threshold is mucus. mucus is not an object like the penis. it cannot be separated from the body. it is neither simply solid nor fluid. it has no fixed form. it is porous. mucus expands but not in a shape. mucus is both mobile and immobile, permanent and flowing.

through *feeding each other*, objects were used as a catalyst for relationship building. factors of chance and undecideability still continue to affect the shape of the end form.

the bowls are still out there. i have no idea where.

jane rendell and pamela wells

between

between: healing quilt

i operate as pivot.
objects made as catalysts, as a vehicle for fluid energy.
hair and tea, poetry, plastic and satin ribbon
9 baby quilts fit together to create a larger space.
(we are sewn together with invisible knots)
i fast as they spend 24 hours with each bestower.
then i give them away.
the receivers deciding when they will be given again.

between: the angel

the angel is that which unceasingly passes through the envelope(s) or container(s), goes from one side to the other, reworking every deadline, changing every decision, thwarting all repetition.[24]

24 Irigaray, *An Ethics of Sexual Difference*, op. cit., p. 15.

between: a space of transformation

rosi braidotti and luce irigaray are, for me, the two feminists where space and subjectivity are most closely linked. for braidotti, the nomadic subject is an important 'theoretical figuration for contemporary subjectivity'. the nomadic subject in braidotti's writing describes an epistemological condition, a kind of knowingness or unknowingness that refuses fixity, that allows us to think between, or to think 'as if'.[25] for irigaray as well, female subjectivity is a spatial condition. the spatiality of the female body metaphorically and strategically describes new forms of cultural exchange between subjects. the 'between' is important here as a way of imagining these exchanges as new occupations of space. the 'between' is offered to us as a place of transformation.

25 R. Braidotti, *Nomadic Subjects*, New York, Columbia University Press, 1994, p. 1 and p. 5.

jane rendell and pamela wells

figure 9.8 pamela wells, *healing quilt*, 1995.

irigaray's writing also offers women a utopian position. her work suggests an alternative and celebratory way of viewing female movement in terms of the 'angel'. the angel circulates as a mediator, as an alternative to the phallus, who rather than cutting through, goes between and bridges. the angel cannot be represented in patriarchal terms since she rethinks the organisation of patriarchal space and time. for irigaray, men have confined women as and in the spaces of the male symbolic systems of law and language, in order to deny their angelic and/or nomadic status. irigaray's mode of operation is suggestive, she is providing us with the opportunity to imagine new possible relations that women might have with space. the most interesting aspect of the angel here for me, is how s/he raises the importance of connection between people. as the 9 baby quilts pass hands for 9 days and then are given to 9 other people. they move between subjects, creating a web of connections. a new social order of anticipation. 9 is the number of change.

beyond

beyond: u r what u eat

bite sized positive affirmations.
phrases on chocolate pieces
'believe in yourself'
'don't give up'
'feel free'
eat it to become it

beyond: jouissance

if there is a self proper to women, paradoxically it is her capacity to depropriate herself without self interest: endless body, without 'end', without principal 'parts'; if she is a whole, it is a whole made up of parts that are wholes, not simple, partial objects but varied entirety, moving and boundless change, a cosmos where eros never stops travelling, vast astral space.[26]

26 H. Cixous, 'Sorties', op. cit., p. 44.

beyond: space of potentiality

irigaray has argued that 'any theory of the subject' has always been appropriated by the masculine. constructions of the self that have important ramifications for theories of identity and desire, in the work of freud and lacan, for example, have been based on the male subject. when women submit to such theories they either subject themselves to objectification by being female, or try to re-objectify themselves as a masculine subject. in *speculum* irigaray states that she criticises "the exclusive right of the use(s), exchange(s), representation(s) of one sex by the other". irigaray argues that the female body should not remain the object of men's discourse, but become the subject of women's discourse. she asks women to claim their own morphology, also inviting the male subject to redefine himself.[27] in *u r what u eat*, the artist, like irigaray, invites the user to redefine themselves – to become the subject of their own making.

27 L. Irigaray, Je, Tu, Nous: Towards A Culture Of Difference, London, Routledge, 1993, p. 59. See also L. Irigaray, *Speculum of the other woman*, (trans. Gillian C. Gill), (New York: Cornell University Press, 1985), especially p. 133.

jane rendell and pamela wells

figure 9.9 pamela wells, *u r what u eat*, 1994 and on-going.

u r what u eat *is about transubstantiation. you eat it, you become it.*

spinning: a space between women

irigaray notes that when her mother goes away, the little girl does not do the same things as the little boy. "she does not play with a string and a reel that symbolize her mother. because her mother is of the same sex, as she is and cannot have the object status of a reel". instead the little girl is distressed. she plays with dolls – a different kind of object from the reel. she dances, 'this dance is also a way for the girl to create a territory of her own in relation to her mother'.[28] in her dance she spins around destabilising existing connections between herself and her place, making new ones between herself and her (m)other.

imagine being five again. imagine spinning round and around in the middle of a room. only stopping when the furniture, walls and floor begin to revolve around you, when everything around you slips out of place. this is the place of prepositions: a space inhabited by angels.

architecture is created here through the relationships formed between women, between mother and daughter, between artist and writer, between theorist and practitioner. the use of the preposition is a feminist tactic deployed to make connections between two things. the topographies of between, the morphologies of prepositions are transformative. although these kinds of space follow a specifically feminist trajectory in taking up irigaray's notion of the daughter spinning to make room between her and her mother, men also have access to this space: 'a vital subjective space open to the cosmic maternal world, to the gods, to the present other'.[29]

28 Irigaray, 'Gesture in Psychoanalysis', *Sexes and Genealogies*, op. cit., pp. 97–8.

29 Ibid.

i wear a compass around my neck.
but i am not interested in where north is.
i wear it so as not to get lost conceptually.
i am interested in the juddering needle, in the slippage,
like the vertigo you feel when the train next to you pulls away.
this subtle jolting causes me to focus where i am going.
disorientation helps to position me.
likewise i think prepositions are navigational as well as transformative.
an overlooked part of speech, they are crucial.
they direct our stance, our proximity, even our gaze.
this issue of overlooking interests me.
there are things that can only be seen with peripheral vision.

jane rendell and pamela wells

a conversation between us: from wolverhampton to london, beyond practice and theory

pamela wells: so how does what you've been saying relate to the rest of this book?
jane rendell: as far as i understand it, jonathan has asked contributors to re-locate architecture both as subject and as matter ... to me this means re-defining architecture through other disciplines and practices. for example, the conceptual space of theory, the 'non-functionally-determined' space of art practice, the choreographic space of relationships between people that many feminists are interested in.

and what does my work have to do with this?
i think that there are inspirational moments in your work that place a different emphasis on the making of architecture, for example valuing the space of relation-ships made between people, over the building as a object-like thing.

how exactly?
if critical theory is a critique of capitalism, allowing an emancipatory moment, feminist critical theory imagines the world from a different perspective, the perspective of an as-yet-unrealised female subject. many of the patterns within your working processes are analogous to irigaray's theoretical discourse concerning the shape of the female body. of course it is important to recognise that the use of a feminine morphology is strategic rather than literal. but to put this more directly, your work decorating plastic with beads transforms it into something precious. this can be used both as a feminine strategy to re-value the decorative, but also to re-focus our attention architecturally on the relationship between materials. how can surface decoration transform the sub-stance that lies beneath?

do you think this is a radical departure? i mean what would a practising architect think of this? how could they relate it to their practice?
we should consider carefully what we mean by the term practice. first, architectural practice is often taken to be the making of perfect objects. but practising is also about trying to get it right but often getting it wrong. second, practice intends to answer a set of aims. critical thinking questions the values of the aims themselves. finally, and most contentiously, i would argue that thinking is also a practice. it is something we do. we make ideas. unless we understand thinking as a form of prac-tice, and practice as a thoughtful process it is impossible to make a relationship between the two.

how does feminism relate to this discussion?

feminism makes it very clear that the relation of theory and practice depends on the particular – on history and geography – there are no universal rules. historically, it is only by acknowledging the work of earlier feminists that we can operate from 'behind'. rather than having to work in direct reaction to dominant male models – either by copying or by overtly attacking – we can adopt more subtle strategies. we are able to be more listening, more empathetic. it is only in this state of mind that we can be ourselves and open ourselves up to the other. to transform as well as transgress.

so what about geography?

the ability and desire to make connections with new things depends on position. recent feminism makes a strong argument for understanding knowledge as situated – that we know things differently depending on where we are. first in one place then in another, we are both stationary and in motion. i think it is easier to make connections with another when in motion, when you are out of your place.

so these angels, do they really exist?

well, we wouldn't be able to have this conversation without them.

jane rendell and pamela wells

SECTION 3

body

---

matter

bauhaus dream-house: forming the imaginary body of the ungendered architect

The body and consciousness of the architect acts as matter or material for the process of architectural education. The body-images of students and teachers, the space-images of educational rituals and the text-images of publications are the subject matter through which the architectural discipline and the architectural profession reproduce themselves. The essay relates the production of utopian gender identity through curricular and non-curricular rituals at the Bauhaus to the formation of the collective unconscious in contemporary architectural education.

1 LACK

1 K. Silverman, *Male Subjectivity at the Margins*, London, Routledge, part quoting Slavoj Žižek, The *Sublime Object of Ideology*, London, Verso, 1989, p. 118, 1992, p. 6.

Through fantasy then, "we 'learn how to desire' ".[1]

In psychoanalytic theory from Sigmund Freud onwards, Lack is the void on which individual human identity and desire is built. Crudely, Lack is experienced by the infant in the moment of conscious separation from the mother, when the infant becomes aware of its own existence as an independent entity. Jacques Lacan describes the recognition of this moment as the mirror or Imaginary stage of identity formation because of the frequent role of the mirror in crystallising this experience of separation for the child. Desire (for the no longer achievable unalienated plenitude associated with the mother) and Lack (of that unity and plenitude) are born at the same time.

Lack is exacerbated further in a second stage of development, the entry into the patriarchal, or Symbolic order, where gender differentiation occurs. Here the male child, in recognising his sexual difference to the mother, enters 'daddy's world' and so joins the sexual and cultural authority of patriarchy, with its association of masculine identity with strength, stability, activity and integrity. Unlike the female, this experience again confronts the male with Lack as he separates from the mother for the second time. Masculine desire for an unalienated plenitude thus becomes doubly intense and doubly futile. In defence, the male represses his double experience of Lack by projecting it on to the female. 'Mummy's world' becomes culturally inferior to that of the father. The female from then on has no plenitude, no stability and no completeness; instead she is expected to represent weakness, instability, obedience and multiple identities.

In her book *Male Subjectivity at the Margins*, Kaja Silverman uses Freud, Lacan and Althusser to explain the formation of masculine identity within institutions including and exceeding the family. She identifies patriarchy as the main unconscious belief system regulating cultural reproduction and coins the term 'dominant fiction' to

Katerina Rüedi Ray

describe its function. By stating that the dominant fiction is 'the ideological reality through which we "ideally" live both the symbolic order and the mode of production' she explicitly links patriarchy (the Symbolic order) and class (the mode of production) as the key instruments of social differentiation.[2] The 'dominant' emphasises the role of power and the 'fiction' affirms the role of fantasy in maintaining the social order. The recognition of fantasy or dreaming in social formation is important. For Silverman fantasy is a social activity; it eroticises specific classes and genders of people and, more importantly, specific social practices, usually to serve but sometimes to resist the dominant fiction of masculinity.

2 Ibid., p. 2.

Resistance to the 'dominant' in the dominant fiction can take many forms. Constructed and sustained in the broadest social sense, the dominant fiction can be threatened by events originating far beyond the individual or the family:

> [t]he male subject's aspirations to mastery and sufficiency are undermined from many directions – by the Law of Language, which founds subjectivity on a void; by the castration crisis; by sexual, economic and racial oppression; and by the traumatically unassimilable nature of certain historical events.[3]

3 Ibid., p. 52.

She focuses on historically traumatic events that undermine the truth claims of the dominant fiction:

> By 'historical trauma' I mean a historically precipitated but psychoanalytically specific disruption, with ramifications far beyond the individual psyche. To state the case more precisely, I mean any historical event, whether socially engineered or of natural occurrence, which brings a large group of male subjects into such an intimate relation with lack that they are at least for the moment unable to sustain an imaginary relation with the phallus, and so withdraw their belief from the dominant fiction. Suddenly the latter is radically de-realised, and the social formation finds itself without a mechanism for achieving consensus.[4]

4 Ibid., p. 55.

She asserts that:

> At those historical moments when the prototypical male subject is unable to recognize 'himself' within its conjuration of masculine sufficiency our society suffers from a profound sense of 'ideological fatigue'.[5]

5 Ibid., p. 16.

Silverman identifies war as a key historical trauma that profoundly destabilises the dominant fiction, shattering the mirror that patriarchal society normally holds up to

Katerina Rüedi Ray

itself and in which it uncritically views itself. Instead, the collective experience of death and the dissolution of inherited social order creates a collective crisis of masculinity. By confronting society with a repeated external manifestation of Lack, war loosens the sign systems that normally bind society together. For the male in particular, war trauma reconnects the collective and conscious experience of social crisis to the individual and unconscious original double experience of Lack.

2 CULTURAL CAPITAL

6 M. S. Larson, 'The Production of Expertise and the Constitution of Expert Power', in T. L. Haskell (ed.), *The Authority of Experts*, Bloomington, Indiana University Press, 1984, pp. 35–6.

[The] effects [of professional education] are measured in the non-physical constraint of accepted definitions, or internalised moral and epistemological norms. It is in one sense impersonal, for it makes the most general knowledge claims; yet it is also deeply personal, in that the individual who internalises the general and special discourses of his or her own culture experiences them as natural expressions or extensions of his or her own will and reason.[6]

The double experience of Lack by the male child is repressed through not only a sexual but also through a cultural, social and economic dominant fiction. This process too begins very early in the formation of a child's identity, in the family, but is most clearly represented in the process of education.

The French sociologist and philosopher Pierre Bourdieu focuses on the role of education in identity formation. Culture and education are, for him, constantly fought over by competing groups, each struggling to possess, retain and increase their power through the possession of the main currency of culture – symbolic capital. He introduces the concept of symbolic capital as the regulating system of cultural power. Cultural capital is primarily used to accumulate social and, by implication, economic privilege. It is not freely available or reproducible but is restricted by class, race and gender boundaries.

7 P. Bourdieu, *Outline of a Theory of Practice*, New York, Cambridge University Press, 1971. P. Bourdieu, *Distinction, A Social Critique of the Judgement of Taste*, London, Routledge and Kegan Paul, 1986.

Bourdieu introduces and develops the concept of symbolic capital in his *Outline of a Theory of Practice* and *Distinction*.[7] Garry Stevens, in his book *The Favored Circle* and article 'Struggle in the Studio: A Bourdivin Look at Architectural Pedagogy', discusses Bourdieu's writings on cultural capital within architectural education and clarifies much of Bourdieu's dense language and argument. I have therefore added his interpretation to my own readings of Bourdieu's texts.[8]

8 G. Stevens, *The Favored Circle, The Social Foundations of Architectural Distinction*, Cambridge, Mass., MIT Press, 1998. G. Stevens, 'Struggle in the Studio: A Bourdivin Look at Architectural Pedagogy', *Journal of Architectural Education*, November 1995.

For Bourdieu, cultural capital is inseparable from an individual or a group. It consists of four major types: institutionalised, objectified, social and embodied. Stevens writes:

Katerina Rüedi Ray

Three are quite straightforward. Institutionalised cultural capital consists of academic qualifications and educational attainments, knowing things, and being certified as knowing them. Objectified capital is cultural objects or goods, such as artworks or any of the many symbolic objects produced in society. Social capital consists of durable networks of people on whom one can rely for support and help in life.[9]

9 Stevens, 'Struggle in the Studio', op. cit., p. 107.

The fourth type of cultural capital is embodied capital. Unlike other forms of symbolic capital, embodied cultural capital is attached to the human body. It is represented by the physical attributes and behaviour of the person who possesses it; appearance and behaviour thus become cultural assets. Embodied cultural capital merges representation and corporeality. It is produced and reproduced by emulation, of people, images and practices; and confers traits signifying the cultural value of their 'owners'. The acquisition of high embodied cultural capital depends on a privileged setting, and time and effort, which traditionally only the leisure class have had and afforded. In a patriarchal culture, embodied cultural capital incorporates symbolic systems constructed around gender differentiation, stratification in social class and differences in economic class.

Bourdieu argues that education is a key site that produces and reproduces embodied cultural capital. In *Outline of a Theory of Practice* he introduces the concept of the 'habitus' as a mechanism for this production and reproduction.[10] Bourdieu (author's emphasis) describes how the tasks of the habitus include the classification of the body:

10 Bourdieu, *Outline of a Theory of Practice*, op. cit., pp. 72–95.

In a class society, all the products of a given agent, by an essential overdetermination, speak inseparably and simultaneously of his class – or, more precisely, his position in the social structure and his rising or falling trajectory – and of his (or her) body – or, more precisely, all the properties, always socially qualified, of which he or she is the bearer – sexual properties of course, but also physical properties, praised, like strength or beauty, or stigmatised.[11]

11 Ibid., p. 87.

The habitus forms embodied cultural capital for a specific social group. This corporate identity uses body language, skin colour, gender, clothing, manner of speech, accent and other factors (author's emphasis):

If all societies and, significantly, all the 'totalitarian institutions' . . . that seek to produce a new man through a process of 'deculturation' and 'reculturation' set such store on the seemingly most insignificant details of dress, bearing, physical or verbal manners, the reason is that, treating the body as memory, they entrust to it in

Katerina Rüedi Ray

abbreviated and practical, i.e. mnemonic, form the fundamental principles of the arbitrary content of culture. The principles em-bodied [sic] in this way are placed beyond the grasp of consciousness, and hence cannot be touched by voluntary, deliberate transformation, cannot even be made explicit; nothing seems more ineffable, more incommunicable, more inimitable, and, therefore, more precious, than the values given body, made body by the transubstantiation achieved by the hidden persuasion of an implicit pedagogy, capable of instilling a whole cosmology, an ethic, a metaphysic, a political philosophy, through injunctions as insignificant as 'stand up straight' or 'don't hold your knife in your left hand'.[12]

12 Ibid., p. 94.

Education reproduces the habitus through its selection, stratification and affirmation of traits consisting of not only consciously acquired knowledge but also unconscious physical and behavioural traits. The habitus regulates the production of practices and the reproduction of cultural capital 'without in any way being the product of obedience to rules' and 'without being the product of the orchestrating action of a conductor'.[13] It is 'history turned into nature'.[14] This is normally denied by educators and students – a denial made possible only because the habitus is seldom consciously experienced, as Stevens writes:

13 Ibid., p. 72.

14 Ibid., p. 78.

It is an active, unconscious set of unformulated dispositions to act and to perceive, and much of its power to structure our lives without our realising it derives from the thoughtlessness of habit and habituation that the habitus produces . . . it is the product of a personal history. Because its enculturation starts from birth, it is a product of the material and symbolic conditions of existence of our family, conditions shaped by our class and therefore by the large scale structures of society.[15]

15 Stevens, 'Struggle in the Studio', op. cit., p. 112.

The habitus is ideology at its most personal and effective. Its purpose is not to produce the dominant culture but, rather, to unconsciously reproduce it. Embodied cultural capital is therefore the most difficult type of symbolic capital to acquire, challenge and change. Extreme social crises like war disrupt the 'naturalness' and authority of embodied cultural capital and force an awareness of its 'constructedness' and arbitrariness into the collective consciousness.

Katerina Rüedi Ray

3 WAR

There stands a man, a man

As firm as any oak tree, oak tree,

Maybe he has lived through many a tempest, tempest, tempest,

Maybe by tomorrow he will be a corpse,

Like so many brothers before him, him, him.[16]

(Song composed by Bauhaus students for Lyonel Feininger's feast day)

Throughout Europe the huge losses of the Great War had a major impact on the collective unconscious. Germany was the greatest loser, with enormous casualties, reduced territory, and economic and social problems far worse than those of the victors. The crisis of its dominant fiction was extreme, spanning from social identity to architecture. Architectural forms associated with the old social order were rejected. Bruno Taut wrote:

It was not possible to make use of any pre-war traditions, for that period was perforce regarded as the cause of the misfortunes of the past, and because every achievement of those days seemed more or less to hang together with the origins of the war.[17]

Walter Gropius, war casualty himself, wrote:

Today's artist lives in an era of dissolution, without guidance. He stands alone. The old forms are in ruins, the benumbed world is shaken up, the old human spirit is invalidated and in flux toward a new form. We float in space and cannot yet perceive the new order.[18]

The solution was to create a new kind of human being. Gropius continued:

First man must be constructed; only then can the artist make him fine new clothing. The contemporary being must begin anew, to rejuvenate himself, to achieve a new humanity, a universal life-form of the people.[19]

Bauhaus students responded similarly. Magdalena Droste writes that many 'arrived direct from active service, hoping for the chance to make a fresh start and give meaning to their lives'.[20] T. Lux Feininger observed:

Almost all have been in the army, it is a new type, a new generation . . . these young people are not babies.[21]

16 E. Neumann, *Bauhaus and Bauhaus People*, trans. E. Richter and A. Lorman, New York, Van Nostrand and Reinhold, and London, Chapman Hall, 1993, p. 158.

17 B. Taut, *Modern Architecture*, London, The Studio Limited, 1929, pp. 92–3.

18 W. Gropius, *Ja! Stimmen des Arbeitsrates für Kunst*, Bauhaus Archive, Berlin, File 69, 1919.

19 Ibid.

20 M. Droste, *Bauhaus 1919–1933*, Cologne, Benedikt Taschen, 1993, p. 2.

21 Neumann, op. cit., p. 186.

Katerina Rüedi Ray

The transformation of the new arrivals began by re-enacting wartime experience. Herbert Bayer's description of the (partly fictional) Bauhaus 'entrance exam' resembles that of a battlefield:

> When I saw the first Bauhaus proclamation, ornamented with Feininger's woodcut, I made inquiries as to what the Bauhaus really was. I was told that 'during the entrance examinations every applicant is locked up in a dark room. Thunder and lightning are let loose upon him to get him in a state of agitation. His being admitted depends on how well he describes his reactions.' This report, although it exaggerated the actual facts, fired my enthusiasm.[22]

22 H. Bayer, W. Gropius and I. Gropius (eds), *Bauhaus 1918–1928*, London, Secker and Warburg, 1938, p. 18.

Uniforms, gestures, songs and anthems, evoking military experience, also formed part of the corporate identity at the school. Tut Schlemmer wrote: 'a Bauhaus garment was designed, the Bauhaus whistle and the Bauhaus salute were invented'.[23]

23 Neumann, op. cit., p. 165.

Worship of physical obedience flourished. Ritualised mystical doctrines, in particular Mazdaznan, an ancient Persian religion related to Zoroastrism introduced by Johannes Itten, provided students and masters with rigid rules of dress, movement and diet. Itten inspired students to adopt monastic dress and coiffure. Lothar Schreyer wrote:

> When one day Itten declared that long hair was a sign of sin, his most enthusiastic disciples shaved their heads completely. And thus we went around Weimar.[24]

24 Ibid., p. 74.

Students also established control over identity by constructing precise rules for 'reading' the body. Paul Citroen, a student, wrote proudly:

> When we shook someone's hand we could tell more about him from the handshake, the dryness or dampness of his skin, and other signs, than he would find comfortable. His vocal pitch, his complexion, his walk, every one of his involuntary gestures gave him away. We thought we could see through any person, because our method gave us advantage over the unsuspecting.[25]

25 Ibid., p. 49.

Perhaps the most bizarre example was a ritual instituted by Itten. Citroen wrote:

> There was, among other things, a little needle machine with which we were to puncture our skins. Then the body would be rubbed with the same sharp oil which had served as a laxative. A few days later all the pinpoints would break out in scabs and

pustules – the oil had drawn the wastes and impurities of the deeper skin layers to the surface. Now we were ready to be bandaged. But we must work hard, sweat, and then, with continued fasting, the ulcerations would dry out. At any rate, that's what the book said. In actuality the puncturing didn't go according to plan or desire, and for months afterward we would be tormented with itching.[26]

26 Ibid., pp. 51–2.

Such extremes of self-denial were clearly masochistic in nature. They rewarded pain and obedience with precious praise and a sense of social belonging. At the same time, displacing fears of the disintegration of identity on to physical actions of the body, they made these fears controllable. Citroen continues:

Great demands were made on our self-denial, and if we occasionally sinned when conditions were too hard or hunger or thirst too great, on the whole we felt happy and privileged to have the firm support of our doctrine, to know the right way so that we did not, like the others, collapse in the general chaos.[27]

27 Ibid., p. 48.

Weakness and denial acquired high symbolic value.

Collective identity was also reconstructed through Bauhaus festivals and theatre. Festivals in particular were greatly beloved. Felix Klee wrote:

My dear friend, you have no idea how important festivals were at the Bauhaus – often far more important than the classes. They made the contact between master, journeyman and apprentice far closer . . . The masters radiated their influence on the students in the most positive way. They could develop all the more freely because they had enough time and were not hindered in their personal development by an overly rigid schedule. And there was a reciprocal action by the students on the teachers. One could call it a living 'give and take' such as I have never again come across to such an extent.[28]

28 Ibid., p. 44.

There were many kinds, including the traditional Kite festival, Lantern festival and Yuletide festival, and events specific to the Bauhaus such as the Metallic festival, White Festival and the Beard, Nose and Ear festival. There was even a festival to celebrate Gropius' birthday. Festivals were powerful in creating embodied cultural capital because they were non-curricular; through the living 'give and take' masters and students 'could develop all the more freely' because they were not consciously constrained by an 'overly rigid' identity implicit in the standard curriculum. 'Bauhäusler' participated enthusiastically in such rehearsals of identity and through them learnt to desire and enact multiple identities.

Katerina Rüedi Ray

Through the Bauhaus theatre, in contrast, Bauhäusler learned to desire a singular, more 'overly rigid' identity. The theatre was central to the formation of identity at the school. It was important enough to be singled out just before the conclusion to the seminal 1923 essay 'The Theory and Organisation of the Bauhaus', as the embodiment of a 'higher unity' parallel only to that of architecture.[29]

In the catalogue of the 1938 Bauhaus exhibition at MoMA, still one of the most influential Bauhaus publications, Schlemmer's description of the stage workshop at Dessau formed the longest text after Gropius' 1923 essay.[30] The choice of figures from Schlemmer's Triadic Ballet for the front cover of the catalogue underlined the Bauhaus' interest in reinventing not only objects but, much more importantly (author's emphasis), human beings, actions and spaces:

> if we go so far as to break the narrow confines of the stage and extend the drama to include the building itself, not only the interior but the building as an architectural whole – an idea which has especial fascination in view of the new Bauhaus building – we might demonstrate to a hitherto unknown extent the validity of the space-stage, as an idea.[31]

Whereas the workshops produced the design of products for the new age of mass-media, the theatre designed a new identity for their producers and consumers. Teaching in the theatre workshop recognised that the new ideology had to extend beyond the curriculum to reconstruct spatial and social behaviour. It had to take place through fantasy (theatre) before it could take place in reality (architecture).

In fact, because students took the theatre workshop before the architecture course, in the second and third years of the curriculum, and the architecture course did not begin until 1927, the theatre formed the first real Bauhaus experiments with space and programme. The spatial and figurative dream-imagery of the theatre workshop preceded the constructional and programmatic invention of the building department. Theatre came before architecture; embodiment correctly came before construction.

The theatre was a legitimate, institutional extension of Bauhaus design principles to the human body itself. It formed the clearest, most consciously articulated mirror-image for the Bauhaus community. In allowing the body of the student to act and be acted upon by the institution, the Bauhaus theatre also dissolved the division between the collective and the individual through which institutional life distinguishes itself from personal life. It indirectly sanctioned extra-curricular regimes of bodily control and formalised the living 'give and take' of the festivals.

However, the body in Bauhaus theatre had a specific identity. Whereas in traditional western theatre the figure had remained an instrument for representing nat-

29 Bayer, Gropius and Gropius, op. cit., pp. 20–9.

30 Ibid., pp. 162–4.

31 Ibid., p. 162.

Katerina Rüedi Ray

uralistic illusion, the Bauhaus theatre exposed the body as an automaton – a focus for the assembly of form, light, movement and, only later, speech. This sensibility laid the ground for the mechanisation of the actor's body. Costumes during the Schlemmer period were derived from abstract, geometric studies, inspired by mechanical parts.

Specific references to gender were either erased or both genders were combined in the same figure. Actions were largely confined to silent performance and pantomime; words were a separate element to be added later. Schlemmer wrote:

> Let us consider plays consisting only in the movements of form, colours and lights. If the movement is purely mechanical, involving no human being but the man at the switchboard, the whole conception would have the precision of a vast automaton.[32]

32 Ibid.

The actor's appearance and gestures were ideally to be transformed into mechanised, abstracted and gender-neutral form.

In the Bauhaus theatre, the multiple identities and gender differences explored in the festivals began to be lost, to be replaced by a singular, apparently gender-free but ultimately male-directed and enacted identity.

4 LAW-OF-THE-FATHER

> All this garrulous attention which has us in a stew over sexuality, is it not motivated by one basic concern: to ensure population, to reproduce labour capacity, to perpetuate the form of social relations: in short, to constitute a sexuality that is economically useful and politically conservative?[33]

33 M. Foucault, *The History of Sexuality Volume 1: An Introduction*, trans. R. Hurley, London, Penguin, 1981, pp. 36–7.

The return to tradition was gradual but irreversible. The androgyny of the theatre was but one manifestation. From 1923 onwards, with the growing focus at the school on standardisation, mass production and collaboration with industry, Gropius affirmed that 'the artist of today should wear conventional clothing' – understood as male clothing.

Patriarchal values had indeed been present at the school from the beginning. The veneration of father figures began already with Itten. Citroen wrote that:

> Itten exuded a special radiance. One could almost call it holiness. We were inclined to approach him only in whispers; our reverence was overwhelming, and we were completely enchanted and happy when he associated with us pleasantly and without restraint.[34]

34 Neumann, op. cit., p. 47.

Katerina Rüedi Ray

Gropius too became a figure of worship, not only during his leadership but thereafter. It was Gropius, not Hannes Meyer or Mies van der Rohe, who was credited with Bauhaus successes and became its symbolic figurehead.

Women were not accorded such treatment. They faced obstacles when they tried traditionally male areas of work. Brandt later wrote of her entry into the metal workshop:

> At first I was not accepted with pleasure – there was no place for a woman in a metal workshop, they felt. They admitted this to me later on and meanwhile expressed their displeasure by giving me all sorts of dull, dreary work. How many little hemispheres did I most patiently hammer out of brittle new silver, thinking that was the way it had to be and all beginnings are hard. Later things settled down, and we got along well together.[35]

35 Neumann, op. cit., p. 106.

Weimar legislation had given women equality of access to study. In 1920, therefore, there were 78 male and 59 female students at the Bauhaus whereas Gropius had originally anticipated 100 men but only 50 women. As the two genders continued to apply in equal numbers, the entry of women students at the Bauhaus was restricted, first via higher fees (180 marks for women and 150 marks for men) and second, in a 1920 decision by Gropius and the Council of Masters via differential admission:

36 W. Gropius, Minutes of the meeting of the Council of Masters, September 1920, Bauhaus Archive, Berlin, file Meisterrat, 1920.

> selection should be more rigorous right from the start, particularly in the case of the female sex, already over-represented in terms of numbers.[36]

Nevertheless female students were grateful. Käthe Brachmann, a student, wrote in the Bauhaus student magazine *Der Austausch* in 1919:

37 H. Dearstyne, *Inside the Bauhaus*, D. Spaeth (ed.), New York, Rizzoli, 1986, p. 49.

> So we women, too, came to this school because we, every one of us, found work to do here, which we must not neglect! May no one begrudge us this work! Thanks to those who already accord it to us![37]

Droste noted Gropius' reluctance to conduct any 'unnecessary experiments' (a euphemism for rejecting equal access to female students) and his recommendations that women should be sent directly from the introductory course to the weaving work-shop, with pottery and bookbinding as possible alternatives.[38] In particular, she identi-fied the fear of the 'feminisation' of architecture at the Bauhaus:

38 Droste, op. cit., p. 40.

> much of the art then being produced by women was dismissed by men as 'feminine' or 'handicrafts'. The men were afraid of too strong an 'arty-crafty' tendency and saw the goal of the Bauhaus – architecture – endangered.[39]

39 Ibid.

Katerina Rüedi Ray

She added that 'no women were to be admitted to study architecture' at the Bauhaus. Indeed, the building department had no female students at all.

The construction of sexual difference at the Bauhaus was overt in admissions policies and academic progress, but it was far more deeply embedded in the legitimation of artistic ability. Gropius, in a crucial statement as part of his first address to the school, made it absolutely clear that the experiences of male students made them better artists than female students:

> *the awakening of the whole man through trauma, lack, terror, hard life experiences or love lead to authentic artistic expression. Dearest ladies, I do not underestimate the human achievement of those who remained at home during the war, but I believe that the lived experience of death to be all-powerful.*[40]

40 W. Gropius, Gropius' first lecture to the Bauhaus, trans. K. Rüedi, Bauhaus Archive, Berlin, File 18, 1919, p. 3.

This was direct recognition that the experience of suffering, and in particular war trauma, was for Gropius the driving force of artistic creativity and an exclusively masculine right and privilege. The importance of Gropius' statement lay in his recognition that trauma and lack not essentially female experiences but that their symbolic value is constructed by men and accepted by women. The traditional association of lack and trauma with weakness and femininity meant that at the Bauhaus male students adopted such traits only if they carried high symbolic capital through association with integrity (the awakening of the whole man), essentialism (authentic artistic expression) and the exclusively masculine experience of war.

CONCLUSION

> *If ideology is to successfully command the subject's belief, then it must necessarily intervene at the most profound level of the latter's constitution.*[41]

41 Silverman, op. cit., p. 8.

The protection of architecture was essential not only to the cultural but also to the economic supremacy of men. The province of Saxony-Weimar, the Bauhaus' home during its first five years, was predominantly an agricultural and artisanal economy. The mystical 'arty-crafty' beginnings of the school therefore initially aligned with local interests. However, as the Weimar Republic tried to modernise, a tension grew between local 'craft capital' and national 'industrial capital'. Initially organised around a series of craft workshops, the school therefore later shifted to produce prototypes for industrial production.

Katerina Rüedi Ray

The post 1923 shift to gender-neutral self-imagery and exclusion of women from 'masculine' activities at the Bauhaus paralleled the Bauhaus' new home in the industrial city of Dessau and the school's affirmation of mass production. Economically valued industrial production and culturally valued androgynous identity aligned class and gender interests to favour men. Masculine monopoly was effected overtly through the school admissions policy and covertly through the formation of a new collective unconscious identity – the universal subject of modernism.

The Bauhaus also experimented in turning cultural capital into an economic sphere in its own right. As the school was forced constantly to justify itself to its political paymasters through public exhibitions and publications, 'image capital' became essential not only to its political but also to its economic survival. The Bauhaus was the first to introduce advertising and graphic design as an educational subject and career. It produced many commercial exhibitions for trade fairs and catalogues of products for mass-manufacture, and this eventually led to commissions from manufacturers themselves. Finally, 'image capital' became essential to its cultural survival. The school began an independent publications programme, through its own and then a commercial press. This 'image capital' fully legitimised it in the European press and, far more importantly, in the exhibition and publication of Bauhaus work in the USA. It eventually made the Bauhaus the most renowned twentieth-century design school.

The positive lessons of the Bauhaus legacy extend beyond the school and design education. Silverman's model of the dominant fiction and Bourdieu's concept of embodied cultural capital and the habitus, spanning the personal and the political, the visual and the verbal, the contemporary and the historical, recognise the importance of institutions, bodies and images in the formation of collective identity. Their work has far-reaching implications both for the study of institutions and their embodied cultural capital because it identifies mechanisms through which large, seemingly impersonal social structures act on specific individuals to reproduce the collective unconscious.

This implies that study of the self-presentation of cultural institutions in times of historical trauma, including that of schools and professional organisations, is fruitful for the analysis of utopian impulses in architecture. Such work might identify the moments of friction within dominant modes of representation: the dialectic within dream-images; the points of resistance within politics and the economy; the misrecognition within the habitus; the ruptures in the integrity of embodied cultural capital; and the cracks in the masculine fiction. This may lead to a re-evaluation of the utopian in the institution of architecture. Bauhaus House-of-the-Father then once again becomes Bauhaus Dream-house.

Katerina Rüedi Ray

black matter(s)

Such as? Does it?

A NARRATIVE IN SOME SEGMENTS

The following chapter is not really a chapter at all. Rather, it is a loose collection of narratives, some fragmentary, others more complete, centred around the concept of matter (stuff) and how stuff matters. Much of the contemporary discourse surrounding issues of race, identity and difference locates itself quite firmly (and perhaps necessarily) in the realm of theory, in historical models and analyses, and in socio-political thinking. Yet blackness, unlike say, gender or sexuality, remains steadfastly *material*, at once visual and superficial. To state one's 'blackness' is not the same as stating one's ethnicity. To be 'black' is not the same as being Indian, or Asian or even European. It is this surface quality of blackness, its role as a visible, marked arbiter of difference, rather than the social, cultural and political roots of racial attitudes which interest me here. Could the idea of blackness be examined at the level of matter? Could the treatment, form and aesthetic of certain material(s) and spaces be firmly rooted in a cultural reading of the black experience – or, even better, *a* black experience, given that there are many. The segments that follow pick up on this thread, each positing an idea of how blackness and the experience of it, from scars

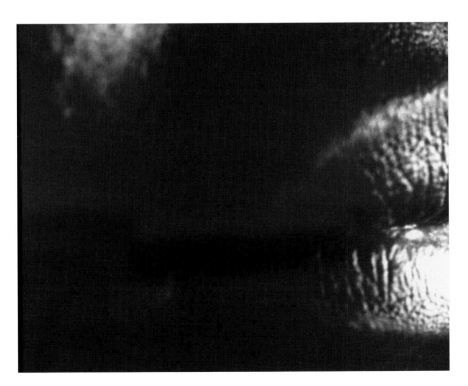

Figure 11.1 *Classical Mouth.*
Photograph, Lesley Naa Norle
Lokko, 1994.

Lesley Naa Norle Lokko

on the body to scars in the landscape, might be read as spatial and architectural gestures in their own right. The segments attempt to shift the embryonic discussion(s) between race and architecture from a position of lack (as in lack of influence, lack of historical references, lack of power, etc.) to a position of strength. Might there be other ways to tackle the thorny issues of representation in the built environment? Could the shift from subject (race) to matter (space) provide us with *a* way – one out of many, perhaps – forward?

The subject, in blackness, really *is* the matter. In both senses of the phrase.

SEGMENT ONE   TUESDAY, 27 JULY 1999 (at 'home' in Chicago, 5.45pm)

the gestures and nod became a polite greeting for the head of the black man, now among them. To eyes accustomed to the radiance above water his blackness was a blow, pure hardness against dissolving light, his head a meteorite fallen between them into the sea, or a water-smoothed head of antiquity brought up from the depths, intact; basalt blackness the concentration of time, not pigment.[1]

1 N. Gordimer, *A Sport of Nature*, New York, Alfred Knopf, 1987, p. 145.

SEGMENT TWO   THURSDAY, 17 JUNE 2000 (Islington, London, 6.15pm)

he had come between them, he came back, the man who had appeared so black, so defined, so substantial from out of water running mercurial with light. He had come between them, paling them in the assertion of his blackness, bearing news whose weight of reality was the obsidian of his form.[2]

2 Ibid., p. 193.

Figure 11.2 *Classical Foot.* Photograph, Lesley Naa Norle Lokko, 1994.

Lesley Naa Norle Lokko

SEGMENT THREE   FLESH AND THE WORD – THE SCAR

'Scar' isn't quite right. It does not quite fit. In material terms, the word describes that which has been left behind. An after-word. It's about repair – about the body repairing itself. The word describes the material practice at the site of an injury, what the epidermic layers do – the way two halves or fragments of the body come together, skin stretching to meet skin, puckered sometimes, shiny and damaged. No one likes a scar. Scars are sometimes called keloids, the medical term for a hypertrophic scar. Persons of African descent, like myself, are prone to keloids, to the puffy, darkened welts that appear when scar tissue produces too much collagen and an overgrowth occurs. These thickened scars are 'raised and unsightly'. They are imperfect, super-scars. These are even less liked. In fact, if you are unlucky enough to suffer a tend-ency towards keloids, you may call a toll-free number, inside or outside the continental USA (1-800-952-5884), and purchase Scar-so-soft™. It will get rid of your unsightly scar, quickly, easily and 'naturally'. There's even a website: http://www.scars-keloids.com, should you wish to order on-line. But the type of scar described above does not really describe the practice of scarification, from the Greek skariphasthai, to scratch an outline. Here, scar-making is not accidental or the result of injury.

Scarification is one of many traditional African cultural and aesthetic practices of bodily decoration, where the body is used quite literally as the site of adornment – a human canvas of sorts. Here, however, the African epidermic propensity towards keloids is a natural advantage. After cutting or pricking the skin, ash is rubbed into the open wound, irritating it and encouraging the overgrowth that results in a keloid. Scarification operates in a number of interesting ways. First, as in the essentially anti-Romantic arts of medieval Europe, traditional African body decoration and sculpture (for, in a sense, that is what scarification is) have a symbolic, as well as aesthetic purpose. Scarification rituals elevate the human above both the merely natural and the merely realistic. As 'civilising marks', scarification separates the human from the less-than-human, from the animal or natural worlds. Second, body modification practices function as multiple border markers: these practices often occur at rituals that celebrate the accession from one stage of life to the next – from childhood to adolesence, or from young adulthood to marriage and parenthood. Third, scars are often used to mark members of a tribal or ethnic group, a way of distinguishing one's self from outsiders. An identikit of sorts.

SEGMENT FOUR   TUESDAY, 27 JULY 2000 (at 'home' in London, time unclear)

A little 'something' extra about the process, and about the process of making in particular, is required here.

Jonathan Hill has asked me to construct a paper, quite literally, to fashion my 'stuff' from the spoken to the written, from the context of my imagination to the bound and somewhat blank context of a book, sites unknown. As I am interested, obsessed even, by the attempts to blur those distinctions (i.e. between the written, spoken and visual), this poses an interesting, if not uncommon, challenge. As architects, we are all too familiar with the transformative and often surprising processes by which one's thoughts are realised: from idea to sketch to construction drawings and finally (and hopefully) to building. As writers or thinkers, however, the transformations are less clear. This difference has been on my mind lately. To think about the process of thinking (or drawing, speaking or writing) at the same time as one is attempting to 'do' it, is difficult. As Beatriz Colomina has stated so eloquently, 'if you think about how you ride a bicycle, you may fall off'.[3]

3 B. Colomina, 'Battle Lines: E.1027', in F. Hughes (ed.), *The Architect: Reconstructing Her Practice*, Cambridge, Mass., MIT Press, 1996, p. 4.

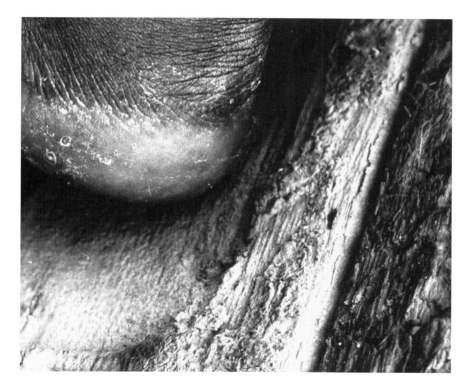

Figure 11.3 *Classical Foot.* Photograph, Lesley Naa Norle Lokko, 1994.

Lesley Naa Norle Lokko

SEGMENT FIVE   FRIDAY, 4 MARCH 2000

(Campbell Hall, University of Virginia, Room 153, 3:24pm)

Black Matter(s) is a 'visual text', one that attempts to provoke, rather than instruct, the viewer. The juxtaposition of image, text and speech is important, in some places more important than content. I'm interested in landscapes, yes, but primarily those in the mind's eye.

SEGMENT SIX   IN LONDON, 2000

It is the thing that is most perceptible and least material. It is the archetype of the vital element. It is the first condition and the hallmark of art, as breath is of life: breath, which accelerates or slows, which becomes even or agitated according to the tension in the individual, the degree and nature of his emotion. This is rhythm . . . it is composed of a theme – sculptural form – which is set in opposition to a sister theme, as inhalation is to exhalation, and that is repeated. It is not the kind of symmetry that gives rise to monotony.[4]

Imprisoned by four walls
(to the North, the crystal of non-knowledge
a landscape to be reinvented
to the South, reflective memory
to the East, the mirror
to the West, stone and the song of silence)

I wrote messages, but received no reply.[5]

4 L. Senghor, 'Ce que l'homme noir apporte', quoted in Nordey, source unknown.

5 O. Paz, 'Envoi', quoted in H. Lefebvre, *The Production of Space*, Oxford, Blackwell, 1991, p. 3.

SEGMENT SEVEN   SUNDAY, 5 NOVEMBER 2000 (Birkenhead Street, London)

Memory: the power or process of reproducing or recalling what has been learned and retained, especially through associative mechanisms; a capacity for showing effects as the result of past treatment or for returning to a former condition. The precise relationship between memory and architecture is difficult to define. The word itself suggests an intangibility, an immateriality, a certain presence in the mind's eye . . . clearly a phenomenon that is more cerebral than physical. Architecture, although rooted in the cerebral, is traditionally made manifest in the material, physical world. In

Lesley Naa Norle Lokko

Black Matter(s), I propose to look at the question of 'sites of memory' through the eyes of the one group in the United States for whom memory – both literally and conceptually – remains problematic: African–Americans. Within African–American culture, memory plays a crucial, fragmented and often contradictory role, not least because '[it] is also a struggle of memory against forgetting'.[6] Severed from the mother culture(s) through slavery and colonialism, notions of 'self', 'home' and 'place' have become hotly contested terrains in which memory plays an increasingly complex role. Who remembers what? And how?

6 bell hooks, *Yearning: Race, Gender and Cultural Politics*, New York, Turnaround Press, 1991, p. 148.

In many traditional African cultures, there is one site into which many of these issues – memory, history, language, home, self and place – collapse: the body. Oral history, bodily art practices, tribal affiliations, architectures based on social – as opposed to formal – relations are all manifestations of a deep, spiritual and aesthetic covenant with the body as the primary site of memory and expression. Ironically, in the history of African–Americans in the United States, it is again the body that has been the primary site of experience and pain. *Black Matter(s)* is a visual and text-based exploration of the black body as the repository of this history. Through a combination of photographs, texts and photo-montages, the project offers a re-interpretation of both 'site', 'self' and 'space' as these relate to the African–American experience. It uses the traditional and familiar tools of architectural investigation – scale, form, material, occupation, programme, etc. – to suggest new and often unexpected relationships between race, space and architecture.

SEGMENT EIGHT   THURSDAY, 18 MARCH 1999 (driving south towards Tuskegee, Alabama)

This is my first trip to the South. The South. I love the sound of the word, rolling it around in my mouth, repeating it again and again to myself as we drive. We are taking five African–American students on a visit to Tuskegee University in Alabama. We drive from Atlanta to Tuskegee via the Martin Luther King historic district, several identical sites of the 1996 Olympic Games and acres and acres of red clay soil along the side of the freeway that remind me of home. It is March and it is very, very hot. My partner is driving and I am thinking about my paper, about coming to the South, about the term 'landscape' and about African–Americans and wondering what the students are thinking, if at all. They are all asleep.

'Look,' I say to him, excited. 'The soil. It's red, like in Ghana.'

'Mmm.' He says. I turn back to the landscape, pleased. I hadn't expected this link.

Lesley Naa Norle Lokko

Figure 11.4 *The South,*
Tuskegee Institute, AL.
Photograph, Lesley Naa Norle
Lokko, 1998.

Lesley Naa Norle Lokko

SEGMENT NINE   FRIDAY, 19 MARCH 1999 (Days Inn Motel, Montgomery, Alabama)

Coming to the issue of the black American landscape as something of an outsider (first as an African, and second – and perhaps more noticeably – as a European),[7] it occurs to me that my own interpretation of events, places and this particular history is spatially marked in an interesting, albeit subconscious, way. In writing this paper, during the difficult process of thinking, drawing, editing, re-thinking and re-drawing, I was acutely aware of the literal, metaphorical and physical spaces I entered and exited as the project unfolded. Beginning at the beginning, with the body and examining its material presence at 10:1 and 1:1, passing through real and imagined landscapes from Alabama to Accra and back again, moving back and forth in time and place, the idea of 'position' – i.e. inside or outside, margin or centre, here or there – and 'direction' – coming or going, forward or backwards, circumlocating the subject or 'going straight at it' – became much more than the organisational tool I initially imagined as an aide to reading the various pieces. It comes to me slowly that the condition of being 'foreign' or 'exterior' to the subject, or imagining oneself in the third dimension (as opposed to the third person) is important in a number of ways. 'Space' slips into the text via a network of connected peoples and places, some real, some not. Similar, in other words, to the 'map' that black Americans have constructed for themselves out of their fragmented history.

[7] Brought up in Ghana, West Africa and later educated in the UK, I have retained a strong British accent.

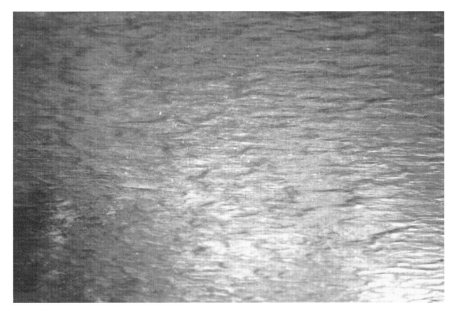

Figure 11.5 *Water, Martin Luther King Jr. Memorial, Montgomery, AL*. Photograph, Lesley Naa Norle Lokko, 1998.

Lesley Naa Norle Lokko

Figure 11.6 *Standing at the Martin Luther King Jr. Memorial, Montgomery, AL*. Photograph, Lesley Naa Norle Lokko, 1998.

SEGMENT TEN   ON BODIES

8 hooks, op. cit., p. 149.

To be in the margin is to be part of the whole but outside the main body.[8]

In many traditional African cultures, there is one site into which many of the issues that are the focus of my investigation – memory, history, language, home, self and place – collapse: the body. Oral history, bodily art practices, tribal affiliations, architectures based on social – as opposed to formal – relations are all manifestations of a deep, spiritual and aesthetic covenant with the body as the primary site of memory and expression. Appropriately too, within the history of African–Americans in the United States, it is the body that has been the primary site of experience and pain. Quite aside from the familiar descriptions of 'bodies in space', the 'active user' and discussions of architecture as the 'envelope' of the body, I want to suggest that the fractured history of African–Americans, perhaps more so than other black Diasporic cultures, dramatically opens itself to the notion that memory, place (landscape) and space are awkwardly tied, like the three-legged runner, by the 'black' body and all it has seen.

The very idea of the 'body' in discourses of race – and here I refer to all discourses: African, African–American, Black British, Carribbean, etc. – is, of course, charged. From Sarah Baartjie – the Hottentot Venus – to Robert Mapplethorpe to Mike Tyson, images of the black body – whether naked, clothed, situated or siteless

– have dominated the ways in which peoples of African descent are seen, are regulated (spatially and otherwise) and, crucially, are recognised. For blacks in the global Diaspora, a persistent sense of 'out of place-ness' accompanies each and every move. Out of Place. Of Place.

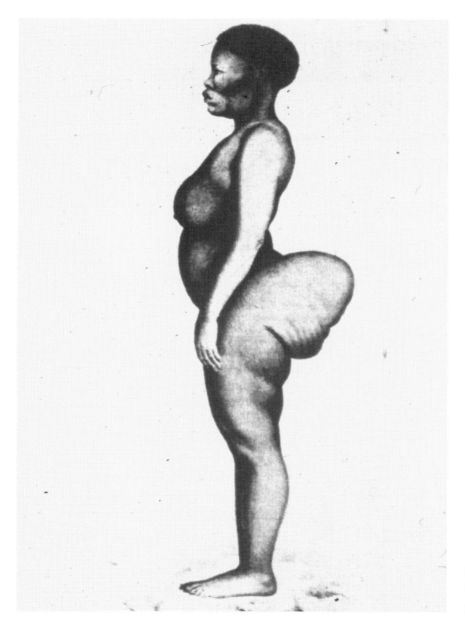

Figure 11.7 *The Hottentot Venus. Reproduced with the kind permission of Sanford Kwinter.*

Lesley Naa Norle Lokko

SEGMENT ELEVEN   1968–1976 (Ghana–Scotland)

Growing up in Ghana, in West Africa, some of my earliest memories intertwine the body and landscape in ways that I have only recently begun to understand. We (my siblings and I) left Ghana each 'summer', to spend the three months from June to September, which constitute the rainy season in the tropics, with my mother's family in Dundee, Scotland. At first there was only the excitement of the trip, of crossing the dusty, cracked tarmac at night (always at night) to the waiting Douglas McDonnell DC-10 or later, more glamorously, a Boeing 747, and the strange, suspended sensation of leaving the muffled red heat of Accra in one breath and awakening to the damp green coolness of England in the next. But then, upon arrival in London, something else changed: the colour of the human landscape around us: at home, in Africa, it was black. On 'holiday', in Europe, it was white. This visual, tactile (matter) difference, more than anything – more than the cold, the damp, the backdrop of Cockney English rather than any of the Ghanaian languages – signified our arrival. What I remember most vividly about leaving the airport in both directions, either arriving on holiday or going home, was the silent landscape of flesh everywhere – black skin at home, white skin abroad. And yet there were other differences, more spatial ones. The specifically African acceptance of flesh, the closeness with which people move in and around one another marked a number of spatial boundaries that were not to be found in Europe,

Figure 11.8 *Crowd. Source unknown.*

anywhere. If one were to have asked me then, somewhere between the ages of seven and ten, what I remembered about either place, it would have been this: the fusion of corporeal differences into a kind of landscape. Density, of colour, texture and form on the one hand and a corresponding sparseness, a visual 'apartness', on the other.

Years later, armed with a more sophisticated understanding of such differences, I am standing on a street corner in downtown Johannesburg, South Africa. All around me Africans (black Africans) are walking: to and from work, to the taxi ranks via the street vendors and to the train stations. They too have formed a kind of landscape: the same closeness, the packing of flesh into impossibly tight 'combis' (minivans), the proximity of one to the other in bus queues and shop-fronts. It comes to me slowly that whites here do not walk – they drive, as in America, in ones and sometimes twos. The odd figure of a businessman, a tourist, a backpacker . . . these stand out in sharp contrast to the moving walls of black Africans around them. I wonder what a child might make of this.

SEGMENT TWELVE   FRIDAY, 26 MARCH 1999 (Campbell Hall, Room 153
                        3:44pm)

When memory goes a-gathering firewood, it brings back the sticks that strike its fancy.[9]

What is the relationship between memory and architecture? A precise definition does not come easily. The word 'memory' itself suggests an intangibility, an immateriality, a certain presence in the mind's eye: clearly a phenomenon that is more cerebral than physical. Architecture, although rooted in the cerebral, is traditionally made manifest in the material, physical world. The question of memory in African–American culture is problematic because, as hooks has stated so eloquently, 'our struggle is also a struggle of memory against forgetting'.[10] Severed from the 'mother' culture(s) through the experiences of slavery, colonialism and imperialism, notions of 'self', 'place' and 'home' are fiercely contested terrains in which memory plays an increasingly fragmented role. Who remembers what? And how?

In Kirk Savage's excellent essay, 'The Politics of Memory: Black Emancipation and the Civil War Monument', Savage tackles the thorny issues of the monument, perhaps the most expedient route to collective memory. There is probably no better starting point from which to interrogate the politics of memory, race and the American landscape. Race precipitated the Civil War and race finally ended it: how telling

9 B. Diop, quoted in T. T. Minh-ha, 'Mother's Talk', in O. Nnaemeka (ed.), *The Politics of (M)Othering: Womanhood, Identity and Resistance in African Literature*, London and New York, Routledge, 1997, p. 26.

10 hooks, op. cit., p. 148.

Lesley Naa Norle Lokko

11 For a truly insightful account of the role of the monument in the shaping of collective memory, see K. Savage, 'The Politics of Memory: Black Emancipation and the Civil War Monument', in J. R. Gillis (ed.), *Commemorations: the Politics of National Identity*, Princeton, Princeton University Press, 1994, pp. 127–49.

that, as Savage recounts, the black scholar Freeman Murray could count only three monuments depicting black soldiers. 'Public monuments do not arise as if by natural law to celebrate the deserving; they are built by people with sufficient power to marshal or impose public consent for their erection.'[11] Put quite simply, blacks did not possess the financial or cultural clout necessary to validate their perspectives and thus legitimise not only their material struggle in the war (blood, guts and glory), but the equally important and vicious ideological role that race played – and continues to play – in the collective national memory. To 'read' America through its Civil War monuments is a troubling exercise in editorial control and underscores perfectly the

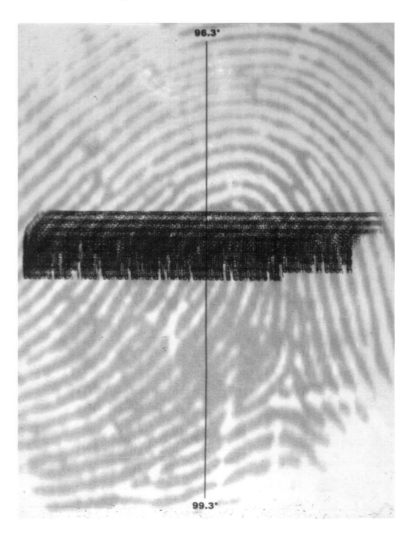

Figure 11.9 Lesley Naa Norle Lokko, *Cultural Weapons Project*, given to my graduate students at Iowa State University, Ames, IA, 1997. Photograph, Lesley Naa Norle Lokko.

Lesley Naa Norle Lokko

complexities of race and power that have dogged this nation since birth. As always, the question of representation is paramount: how to represent the (awful) contradictory impulses of slavery and democracy. How to represent warfare — not 'which heroes or which victories ought to be celebrated, but what ideas deserved representation. Ideas of warfare itself — organised violence and destruction — were unfit for representation'.[12]

But — and here's the rub — race is neither invisible, nor nameless. On the contrary, in fact. One could persuasively argue that the opposite is true: that African–Americans have been so named, made visible (albeit in very particular ways) that the struggle, to paraphrase hooks, is actually about 're-memory', the process of undoing the narratives and representations that are so easily, carelessly available and re-inscribing one's own. For the architect — black or white — this poses an interesting dilemma. Like the African–American subject, architecture is visible, named. Its formidable presence is all around us, everywhere, at all scales and in all places. How then to take this history that is characterised by silence and displacement and place it, literally, in, on, around, above, below, between . . . somewhere, anywhere. How then to make out of material, form, space and light a response to the condition, as Cornel West puts it, of 'natal alienation'?[13]

SEGMENT THIRTEEN   JANUARY 1993 (Swakopmund, Namibia)

dem heroischen Deutschen Soldaten.

In memory of dead Germans (heroes). But this is a British soldier, n'est ce pas? Surveying the familiar bronze sculpture, the flash of recognition is instantaneous, surfacing from some unknown source. War films? School trips? White, noble, upright and strong, sometimes armed, sometimes not . . . perched astride a neo-Classical stone base, it is only the inscriptions that change. From the edge of South West Africa (now Namibia, formerly a German colony) to Montgomery, Alabama, the statues are identical. This suggests a kind of visual fusion — all statues become one, all causes are one (won). 'White and Anglo-Saxon . . . not a neutral individual body but a collective body, conceived with certain boundaries and allegiances.'[14] As a means of establishing a collective (albeit selective) memory and settling it within literal and psychological landscapes, monuments are crucial. They may, however, as Martin Luther King, Jr. famously did, be appropriated.

[12] Ibid., p. 127.

[13] C. West, 'Cultural Politics of Difference', in C. West, *Keeping Faith: Philosophy and Race in America*, New York, Routledge, 1993, p. 16.

[14] Savage, op. cit., p. 135.

Lesley Naa Norle Lokko

Figure 11.10 Lesley Naa Norle
Lokko, *Cultural Weapons
Project,* given to my graduate
students at Iowa State
University, Ames, IA, 1997.
Photograph, Lesley Naa Norle
Lokko.

Lesley Naa Norle Lokko

190

SEGMENT FOURTEEN   WEDNESDAY, 28 JULY 1999 (at home in Chicago).

A place on the map is also a place in history.[15]

[15] A. Rich, 'Notes Towards a Politics of Location', in *Blood, Bread and Poetry: Selected Prose 1979–1985*, London, Virago Press, 1987, p. 210.

For the European navigators who sailed across the Atlantic, America was literally blank space. North America became a continent only very slowly: for the initial explorers, America was a group of islands, similar perhaps to the Azores or the Canaries. With Ferdinand Magellan's circumnavigation of the globe in 1522, what was, in the colonialist eye, essentially blank space became measured space. The determined lines of latitude and longitude, those abstract intellectual inscriptions of measurement across the globe, fixed the Americas well within the boundaries of a European view of the world. Latitude and longitude: pure, Platonic, all-encompassing expressions of perfect spherical geometry. The history of the relationship between geometry, property and divinity needs no further elaboration here, except to note that the European 'discoverers' of the 'New World' were driven by an unshakeable belief in the power of geometry and mathematical measure. As Dennis Cosgrove has noted, 'measuring and mapping, imagining the landscape in the mind or inscribing it on to paper are more rapid, less dangerous and more secure ways of coping with unknown space than penetrating the Appalachian forests with axe or trekking the featureless grasslands . . . in the settlement of America, each community faced the need to balance the freedoms and physical dangers offered by immeasured space against the safety and social constraint offered by measure, rule and boundary'.[16]

[16] D. Cosgrove, 'The Measures of America', in J. Corner and A. McLean (eds), *Taking Measures Across the American Landscape*, New Haven, Yale University Press, 1996.

How can this history be measured, recorded, represented against the experience of black America? This is not a community balancing 'freedom' and 'physical dangers', trekking courageously into the wilderness. For Africans arriving in the United States and Europe as dislocated, violently separated communities, theirs is an entirely different kind of history. In place of the myths of establishing oneself at the edge of the unknown, as various cultures arriving in the 'New World' had done, their task was to make sense out of senselessness, re-make history, re-make culture, and forge different relationships to the land. To recognise other histories, other peoples, other languages and sounds and, crucially, other ways of occupying the same space requires, in addition, the ability to recognise those places in the very construction of the majority history and culture. Speaking of literature but applicable to place- and space-making, Toni Morrison explains [American] 'knowledge holds that traditional, canonical American literature is free of, uninformed and unshaped by the four-hundred-year-old presence of, first, Africans and then African–Americans in the United States'.[17] Her argument focuses on the ways in which American society relegated its contradictions

[17] T. Morrison, 'Romancing the Shadow', in T. Morrison, *Playing in the Dark: Whiteness and the Literary Imagination*, Cambridge, Mass., Harvard University Press, 1992, p. 4.

Lesley Naa Norle Lokko

18 Ibid.

and internal conflicts to a 'blank darkness',[18] effectively silencing the black experience and collective memory. If cultural identities are, as she argues, [partly] formed and informed by a nation's literature, then what are we to make of the problematic forced construction of 'America' as a new, free, democratic and – essentially – white man?

Historical analysis, as Tschumi states, 'has generally supported the view that the role of the architect is to project on the ground the images of social institutions, translating the economic or political structure of society into buildings or groups of buildings. Architecture, therefore, was first and foremost the adaptation of space to the existing socio-economic structure.'[19] What, then, are the available options that might make it possible to search, spatially, for the hidden agendas in architecture that consolidate and articulate one set of narratives over another? The museum and the art gallery are not the only available architectural explorations – and never have been.

19 B. Tschumi, *Architecture and Disjunction*, Cambridge, Mass., MIT Press, 1994, p. 5.

surplus matter: of scars, scrolls, skulls and stealth

matter

3 . . . Used as a vague designation for any physical substance not definitely particularized, e.g. applied in Physiology to the fluids of the body, excrementitious products, etc. Often with qualifying adj., as in **colouring**, **extractive**, **faecal**, *etc.* **matter**

4 spec. (= corrupt matter). Purulent discharge, pus.

OED., 2nd edition, vol. IX, Oxford 1989.

2 Surveying the way form has been conceptualised, Martin Jay writes: 'Form has been synonymous . . . with the most substantial essence of a thing . . . . Here formal value has carried with it a metaphysical charge . . .' M. Jay, 'Modernism and the Retreat from Form', in M. Jay, *Force Fields: Between Intellectual History and Cultural Critique*, New York and London, Routledge, 1993, pp. 147–57; 148.

To write under the title *Subject/Matter*[1] is already, and in a very particular way, to be positioned. Two readings immediately come to mind. On one hand Subject:*Matter*, that is 'matter' as the subject of inquiry, that to which the text is to be addressed, its target or destination. And we should note that it is *matter* that is at issue, and not material; for however generally the latter may be taken it always seems already too determined, achieved and nameable to equate with matter. Material is dignified, a work of culture with a history – it is wood, cloth, stone or metal. And, on the other, the title, when read as Subject/Matter, immediately recalls the idealist oppositions Subject/Object and Form/Matter whereby form comes to be identified with the subject who actively and with intention bestows it upon matter and hence elevates it into the realm of meaning (its 'content') and hence 'life'.[2] Upon the regulated balance or commensurability of the terms in the Form/Matter dyad, architectural doctrines such as 'fitness for purpose' or 'economy of means' would then rest. However, where matter, in form, becomes marked by lack (through, for example, mutilation) or excess, the 'good form' to which these maxims point fails. In an apparent exchange of properties, matter's supposed passivity is cast aside and it seems to emerge, in its texture as 'matter', into visibility as it proliferates and encrusts, or leaches, twists and folds with slow and fluid momentum under itself. The ease with which that very particularly weighted word 'cancerous' comes to commentators when describing this

Figure 12.1 Hans Holbein, *The Ambassadors*, 1533. Copyright National Gallery, London.

Mark Dorrian

194

grotesque profusion (when speaking, for example, of certain kinds of ornament) is due to its signifying a condition in which the production of the matter of the body becomes unregulated. And is not the reason why cancer appears as the most monstrous of diseases because in the revolt of matter (and this motif – the hubris of matter as the inauguration of monstrosity – has a long and gender-specific history),[3] the body turns against itself and so its organic unity comes apart?

It is important to recognise that formlessness, thought in its widest sense, cannot be considered a unitary notion. It is patterned by differing temporalities and valencies that are inscribed within concepts such as the amorphous (that which is beyond, or outwith, form); the unformed (that which is yet to come to form); the deformed (that which has departed, or 'fallen', from form); and the anamorphic (a term, meaning 'back to form', which infers a play between form and deformation). Something of this temporality can be illustrated in the historical emergence and deployment of the categories Gothic and Baroque: E. H. Gombrich has noted how, during the course of the eighteenth century, they came to stand respectively for the unformed and the deformed, in opposition to the 'good form' of the Classical: 'Gothic,' he writes, was 'increasingly used as a label for the not-yet-classical, the barbaric, and *barocco* for the no-longer-classical, the degenerate.'[4] If we take the deformed to be lapsarian formlessness, arising that is upon the occasion of a 'fall'

3 Aristotle, 'Generation of Animals', in Aristotle, *The Complete Works of Aristotle, I*, ed. J. Barnes, New York, Princeton University Press, 1984, pp. 1111–1218; iv, iii, pp. 1187–95; M. H. Huet, *Monstrous Imagination*, Cambridge, Mass. and London, Harvard University Press, 1993; M. Dorrian, 'On the Monstrous and the Grotesque', *Word & Image*, 16:4, 2000, pp. 310–17.

4 E. H. Gombrich, 'Norm and Form: Stylistic Categories of Art History and their Origins in Renaissance Ideals', in E. H. Gombrich, *Norm and Form: Studies in the Art of the Renaissance*, London, Phaidon, 1966, pp. 81–98; 84.

Figure 12.2 *F-117 Nighthawk Stealth Fighter*. Image courtesy Lockheed Martin Corporation.

Mark Dorrian

from form, then we might, placing the question within the frame of Kantian aesthetics, consider the fall in question to be the *swallow*, the descent that leads from head to gut, from the ideal (form) to the base (matter), from the (in)finite moment of suspension that is Kantian taste (with Kant it is precisely *form* that is tasted, as opposed to concept, etc.)[5] to consumption and dissolution.

And if we sought a moment upon the body where a thematics of both excess and lack of matter converge, to what would we turn? Perhaps our attention would be drawn to the scar. For the scar is the wound that refuses to heal, and in that refusal is an enduring signifier of an absence, surplus matter as a monument erected upon the body. Further, in this act of remembrance, the scar denaturalises the body's surface, drawing attention to and marking its 'materiality'. The scar upon my body is where, through disfiguration, it takes leave of itself, where in welt, scab, encrustation and puncture the matter of my body becomes visible and is articulated in its silence, where it becomes 'pure', that is, *other than me*.

With the scar, we are also consequently speaking about the glyphic economy of the tattoo, of the *tattoo as scar*. The identification is familiar, at least since the European voyages of exploration in the Pacific. The surgeon John Hunter, writing in his *Treatise on Venereal Disease* of 1786, compared the scars left upon the skin by smallpox and venereal disease to unnatural tattoos and artificial impressions marking the body.[6] The ecstatic vision of the worked and tattooed 'savage' body as a 'perverse and monstrous extension of an erotogenic surface'[7] put forward by Alphonso Lingis, however beholden to the consequences of certain binarisms it might remain (the 'savage' body phantasmically projected, in opposition to the western/'civilised'/ classical body, as sexually determined, as 'one with the earth itself', etc.), is eloquent in its reading of the scarred surface as a play of lack and excess of matter: 'The savage inscription is a working all over the skin, all surface effects. This cutting in orifices and raising tumescences does not contrive new receptor organs for the depth body . . . it extends the erotogenic surface . . . it is a multiplication of mouths, lips, labia, anuses, these sweating and bleeding perforations and puncturings.'[8] This dermal topography is neither a map of the body nor, in any straightforward sense, a map drawn upon it; it is rather a redistribution, multiplication and prolongation of the body upon its surface.

The theme of the tattoo punctuates the discourse on architecture in the modern period. Adolf Loos' identification of the tattoo with ornamentation in his famous polemic of 1908, *Ornament and Crime*, is well known.[9] Less so is a passage, written around sixty years before, from 'The Lamp of Beauty' in John Ruskin's *The Seven Lamps of Architecture*, in which the same analogy is deployed. Discussing a particular kind of ornamentation, a disfiguring ornamentation and hence, he tells us,

5 I. Kant, *The Critique of Judgement*, trans. J. C. Meredith, Oxford, Clarendon Press, 1961, pp. 133–4.

6 B. M. Stafford, *Body Criticism: Imaging the Unseen in Enlightenment Art and Medicine*, Cambridge, Mass. and London, MIT Press, 1991, p. 289.

7 A. Lingis, 'Savages', in *Excesses: Eros and Culture*, Albany, State University of New York Press, 1983, pp. 17–46; 43. Elizabeth Grosz considers this text at the outset of her essay 'The Body as Inscriptive Surface' in E. Grosz, *Volatile Bodies: Toward a Corporeal Feminism*, Indiana University Press, Bloomington and Indianapolis, 1994, pp. 138–59.

8 Lingis, op. cit., p. 34.

9 A. Loos, 'Ornament and Crime', in A. Loos, *Ornament and Crime: Selected Essays*, trans. M. Mitchell, Riverside, Ariadne Press, 1998, pp. 167–76; 167–8.

Mark Dorrian

ornament that cannot in truth be called ornament, he suggests that its cost be set down in the architect's contract under the heading *For Monstrification*. 'I believe that we regard these customary deformities with a savage complacency, as an Indian does his flesh patterns and paint . . . I believe that I can prove them to be monstrous, and I hope hereafter to do so conclusively; but meantime, I can allege in defense of my persuasion nothing but the fact of their being unnatural.'[10] As he continues it becomes clear that, for Ruskin, the tattoo is matter without form: it is a disfiguring scar, a traumatic surplus of matter *as* surface. Yet this ornament, to follow the logic of the trope, which is all about surface, which is inessential, which is not grounded in the 'natural' organic body, at the same time has a certain depth in that it punctures the body. We will return to it later and as we'll see, via a consideration of anamorphosis, it is precisely this ornament's character as surface, indeed as *only* surface, that gives it its ability to puncture. One of the tattoos, one of the monsters (designating here something both unnatural and traumatic, where trauma, in its etymological root, is *wound*[11]), that Ruskin confronts will come to be of particular interest to us, something in fact that he interprets as pure surplus matter: the scroll.

When form topples and 'falls', when matter becomes exorbitant through modes of distortion, deformation, liquidation, putrefaction or mutilation, a complex double movement, up and down, is evident. The primary gesture that splits the field of objects into the well-formed and the ill-formed, the normative and the aberrant, is followed by a secondary discrimination that bifurcates the second field, the domain of aberrations, into 'bad' and 'good' parts; that is, a division is instituted between, on the one hand, the (horrific or abject) aberrant phenomena that must be disavowed, and, on the other, those that can be reintegrated with the discourse (concerning nature, the will of the divine, the movement of spirit, etc.) within which the primary gesture (the designation of 'good form') is itself anchored and authorised. Thus the formless aberration can, in its evaluation, even come to *exceed* good form. This economy of recuperation has a long history, and the ambivalence attached to the monstrous figure is only one example: Ambroise Paré signals this characteristic scission, which produces the high and the low, the noble and the base, when, at the beginning of his book *On Monsters and Marvels* (1573), he writes: 'There are several things that cause monsters. The first is the glory of God. The second his wrath.'[12]

So, we have the formless phenomenon serving, in certain historic moments, as a demonstration of the limitlessness or plenitude of creation: it is the monstrous 'wonder', something that has the aura of the divine, or else that serves through its very negativity as an index of the absolutely free character of God's creativity. Ruskin himself uses the latter argument: by the exceptional form (that is, the formless, here rhetorically sublimated) God indicates 'that the adoption of the others was not a

10 J. Ruskin, *The Seven Lamps of Architecture* (1849), London, New York, etc., Cassell and Co., 1909, p. 156.

11 S. Stewart, 'Coda: Reverse Trompe L'Oeil/The Eruption of the Real', in S. Stewart, *Crimes of Writing: Problems in the Containment of Representation*, Durham and London, Duke University Press, 1994, pp. 273–90; 277.

12 A. Paré, *On Monsters and Marvels*, trans. J. L. Pallister, Chicago and London, University of Chicago Press, 1982, p. 3.

Mark Dorrian

13 Ruskin, op. cit., p. 157.

14 Ibid.

15 G. W. F. Hegel, *Aesthetics: Lectures in Fine Art*, vol. 1, trans. T. M. Knox, Oxford, Clarendon Press, 1975, p. 538.

16 M. de Certeau, 'Vocal Utopias: Glossolalias', *Representations*, no. 56, 1996, pp. 29–47; 31.

17 Ibid., p. 30.

matter of necessity'.[13] (Among these exceptional forms we should count those things, he says, [that should be] hidden from the eye, such as the body's intestines or the strange mineral and vegetable aberrations concealed in the earth.)[14] Or again, form that is warped and tortured may point to an excessive content, as in Hegel's discussion of the visual arts in the Romantic era, where content has exceeded the limitations of matter to express it and has thus passed beyond the 'good form' of the Classical whose paradigm is Greek sculpture. Here the movement of spirit is understood in terms of the negation of the material, the corporeal, the individual and the subjective as exemplified in the tortured and suffering body of Christ.[15] And finally, doesn't the divine voice itself come, as inspiration, in the grotesque 'language' of glossolalia (speaking in tongues), a speech in which the matter of language exceeds its form? Michel de Certeau notes that this speech, which 'encloses in a linguistic simulacrum all that is not language and comes from the speaking voice'[16] is already present in *the noises of otherness* that populate ordinary conversations and which, as he puts it, 'represent the *tattoo* of the vocal and interlocutory upon the body of discourse'.[17]

We will shortly see how this double movement that attends the formless works out in a contemporary object (which appears as both god-like *and* horrific). But first we need to recall the Form/Matter duality with which we began. This perhaps finds its most explicit demonstration, and its most extreme theatricalisation, in the kind of anamorphic art known as catoptric or mirror anamorphosis. Developing from the early 1600s (the first manual on the subject was 1630), its popularity grew during the following 150 years: by the middle of the eighteenth century it was widely disseminated throughout Europe as a popular amusement and toy. The technique worked by using curved mirrors to optically correct a distorted image. Viewed without the mirror, the anamorphic image appeared as a radically deformed field of lines, colours and tones that spread, in a circle or an arc, around a central point. The image would be painted or printed upon a flat surface, or, if a conical reflector was to be used, might be painted on the vertical surfaces of a casket within which the mirror would sit. When the mirror, a cylinder or cone of polished metal, was placed upon the central point, and when the anamorphic image was viewed in it, the field of warped and morcellated objects before it was, as it were, magically redeemed, brought back into life and form. In his classic study of anamorphic art, Jurgis Baltrušaitis, discussing a Dutch conical anamorphosis of Venus and Adonis from the eighteenth century, writes: 'Distorted round the mirror, the beautiful classical figures assume a monstrous aspect. The youthful hero is bisected, his head down. His swollen limbs are turned around, his feet are in the air . . . Venus' arms resemble intestines. The whole is a strange whirlwind of scattered pieces and shapeless anatomical débris which are reformed and resolved with precision in the reflections of the cone.'[18] And shortly before, considering a portrait of a woman with a bird: 'The world bursts asunder before reconstituting itself. The heads, the limbs are detached from the body and are then reinstated. Thus the woman who is holding a bird by a thread is split into three pieces . . . The face is upside down and fluid . . . Illumined against a sombre background, the vision seems to emerge from the night . . . The correction in the mirror, wherein true forms are reborn from the chaos, possesses [a] supernatural element.'[19] *In short the mirror is, as it were, the correlate of the Idea through and in view of which base matter (here the anamorphic collapsed and desiccated object-field) is worked upon and uplifted into Form (and thereby also 'life').*[20] In certain portraits the removal of the mirror revealed, occupying the centre of the swirling field of matter, a skull, a death's head.

Of all the objects that technology presents us with today, the one that most obsesses architects is (let's use this word for the time being) an *anamorphe*: the F-117 Nighthawk stealth fighter plane. It comes as no surprise that this aircraft is also a supremely mythical object, in fact *the* mythical object for the contemporary west. Each and every commentary made upon it bears witness to this.

Clothed in the ancient theme of the 'cloak of invisibility' (which always comes as a divine gift), the attributes of the plane are turned into something of the order of a metaphysical token and directive. The surfaces of the aircraft, to which it owes its minimal electromagnetic profile, find a direct correspondence with the gifts in ancient myths that confer invisibility and which always have the nature of a 'skin'. When the F-117 was brought down during the bombing of Serbia, the press reports of what followed drove home the mythic nature of the event. The reporting cast the local farmers' dismemberment of the wreckage as a kind of folklorish eucharist whereby a peasantry wielding rustic knives divided the body of a fallen god. Thus we were told that when the object 'fell from the sky like a meteor . . . all of Europe was lit by fire'. As for where the body landed, '*for all time* this will be The Place Where the Plane Fell Out of the Sky'. Each fragment of the aircraft was sought after like 'a piece of the True Cross'.[21]

It has been said that the stealth fighter is an *anamorphe*. But in what sense exactly? Certainly it might be characterised by a certain formlessness, but the claim can be more precisely delineated in terms of the aircraft's status as an arrangement, a 'spread' of matter, calibrated according to its representation in the mirror, or in this case, upon the radar screen; in constructing the deformed object one moves from its appearance upon the surface of representation back out to the world into which the screen explodes the form and scatters it. As Paul Virilio has written: 'It is somewhat as if the image in the mirror were suddenly modifying our face: the

18 J. Baltrušaitis, *Anamorphic Art*, trans. W. J. Strachan, Cambridge, Chadwyck-Healy, 1977, p. 145.

19 Baltrušaitis, op. cit., pp. 140–3.

20 For comments on the collapsed anamorphic image as the image of death see M. Iversen, 'Orthodox and Anamorphic Perspectives', *Oxford Art Journal*, vol. 18:2, 1995, pp. 81–4; 84.

21 R. Fisk, 'Assault on the Serbs: Into a Peasant Village Falls a Hi-tech Enemy', *The Independent*, 29 March 1999.

Mark Dorrian

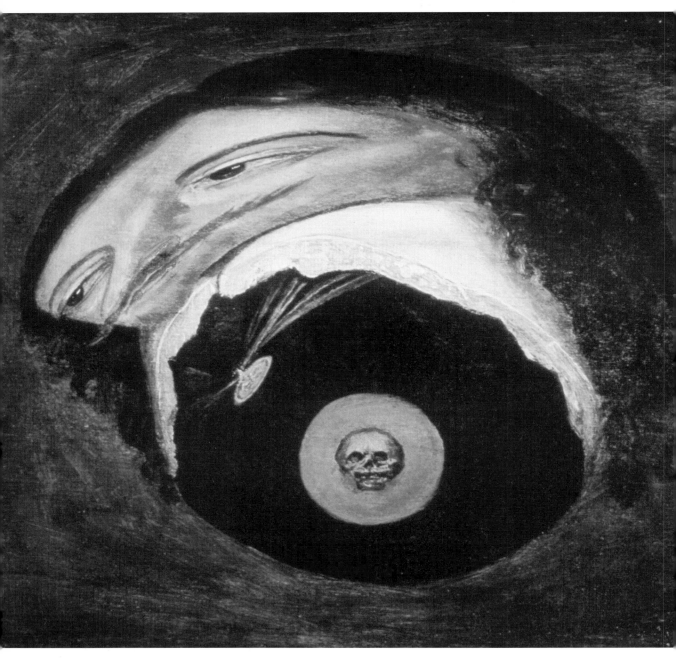

Figure 12.3 Unknown artist, *Anamorphic portrait of Charles I,* after 1649. Statens Konstmuseer. Photograph, The National Museum of Fine Art, Stockholm.

Mark Dorrian

electronic representation on the screen, the radar console, modifies the aerody-
namic silhouette of the weapon, the virtual image dominating in fact "the thing" of
which it was, until now, only the "image".'[22] The contemporary *anamorphe*, however,
inverts the relationship that its predecessor had to the screen and so realises something that is historically quite unprecedented. Where catoptric anamorphosis effects
the *recovery* of the form in the mirror (the form, that is, which in the first instance
was 'presented' to it), its contemporary double *disappears* into the screen. The
notional sequence would be this: a conventional aircraft is presented to the screen;
and then the representation that appears upon it determines the specifics of the
deformation applied to the object. But here the process leaves its antecedent, for
the deformation produces the almost total implosion of the object as representation.
Thus the deformation might be more accurately as *paramorphic*; it remains, like
anamorphic distortion, addressed to a visual point, to an eye, but there is, through
that eye, no imminent return (*ana-*) to form; rather it is put in a position radically
alongside (*para-*) form.

However, the Nighthawk has a paradoxical character and this is fundamental to
its mythic status: in it, opposing properties and meanings coincide. Thus, even while
arguing that the stealth fighter is a *paramorphe*, one is tempted to, at the same time,
acknowledge that two great and antithetical dreams of *form* reach their apotheosis
with this aircraft and in it are figured *simultaneously* in a strangely pure way. The first
dream is that of the departure of form from the symbolic and its elevation into a state

22 P. Virilio, 'Desert Screen' in
P. Virilio, *The Virilio Reader*, ed. J. Der
Derian, Oxford, Blackwell, 1998,
pp. 166–82; 168.

Figure 12.4 *B-2 Spirit Stealth
Bombers*. Image courtesy US
Air Force.

Mark Dorrian

of pure content; which is to say, the total convergence of the 'meaning of the form' with its Idea or task (in this case its invisibility to remote systems of detection) such that the form comes to rest, not merely as a signifier, but as a pure and necessary materialisation of the motivating Idea. If this corresponds to Marinetti's notion of 'speaking without adjectives',[23] a speech purged of all (decorative and excessive) elements which would delay contact with the actual, then it finds its inverse in the other oneiric image presented by the stealth fighter; namely a speech that consists *only* of adjectives. Here, form, by refusing all demands made upon it, is raised into autonomy (the form of the aircraft *against* its flyability; the fact that the plane flies *in spite of* its form). Viewed in this way the form of the aircraft, insofar as it is experienced as a signifier, becomes opaque and impossibly fecund: no longer assured of what it *is*, we can say only what it is like. Thus the F-117 is a kind of split phenomenon: and its status as an object both 'invisible' and 'spectacular' is only the beginning. To architects it offers a sado-masochistic object *par excellence* (to take Slavoj Žižek's characterisation): through it one experiences the simultaneous refusal of the Law (autonomous, non-determined form) together with its absolute assertion ([the *frisson* of] complete technical determination of the object).

Yet in the last instance, what is so striking about the stealth fighter is not its strangeness, but rather a certain and uncanny familiarity. It presents us with the paradox that at the very moment at which we seem to depart from the field of the

23 As Marinetti wrote, in his *Risposte alle obiezioni*, 11 August 1912: 'I believe it necessary to suppress the adjective and the adverb, because they constitute (taken together and individually), the multicoloured festoons, the *trompe-l'oeil swags*, pedestals, parapets and balustrades of the old traditional period'; cited in T. Benton, 'Speaking Without Adjectives: Architecture in the Service of Totalitarianism' in D. Ades *et al.*, *Art and Power: Europe Under the Dictators 1930–1945*, London, Thames and Hudson, 1995, pp. 36–42; 36.

Figure 12.5 *The Phobic 'Thing'*. Image courtesy Lockheed Martin Corporation.

Mark Dorrian

symbolic, we find that we re-enter it (or at least we once again experience its effects) with unprecedented force. The 'semiotically neutral' calibration of the aircraft's form (its determination by technical requirements) seems perversely to deliver us into a well-defined and highly semiotically-charged tradition of 'form-making' (whose objects form a kind of unnameable core around which meaning circulates). The stealth fighter is, in short, the vision of menace projected by science fiction: the monstrous, phobic 'thing' whose semiotic condition is established not so much by systematically eradicating the anthropomorphic as by preying upon it. This connection is made explicit in the orchestration of the weapon's image by the official photographs. Marinetti's well-known aestheticisation of war may today seem to have undergone 'sublimation' into the ecstasies of precision in mathematised space, but as the stealth fighter shows, this is only partly true: at its root as an obsessive image lies an obscene pleasure which technological connoisseurship might disavow and cover over, but which is absolutely congruent with it.

The character of the stealth fighter as a traumatic image can be theorised by reading it in the context of Jacques Lacan's discussion of anamorphosis in his 1964 seminar.[24] Lacan's commentary turns on Hans Holbein's painting *The Ambassadors* (1533) which he, following Baltrušaitis, linked, in its presentation of the symbols of the Arts and Sciences, to the theme of *vanitas*. What is of course the nexus of Holbein's work is the play between, on one hand, the extreme realism of the frontal

24 J. Lacan, *The Four Fundamental Concepts of Psycho-Analysis* (Seminar XI, 1964), trans. A. Sheridan, New York, W. W. Norton and Co., 1978, pp. 79–90.

Figure 12.6 *The Phobic 'Thing'*. Image courtesy US Air Force.

Mark Dorrian

perspectival view of the two ambassadors, the fabrics that clothe and surround them, and the (scientific and musical) instruments that lie between them, and on the other, the strange formless stain that is smeared across the foreground of the image but which, when viewed obliquely, emerges as a skull rising above the now collapsed field of the painting. The world represented in the painting, the world that is interrupted by the anamorphic skull, is extraordinarily fully achieved: as Baltrušaitis writes: 'Everything is astonishingly present and mysteriously true to life . . . The whole painting is conceived as a trompe-l'oeil.'[25]

In Lacan the distinction between 'reality' (our constructed, familiar experience) and the *real* is crucial. The latter is something that is unassimilable by symbolisation, something that resists being knitted into the network of signifiers through which the symbolic universe of everyday 'reality' is constructed. The effect of the real upon this universe is disruptive; the subject experiences the encounter with the real ('an essential encounter,' Lacan writes, 'an appointment to which we are called with a real that eludes us'[26]), which is compulsively returned to, as trauma. Slavoj Žižek associates Hegel's notion of a pre-ontological 'night of the world' with the Lacanian real: he quotes from Hegel's *Jenaer Realphilosophie*: 'This night, the interior of nature, that exists here – pure self – in phantasmagorical representations, is night all around it, in which here shoots a bloody head – there another white ghastly apparition, suddenly here before it, and just so disappears. One catches sight of this night when one looks human beings in the eye – into a night that has become awful.'[27] Figured in this Žižek sees the Lacanian *le corps morcelé*, the fragmented body that is anterior to the assumption of a (phantasmic) unified, consolidated body image and to symbolisation.[28] This horrific and spectral pre-symbolic and pre-ontological 'night of the world' is something prior to 'world', something 'not-yet-worldly': it is 'not the old, premodern "underground" as the dark, lower strata of the global cosmic order in which monstrous entities dwell, but something *stricto sensu* acosmic'.[29]

The spectral presence of the anamorphic skull in *The Ambassadors* appears, in its intrusion into the frontal perspectival 'reality' of the painting, as a phobic image. Its appearance within the painting constitutes the mark of 'the real whose extraction constitutes reality'[30]: the subject's encounter with the anamorphic stain is an encounter with the exhaustion and collapse of representation, and specifically with *its* representation, that with which it identifies. The skull rips across the surface of 'reality', displaying it as a signifier, as contingent, as surface, as 'empty'.[31] The subject is no longer confirmed in the fullness and plenitude of its representations: rather, as Lacan writes, 'Holbein makes visible for us here something that is simply the subject as annihilated – annihilated in the form that is, strictly speaking, the imaged embodiment . . . of castration'.[32] And indeed the appearance of (the anamor-

25 Baltrušaitis, op. cit., pp. 91–3.

26 Lacan, op. cit., p. 53.

27 Cited in S. Žižek, *The Ticklish Subject: the Absent Centre of Political Ontology*, London and New York, Verso, 1999, pp. 29–30.

28 Ibid., p. 35.

29 Ibid., p. 50.

30 S. Žižek, *Looking Awry: an Introduction to Jacques Lacan through Popular Culture*, Cambridge, Mass. and London, MIT Press, 1998, p. 95.

31 See P. Adams, *The Emptiness of the Image: Psychoanalysis and Sexual Differences*, London and New York, Routledge, 1996.

32 Lacan, op. cit., pp. 88–9.

Mark Dorrian

phic skull as) the stain or blind spot within the field of the vision is founded in the anni- hilated subject, that is the subject constituted by lack and desire. The anamorphic stain in *The Ambassadors* materialises the gaze, the gaze that appeared as an object in some primal separation from the subject (symbolic castration) and which now appears, directed back at the subject, in the field of the Other: as Margaret Iversen puts it, drawing a comparison with Roland Barthes' notion of the punctum, the gaze as object 'reverses the direction of the lines of sight and disorganizes the visual field, erupting into the network of signifiers that constitute "reality"'.[33]

If Lacan values the 'anamorphic ghost', the stain that denaturalises the represen- tational space within which the ambassadors stand, he values equally its 'secret meaning', the death's head that emerges upon the collapse of the worldly scene. However, something that is very striking about the painting is that it portrays not simply a straightforward disjunction between two perspectival registers, but rather the *accommodation* of one within the other. For, notably, the anamorphic skull is figured as an object within the 'reality' of the space that belongs to the pictured figures: the index of this accommodation is the shadow that the skull casts across the mosaic floor upon which the two men stand.[34] Here then we seem to have a pic- turing of the inclusion of the real within 'reality'. This is precisely the condition that Žižek sees as lying at the root of the paranoiac construction of the prosecutor- figure[35] (the Other of the symbolic register, that which lies beyond it and 'controls' it: here death as the prosecutor of the ambassadors). And is the character of this prose- cutor, who is at once spectacular and unseen, who cannot be simply named, deter- mined or circumscribed, who (inescapably) sees us (the stain as the gaze of the Other) and whose punishment is imminent, not that of the stealth fighter as it is sup- ported by the discourse within which it is embedded? The theistic quality of the 'para- noid's persecutor' is, as we have seen, equally evident in commentaries upon the aircraft. Insofar as the stealth fighter is experienced as an 'anamorphic ghost' within 'reality' it actualises something of the death of the world, of the subject's symbolic universe. To this extent the death's head is as much the emblem of the Nighthawk as it is of the anamorphic stain in Holbein's painting; as it is, too, of any encounter with the real. The weapon as stain, as anamorphic ghost, is a spectral, unworldly, uncanny object: an object that haunts reality, which opens up a rift, an abyss, within it, and insofar as it resists symbolisation and incorporation within the network of signifiers, is compulsively returned to in search of meaning.

In describing the anamorphic skull in *The Ambassadors*, Lacan famously likened it to a tattoo 'supported' by a penis whose tumescence produced the distortion in the image. The trope of the tattoo bears witness to the anamorphe's equivocal participa- tion in the solidity of the scene portrayed: the anamorphe is something more drawn

33 M. Iversen, 'What is a Photograph?', *Art History*, vol. 17:3, September 1994, pp. 450–64; 457.

34 A shadow that has a markedly different directionality to those cast by other objects. See the discussion in S. Greenblatt, *Renaissance Self-Fashioning: from More to Shakespeare*, Chicago and London, University of Chicago Press, 1984, pp. 17–21.

35 Žižek, *Looking Awry*, op. cit., pp. 18–20.

Mark Dorrian

Figure 12.7 *The Anamorphic Ghost.* Image courtesy US Air Force.

36 Ruskin, op. cit., p. 163.

37 Ibid.

upon this 'reality' than drawn *into* it; yet at the same time it penetrates, scars and punctures (deflates?) it. Where, to return at last to Ruskin, in the various monsters that he groups under the thematic of the tattoo, do we meet the anamorphe? Without doubt this moment appears, most pressingly, in his ruminations upon the decorative scroll, which he figures, in its radical formlessness, as an effusion of pure matter: 'it has no skeleton, no make, no form, no size, no will of its own'.[36] It is something strangely virtual, hardly there, and yet because of this is at the same time more present than the substantial entities around it upon which it has a profoundly unsettling effect. What it brings is death: it too is a death's head, more *skrull* than scroll. Like Holbein's anamorphic skull, this 'wretched film of an existence' *punctures and deflates* the solidity of everything about. It is a vice and ugliness, 'a vile thing' spoiling 'all that is near'.[37]

I am grateful to the Canadian Centre for Architecture in Montreal for the award of a visiting scholarship during which part of this essay was written.

Mark Dorrian

animal architecture

Materiality is the stuff of architecture. Materials and their properties organise both the minute and the monumental architectural feature in the built environment; from the microchip to the high-rise. Architectural materials may range from the plastic or solid to the virtual, dynamic or sensory. In turn, these modes of materiality are developed into architectural forms by the technologies and methods that constitute the design process.

The following discussion explores concepts of matter and form found in architectural design and biological theories of evolution. For example, Darwinian explanations of diversity and modification in biological evolution suggest principles of design that can lead to different descriptions of form and matter in architecture.

In biological evolution, we might say that form is the external characteristics of an organism (its morphology) and is produced as a result of an evolving matter (DNA replication). This is in direct contrast to leading concepts of form and matter in modern architecture, encapsulated by the modernist discourse of 'style', in which formal criteria, such as light, tone, texture, solidity or permanence, are the active agents of design. However, if a concept of active, evolving matter is introduced, a relationship between architectural form and matter is established whereby a design is not exclusively determined by formal criteria, but by its materiality too. Darwin's theory of natural selection is evidence of just such a shift of principles in a 'design' process.

Classical theories of biological evolution, in which form is the only positive and *inherently* transformative constituent, relied upon immutable and eternal principles of matter.[1] Creationist and essentialist theories of the origin of species were therefore challenged by Darwin's principle of natural selection. Contemporary life and biological sciences continue to produce more sophisticated and radical analyses of evolving matter, developing Darwin's general theory of the mechanisms that produce speciation into specialist areas of biological science, including genetics, biotechnology and molecular biology.

However, the same shift is not reflected in the visual arts. Modernist architecture is frequently not informed by such modified concepts of form and matter because material constituents are still perceived to be of less significance for producing real change in design than their formal counterparts. These contrasting concepts of form and matter are particularly evident in architectural design that attempts to work with both modernist and scientific criteria of matter. Analogues to scientific principles of design, such as the transmission of genetic material through DNA replication reflected in Peter Eisenman's Bio-Centrum projects, show a design concept that is informed by theories of matter from genetics. However, the *aesthetic* assessment of these designs resorts to a limited modernist idea of form as the primary means of

1 Aristotelian and Platonic descriptions of matter are generally understood in relation to becoming, inconstancy, inadequacy or simulation. Matter is therefore less desirable than an essential or ideal Form.

Peg Rawes

evaluation. The application of design principles from biological science, which are informed by concepts of evolving matter and form, remain limited.

This discussion will therefore explore a number of theories that reflect a more profound and critical engagement with principles of evolving matter found in the biological sciences. Development of these examples will suggest modes of architectural design that are derived from both the formal and material organisation of biological matter to highlight, in particular, the scope for an evolving and heterogeneous concept of form, rather than a return to a limited 'formalism'. For example, an analysis of the role of architect, user and product in relation to Richard Dawkin's concept of 'memes', suggests a richer and more complex expression of the processes involved in architectural design.

FORM AND MATTER

Daniel Dennett describes how Darwin's theory of natural selection is a materialist concept of evolution. *Darwin's Dangerous Idea: Evolution and the Meaning of Life* analyses Darwin's theory developed in *The Origin of Species*.[2] Natural selection is considered to be a highly successful design mechanism, providing a theory which proved that 'modern species were revised descendants of earlier species – species had evolved', and for showing 'how this process of "descent with modification" had occurred'.[3] In particular, two underlying principles – adaptation and diversity – are analysed to illustrate how the relationship between form and matter (phenotype and genotype)[4] are fundamentally altered as a result.

His argument therefore considers the shift from a static, inert concept of matter found in classical taxonomy inherited from Aristotle's theories of natural science and Plato's concepts of ideal forms to a theory of evolution in which matter is active. Classical systems of taxonomy describe change in morphologies that are derived from a pure ideal form or essence ('eidos' or 'species'). In such systems organisms can only exist as imitations of these ideal and yet transcendental originals. Creationist and classically determined systems of classification opposed to Darwin therefore prove to be limited by principles of fixed and non-evolving matter. Such essentialism claims that a dog, eagle or cat is an imitation of an essential 'dog', 'cat' or 'eagle'. Darwin's theory of natural selection, however, renders untenable a concept of matter that is unchanging and eternal. Instead, natural selection invests biological matter with principles of modification and diversity.

These principles have now become more explicitly developed in modern genetics and microbiology, and are contested in biotechnology research. Mendel's work on

2 D. Dennett, *Darwin's Dangerous Idea: Evolution and the Meaning of Life*, London, Allen Lane, Penguin, 1995. C. Darwin, *The Origin of Species by Means of Natural Selection*, ed. J. W. Burrows, New York, Harmondsworth Press, Penguin, 1985.

3 Dennett, op. cit., p. 39. Darwin did not produce a biological explanation of the origin of speciation, nor did he invent a theory of genes. Genetics, the study of heredity and variation was developed subsequently by Mendel and Bateson amongst others.

4 The genetic make-up of an organism (genotype) is analogous to matter, and the physical constitution of an organism, determined by the genetic make-up and environment (phenotype) is analogous to form.

5 S. Jones, *The Language of Genes: Biology, History and the Evolutionary Future*, London, Harper Collins, 1993, p. 54.

6 K. Kelly, *Out of Control: The New Biology of Machines*, London, Fourth Estate, 1994, p. 478.

dominant and recessive factors of inheritance in peas and the discovery of the structure of DNA's double helix confirmed the basis of natural selection's principles.[5] More recently, developments in molecular biology have shown that Darwin's principle of incrementally changing matter is an incomplete form of evolution, i.e. it is not the only evolutionary process at work.[6] And biotechnology's artificial manipulation of genetic material and its transmission between unrelated organisms, which produce distinctly 'unnatural' organisms, require Darwinian principles of adaptation and diversity to be reformulated.

But, despite recent developments in microbiology and evolutionary biology, Darwinian evolution nevertheless presents significant principles of understanding material change in scientific terms. For architecture, the principle of natural selection and related biological developments provide an analysis of matter and form dramatically distinct from those criteria found in the modernist canon of style.

MATTER AS FORM

Peter Eisenman's laboratory for Bio-Centrum in Frankfurt exemplifies a project that shows how biological matter is represented in architectural design. The extension to a research laboratory at the J. W. Goethe University, Frankfurt is presented as a design that has a direct correlation between architecture and biological design principles, in particular the production of DNA. The processes of DNA production (replication, transcription and translation) are used as 'adaptive' principles of design and further enhanced by the use of fractal (rather than Euclidean) geometry. The building is therefore perceived to reflect a modern adaptive environment and so counteract modernist principles of rigid or fixed divisions of space. Such a strategy, we are told, is a truly interdisciplinary project, suspended between the architectural and biological. The architects' account of the project states (my emphasis):

> Blurring the interdisciplinary boundaries allowed us to explore other formal options that may fall between biology and architecture.
>
> As biology today dislocates the traditions of science, so the architecture of our Bio-Centrum project dislocates the traditions of architecture. While architecture's role is traditionally seen to be that of accommodating the representing function, this project does not simply accommodate the methods by which research into biological processes is carried out. Rather, it articulates those processes themselves. Indeed, it could be said its architecture is produced by those very processes.[7]

7 P. Eisenman, 'Recent Works, Bio-Centrum, Frankfurt-am-Main', in M. Toy (ed.), *Deconstruction II, Architectural Design*, vol. 59, no 1/2, profile 77, London, Academy Editions, 1994, p. 44.

Peg Rawes

The organisation of DNA appears to inform the project on both an organisational and formal level. However, the project description and plans confirm that the design was concerned with producing formal similarities (orthogonal blocks represent splitting, replication and reformation of a new DNA molecule), but failed to make apparent the organisation or evolution possible that DNA replication might offer to the building process. Practical issues of matching the client's needs with the concept and feasibility of the scheme based on biological processes would account for some of these differences. Nevertheless, the project indicates the extent that the claims made for interdisciplinary architecture overlook, or do not use, concepts of modified form and matter in the design process. Each of the processes described in replication or the material transformations that occur in DNA becomes restricted to a blueprint or representational model upon which the design is constructed. In the end, despite the potential sophistication of the project, it is reduced to the limited modernist assessment of representation or form, at the expense of a radically different aesthetic, which is informed by a biological process.

MUTATIONS, ENGINEERING AND SYMBIOSIS

The artist, Thomas Grünfeld, has produced a series of works called *Misfits* that suggest an engagement with debates in genetic and evolutionary concepts of matter. Challenging a rational or 'natural' form of evolution and taxonomy Grünfeld's 'creations' present unnerving speculative visions of, on one hand, extremes of engineering and design and, on the other hand, mutations and faults in an evolutionary process. Each sculpture is constructed by taxidermy, however, the proximity of hair next to feathers, or fur and hair, are so similar in colour that the creature's form can be said to be both similar and heterogeneous at the same time. Biological questions are raised by this 'unnatural' creation and its companions (such as the swan-rabbit, ostrich-bull) because the *Misfits* imply that the traditional understanding of an 'architecture' linking species to species is being revised.

Clearly such objects are informed by contemporary concern with the different kinds of evolution that are being proposed by biologists and developments in biotechnological intervention in cellular and genetic processes. The ability to intervene directly in the reproduction and transmission of genetic material means that the desire to produce blueprints of 'pure types' of genetically coded organisms, the genome project, becomes a highly controversial aspect of modern biology.

Microbiologists and geneticists are now sceptical of random mutation which, under strict Darwinian principles, can only be 'selected' by the environment. Instead,

Figure 13.1 Thomas Grünfeld, *Misfit (St Bernhard) (94/12)*, 1994. The Saatchi Gallery, London. Photograph, Stephen White.

theories of 'directed mutation' are proposed and supported, for example, by colonies of *E. coli* bacteria that appear to self-direct rapid periods of required mutation if placed in stressful environments.[8]

8 Kelly, op. cit., p. 483.

Alternatively, microbiologists, such as Lynn Margulis, have put forward theories of bacterial symbiosis, which dramatically affect the extent that a linear inheritance of genetic material, evolving gradually through successive generations, can effectively produce larger and complex systems. Margulis' provocative notion of symbiosis by capture considers the development of nucleated cells, which are the outcome of kidnapping. 'A process in which membraned cells' incorporated bacteria and thereby acquired the benefits of photosynthesis and respiration without a whole, new evolutionary process.

Microbiology has also suggested that DNA is comprised of viruses (or, that viruses are mutated fragments of DNA).[9] Thus, accounts of symbiotic relationships in microbiology may offer a more radical account of diversity and adaptation in evolution.

9 Ibid., p. 478.

Recombinant DNA research replaces traditional 'mechanistic' biology. The discovery of the DNA helix gave the material basis for genetic inheritance and founded modern genetics. Previously secure deterministic genetic principles have become replaced by research that observes complexity, feedback and non-linear means of exchange. For example, the claim that a gene is a constant and identifiable section of DNA that only transmits information one-way has now been replaced by the observation that information can flow in reverse (i.e. from RNA to DNA). In addition, the identity of genes has been found to fluctuate and depend upon the genome as a whole. Infection and disease have shown that genes can be transmitted horizontally between unrelated species.[10] Thus the use of the DNA helix as a deterministic formal system from which neat formal comparisons can be represented is a highly reductionist approach to design.

10 M. W. Ho, 'The New Age of the Organism', in C. Jencks (ed.), *New Science = New Architecture?, Architectural Design*, no. 129, 1997, pp. 45–6.

Thus, given that the biological sciences have developed theories in which genetic transmission may not follow pure Darwinian inheritance the *Misfits* may now be considered not merely as 'freaks' in the system, but 'organisms' that reflect other kinds of evolution. Most obviously, they suggest the intervention of biotechnology into a 'natural' evolutionary process, but they also allow speculation about 'directed mutation', or evolution as a result of viral or bacterial infection. The *Misfits* may also be considered to be examples of 'affect animals', because despite their obvious differences, they also have molecular similarities, which are discussed in the following sections.

Peg Rawes

Figure 13.2 Thomas Grünfeld,
Misfit (Nandu) (94/13), 1994.
Photograph, Stephen White.

Peg Rawes

BECOMING-MATERIAL

Gilles Deleuze and Felix Guattari's philosophical theories suggest strategies that can inform modern architectural design and challenge the traditional boundaries of knowledge, for example, the divisions between the arts and sciences. In particular, they attempt to produce a mode of thought that is formal, material, scientific *and* aesthetic. Deleuze and Guattari's theory of 'becoming' is also an analysis of biological structures that produce concepts of evolving form and matter.

Classification systems of the natural world that are derived from idealist thought, such as Aristotelian inherited taxonomies, are opposed because they represent a reductive system of positive and negative binary oppositions (e.g. man/woman, form/matter, idea/imitation, sameness/difference, external/internal, macro/micro). Instead, Deleuze and Guattari suggest an aesthetic in which the normative oppositions that produce idealist principles are reversed or revised. Consequently, matter becomes evaluated positively because it is active, internal (and imperceptible), heterogeneous and evolving. The biological sciences are therefore viewed as a particularly good means of understanding relationships between organisms through concepts of a transformative matter and systems of transmission.

Deleuze and Guattari consider the effects of classification in the natural sciences (and psychoanalysis). They identify three distinct systems of knowledge that produce varying kinds of organism. First, 'oedipal animals': domesticated animals that imitate humanist desires. Second, 'state animals': the proper, archetypal animals of science or mythology which display characteristics of species, genus or phylum.[11] Finally, there are 'affect animals': animals that exist as multiples, packs or populations.[12] It is, however, *only* the pack animals that represent a distinct *mode* of biological matter and therefore prevent the norms of classification from being applied. Affect animals resist the singular, 'natural', normative or domesticated system because their external and internal relations reflect *multiplicity*; they are irreducible to the singular, both internally, as a complex organism and externally in their behaviour. A more profound expression of an evolving organism is therefore perceived in complex or multi-cellular organisms that operate as packs or groups, such as the wolf; or the activities of simple, single-celled organisms (e.g. bacteria, viruses) that function at the level of magnitude or quantity.

This complex critique of taxonomy evaluates the kinds of matter and form that existing classifications imply and also provides an alternative mode of classification; the 'affect' animal. We might therefore suggest that the modern architectural canon, its institutions (educational, professional and regulatory) and paradigms of design might then be considered royal, state or archetypal. Nevertheless a royal architecture

11 Species = group of organisms that breed with members of group and have similar characteristics. Genus = group of organisms, containing several species that have common structural characteristics. Phylum = major division of organisms, containing species with same form (e.g. Arthropoda).

12 G. Deleuze and F. Guattari, *A Thousand Plateaus: Capitalism and Schizophrenia*, London, The Athlone Press, 1986, pp. 240–1.

Peg Rawes

remains a limited form of assessment in which buildings (e.g. the Guggenheim Museum in Bilbao by Frank Gehry, or the Lord's cricket ground media centre in London by Future Systems) are identified as archetypes of modern design. In each case the canonisation of a design tends to negate its use of adaptive, or evolution-based technologies and materials, because of the need to attribute a 'singular' and external form to the project.

'Affect' architecture on the other hand is determined by both modes of internal and external organisation and material. For example, the combined effects of the architect and user in the domestic space or, self-organised, shanty housing in cities in developing countries, such as Rio de Janeiro or Delhi.

INSIDE/OUTSIDE

Having deconstructed how the exterior form is produced by systems of taxonomy Deleuze and Guattari analyse the *internal* biological structure – the molecular. 'Memories of a Molecule' revises the opposition between the principle of the singular, ideal and homogeneous formal characteristic versus the multiple, heterogeneous material properties. Instead, the imperceptible, internal structure of an organism is a multiple and continuous system of material processes which are, in turn, reflected in the heterogeneous external form. They write:

> Memories of a Molecule. *Becoming-animal is only one becoming among others. A kind of order or apparent progression can be established for the segments of becoming in which we find ourselves; becoming-woman, becoming-child; becoming-animal, -veget-able, or -mineral; becomings-molecular of all kinds, becomings-particle. Fibers lead us from one to the other, transform one into the other as they pass through doors and across thresholds.*[13]

13 Ibid., p. 272.

Now the relationships between organisms are not based exclusively upon the 'having' or 'not having' of external properties, such as feathers or scales, but on groupings of an internal molecular structure. Thus a relationship between seemingly unrelated species and genus is made possible. The unclassified hybrid or mutant becomes legitimate as a singular *mode* of biological organisation (i.e. not an impure version of the normative royal or mythical creature) because cellular activity, such as osmosis, is shared by utterly distinct organisms and species.

The morphology of an organism also has a different representational value. Rather than a formal relationship based upon the similarity of one organism to another, the relationship between two independent bodies is realised through a material consistency that produces formal difference rather than repetition of the same characteristic. Given the extent that modernist design gives precedence to *similarity* between forms this is an interesting alternative. A concept of form arises that is not determined by imitation of a morphology, but *difference*; form is produced *as a result* of the material structure existing between organisms, not an imposed design.

Deleuze and Guattari's theory of the molecule as a material aspect of form therefore introduces an alternative aesthetic in which form and matter might function. First, they propose a different mode of relations between organisms to challenge orthodox principles of classification. A critique of the singular, normative type provides the scope for considering adaptive and evolving modes of form, rather than a chronology of preconceived styles. Second, internal structures are the organising principle that produce external formal relations. These biological structures act through flow, exchange and transmission, rather than rigid or static material properties. Form is generated not from an external idea but from an internal system of complex material relations to resist the emphasis placed on external form. Finally, form is produced through difference, not similarity. Hence, form, matter and representation in design are invested with difference and evaluated independently from reductive formalist aesthetics.

This concept of matter is a highly abstracted description of molecular activity. It is a general principle of design but one that can be made more concrete by examining different kinds of 'building' in organisms across the classes, from protozoa, invertebrates to mammals. Zoologist Michael Hansell writes:

> The distribution of the builder through the phyla is also apparently unpredictable: there are pockets of talent, as in the gastropod molluscs and areas of excellence, like the birds. Impressive builders occur even among the protozoa and a number of very capable species are scattered throughout the lower metazoa. Even lowly species of animal respond throughout their lives in various ways to a variety of stimuli as they move about feeding, reproducing, etc. Artefact builders serve to remind us that the organisation of even simple animals is marvellously intricate.[14]

14 M. H. Hansell, *Animal Architecture and Building Behaviour*, London, Longman, 1984, p. 45.

Animal Architecture and Building Behaviour considers the relationships that link diverse groups of organisms. For example, in the production of secretions: a species of amoeba that builds a portable shell using 'cement' it secretes and grains of sand picked up from the environment; a flagellate that builds a protective cage of silica rods inside which the organism lives;[15] or invertebrates and vertebrates that produce mucus, which usually contains 'muco-proteins', which aids locomotion, prevents friction and dryness, or lubricates air and alimentary passages.[16]

15 Ibid., pp. 6–8.

16 Ibid., p. 47.

AFFECT ARCHITECTURE

Architecture may therefore be perceived as a complex system that is determined by various modes of materiality and through which internal and external forms are generated. The NOX project, Off-the-Road/103.8MHZ, 1998, is an example of 'affect' architecture. Taking sound as the basis for connection between the built form, it proposes a scheme built in Eindhoven, not upon visual spatial awareness, but resonance. The urban environment becomes constructed through relations of sound that are local, minute, imperceptible and continuous:

> The space between highway and residential area is utilised to create a zone of transition, by turning it into a field, a medium, a system characterised by wave patterns. Instead of distributing typologically differentiated images, the 208 houses follow the exact inflections of the sound patterns, creating a complete differentiation within one volume.[17]

17 NOX, 'Off-the-road/103.8MHZ: Housing and Noise Barrier, Eindhoven, 1998', in S. Perella (ed.), *Hypersurface Architecture II, Architectural Design,* vol. 69, no. 9/10, profile 141, Chichester, Academy/John Wiley and Sons, 1999, p. 53.

18 M. Novak, 'Eversion, Brushing Against Avatars, Aliens and Angels', ibid., p. 74.

Alternatively, Marcos Novak develops a kind of engineering or mutation of technological devices in order to generate radical architectural concepts. Taking the notion of sensors (e.g. infra-red or digital sensors), which make an 'inaccessible region of reality' available to us, he produces the concept of 'sensels'. Like 'pixels' (picture elements), 'voxals' (volume elements) and 'texels' (texture elements), 'sensels' are digital analogues of 'shape'. They provide a sense of shape that is not immediately available to us; a 'sense-shape' that is 'exact but invisible, a region of activated, hypersensitive space'.[18] Thus, a sensel is a digital material through which we can produce 'sensed-form' across a number of bodies in a field or space.

PRODUCTION

Both architectural and biological matter are in some way assessed by debates of authorship, design, classification, evolution and boundaries between the artificial and natural. For example, the role of architect as sole author becomes reduced if the materials s/he uses, such as 'smart' plastics, polymers or electronically responsive environments, independently regulate or evolve an environment without the direction of the architect. Or can the modern architect convincingly be said to be 'author' of a design when built projects rely upon the expertise and skills of structural engineers in order to be realised?

Richard Dawkins' neo-Darwinian theory of the 'meme' introduces a means by which to reconsider the role of the architect, user and building in architectural design. Memes

Peg Rawes

are cultural units of transmission, or analogues of genes.[19] Their evolution imitates the process of genetic modification. Thus a meme is a unit of transmission that undergoes evolutionary change and diversification as it is transmitted between carriers.

19 R. Dawkins, *The Selfish Gene*, Oxford, Oxford University Press, 1976, p. 206.

A meme is generally understood to be a concept, or a complex 'idea', that is identified over a period of time or duration. As in the Darwinian principle of random adaptation any unit can transmit and therefore diversity is assured. In addition, memes may, as genetic modification occurs, operate at different speeds, exist for different durations and seek different desirable environments.

Communication skills (design, writing, speaking, hearing, etc.) are the fundamental memes of transmission. These 'technologies' of cultural evolution provide the mechanisms, tools and structure through which transmission may occur. As a structure of transmission the built environment is also a meme carrier. Memes are always embodied in some form, be it a deep throaty voice in a body, a digital rendering or a tower block within a city. They are therefore intimately related to a materiality.

Memes can also be linked and replicate together, for example the two memes of 'matter' and 'form' in design have been shown to have an intimately related genealogy in this essay. In this sense they are analogous to the complexity of the genome. They are also inherently defined by degrees of mutation, which may occur, by processes of addition, modification, invention and adaptation. There are therefore no 'pure' memes as such.[20]

20 Dennett, op. cit., pp. 347–55.

In architectural education the institution is probably still the most significant and powerful site of exchange. Thus the institution becomes one of the most potent 'meme pools' in architectural design, containing both the orthodox, conservative, fashionable and resistant memes. The studio system hones these systems of transmission further still, so that memes such as deconstruction, cybernetics, feminism, modelling techniques, behavioural systems, become absorbed and adapted as successive generations of architects are educated.

Increasingly, electronic modes of communication (computer-aided design, e-mail, internet) are providing the most prolific modes of transmission (although not necessarily the most interesting or effective) and are perceived to be most suited to the viral tendencies of the meme. Computational communication is a particularly well adapted set of memes because its 'software' features correlate to the transmission of genetic code. For example, a rendering may contain a digital materiality (an algorithm) which is analogous to the genetic code observed in biological evolution. Algorithms introduce 'unintelligent thinking' into design by taking a set of simple commands that can be replicated easily to generate complex systems.[21] Despite its mechanical procedure, an algorithm introduces results that are not goal driven, and when used in computer-aided design enables the production of virtual or speculative space.

21 Ibid., p. 50.

Peg Rawes

This computer-based transmission and evolution of ideas also introduces perhaps the most controversial aspect of Dawkins' meme theory – the extent to which it is dissociated from the bodily organism. The theory is, at its most extreme, considered to be wholly anti-humanist because it implies that the designer is only currently the most effective or suitable conduit (brain) for ideas. In addition, the effectiveness of the algorithm meme to translate evolutionary principles into computer-aided design exacerbates fears that design is not necessarily a humanist experience. Nevertheless, the algorithm is one of the most radical principles coming out of Darwinian evolution.

Less controversially, meme theory reflects the change in status of the designer and the shift from the 'top down' hierarchy to one of 'bottom up' evolution, and networks of exchange. The canon of architectural evolution shifts from recording the singular achievements of 'Frank Gehry' or 'Richard Rogers', to reflect the real professional context of sets of memes that are shared between a group of individuals, such as 'museum', 'audience', 'force', 'access'. Thus a more sophisticated and realistic expression of the processes involved in design is generated – e.g. a 'Gehry meme' (now similar to a brand?) – and the perception that the product is determined by one sole author becomes redundant. Alternatively, the process from drawing to the realisation of a building may be observed as a collection of related memes transforming during the course of a project.

A consideration of memes, therefore, reflects a more pragmatic expression of the process of architectural design. The roles of author or critic become components in a more complex system, not sole originators of design. Likewise the user becomes an active agent in the construction of architectural meaning.

CONCLUSIONS: A NEW AESTHETIC?

This discussion comes from an interest in the scope of design in modern architectural practice. In particular, it has explored the value attributed to *material* constituents of architectural form that uses principles of biological evolution. Contemporary architectural practice and education is assessed in relation to a number of issues. First, a concern with an *interdisciplinary* architectural practice and the extent to which the use of concepts of matter, design, form and system, which are drawn from the biological sciences, provide alternative modes of design. Second, a critique of architectural practice and theory that is limited to modernist principles and fails to properly assess the interdisciplinary nature of architectural design.

Modern architectural design may use a number of different concepts of matter deriving from biological science and aesthetics. Materiality produced within the biological sciences offers a productive means for extending the limitations of form found in modernist architectural design. As a result a concept of form is modified from a mode of representation and homogeneity into a concept that is heterogeneous and dynamic. In addition, biological discussions of matter suggest ways in which to evaluate architecture as a system that incorporates complex and transformative modes of realisation. Thus, when architectural design is successfully interdisciplinary, different concepts of matter and form are introduced both as internal and external forces. Such architecture reflects modal and dynamic systems in which the role of the designer, user and product become evolving and interrelated.

Peg Rawes

nanotechnology – the liberation of architecture

Gathering the objects into a pile on the dresser, she unscrewed the hair brush handle and removed a plastic panel from the rear of the brush head . . . A grey paste oozed from the handle, directed by a reference field within the head. Like slime mould it crept across the table top . . . The resulting pool of paste and deconstructed objects was contracting into a round convexity. Nano was forming an object within that convexity like an embryo within an egg.[1]

I would have said that a couple of important benchmarks [towards full nano technology] are the first successful design of a protein molecule from scratch – that happened in 1988 – and another one would be the precise placement of atoms by some mechanical means [it has been] . . . At present I would say that the next major milestone that I would expect is the ability to position reactive, organic molecules so they can be used as building blocks to make some stable 3-dimensional structure at room temperature.[2]

1 G. Bear, *Queen of Angels*, London, Legend, pp. 290–2.

2 K. E. Drexler, *Mondo 2000*, no. 9, p. 97.

The design and architecture of our built environment is stupid. Inertness of thought and inertness of practice has been prompted by inertness of product.[3] Currently, the designer transverses rocky ground between the fluidity of the concept sketch and the discernible parameters of construction. He or she is forced into choices from an incredibly limited palette. If, for a moment, we consider the brick, we can see that many of its perceived advantages are intellectually unsustainable. Its merits, we are told, are its variety of colours, its human scale, its simple jointing methods and its procurement advantages; in fact its merits do not include a capacity to keep water out. The use of brick in building necessitates many preventative methods including damp proof courses and even the provision of another wall 75mm behind to stop water travelling to the inner face and allow space for insulation. A house within a house is a silly idea for the beginning of the twenty-first century.

The hand is gloriously adaptable; it can hold pens, play pianos, test the thinness of paper and pick noses; these are just a few of the many uses in its infinite repertoire. It is the mental software you run on it that makes it into new tools. It is a biological machine; a meat tool but it cannot change topological form. What hopes have we in real space and real time of escaping material stupidity? Is it possible to design materials that change their innate qualities and topologies? The answer could be nanotechnology.

Imagine a world where all is possible, where fabrics pump themselves dry if you get splashed or step in a puddle, where objects can change their form and function many times a day, where anyone can make anything, anywhere, anytime, and where immortality is assured. This is not some fairy tale world but could be our near future, a utopia of super abundance with infinite supply and flexibility of material.

VAT NANO AND NAT NANO

To have total dominion over matter has always been within the province of the gods or at least a Renaissance alchemic magi or two. The twenty-first century will not bring us spells and incantations but magical molecular nanotechnology. Until recently advances in material science had been conditioned by hard engineering, which develops materials that rejoice in their capacity for inertia: low expansion, low contraction, high impermeability and such like, creating specific materials for different jobs. Until now our ability to 'birth' hybrid material, whether organic or inorganic, has been limited by a 'top down' approach: that is the process of dissection of the whole to smaller and smaller parts. As with some theories of consciousness, a 'bottom up' approach has led to new insights; in this case, towards the creation of hybrid mater-

3 This is both a comment on architects and architecture. First, architects are normally trained from generation to generation, by a simply conditioned reflex to please the tutor. The uncareful student inherits the tutor preoccupations and dogmatic stupidity. This sycophancy has immediate short-term benefits, such as the gaining of serf-like employment and validation by professional bodies. This aspect of architectural education has left the profession sorely lacking in evolving cultural and scientific validity. Architecture schools are cocooned in their highly specific spaces and illegitimate aspirations, little or no contact is explored within and without the wider institutional context. Where is the genetic engineer, the mathematician, the quantum physicist, the A.I. pioneer and the neural biologist in the architectural debate? Second, when architects talk of smart buildings these are normally the same old stuff but with a selection of simple prosthetics such as light sensors and small electric motors, their smartness is usually the smartness of the trickster.

Neil Spiller

ials and the ability to reconfigure those materials continually. This 'bottom up' approach has become possible as our dexterity at microscopic levels has increased.

Currently nanotechnology is more theory than practice, but as time goes by, more and more of its applications are being understood and achieved. Nanotechnology (nano) is the creation of K. Eric Drexler and is based on the premise that if we can make self-replicating machines small enough, in the end we will be able to create molecular sized factories and manipulate matter atom by atom, reconstituting and creating anything.[4] There are two types of nano: wet and dry. Dry is the design of minute but traditionally mechanical devices such as gears, bushes, pumps and levers assembled from small quantities of atoms to create molecular sized factories. Wet nanotechnology utilises the replication potential of biological cell division and DNA as its machinery. Who needs more hardware when we have all the wetware we need? The implications of these types of technology are devastating. Much has been written of the affects of the 'wired' world of cyberspace but these will blend into insignificance compared with the surreal and magical consequences of nano.

Nanotechnology requires a gestation period, but its gestation is exponential; it would accelerate as one assembler assembles another: so two becomes four and four becomes eight. This is the same pattern as bacteria and, indeed, a similar speed of reproduction as bacteria could be achieved, that of a generation every twenty minutes. This amazing reproductive potential gives rise to what is known as the 'grey-goo' problem, that is, a fear that should this technology escape control, perhaps by viral infection in its soft- or bioware, it could overrun the Earth in a matter of hours or as Rudy Rucker puts it 'the whole planet could end up as a glistening sludge of horny can openers'.[5]

The gestation period could also require a structure analogous to the womb; to cosset and hold wet raw materials which may be ducted into the womb space or be present before the nano is activated. It is theoretically possible to grow anything in a nano 'vat' or 'matter compiler', as these wombs are called. Drexler describes the growth of a rocket engine. His description conjures images of foetal development: 'Then the vat's pumps return to life, replacing the milky fluid of unattached assemblers with a clear mixture of organic solvents and dissolved substances – including aluminium compounds, oxygen rich compounds to serve as assembler fuel. As the fluid clears, the shape of the rocket engine grows visible through the window, looking like a full-scale model sculpted in translucent white plastic. Next a message spreading from the seed directs designated assemblers to release their neighbours and fold their arms. They wash out of the structure in sudden streamers of white, leaving a spongy lattice of attached assemblers, now with room enough to work. The engine shape in the vat grows almost transparent, with a hint of iridescence.'[6]

4 K. E. Drexler, *Engines of Creation*, Oxford, Oxford University Press, 1990.

5 R. Rucker, *Mondo 2000*, p. 96. This quote is taken from Rucker's introduction to an interview with Eric Drexler entitled 'Vulcan Logic on the Road to Lilliput'.

6 This quote is a small part of Drexler's description of growing a rocket engine. Drexler, *Engines of Creation*, op. cit., pp. 60–3.

Neil Spiller

225

This technology will create opportunities for architecture and product design so they can cater for our fluctuating functional and aesthetic requirements. The products of this technology will be soft, responsive, wet and smart and they will be grown, grafted and bred.

Nano can be used to rejuvenate and sustain the longevity of the body's organs and blood highways. How will this fundamental leap in human and technological evolution affect the products on which we have such dependence? Product design is the provision of prosthetics that expand our normal limited human dexterity in coping with the modern mechanistic world. A simple but radical result could be the ability of objects to reflect Heidegger's concept of 'worlding' at the moment of their creation. An object, according to Heidegger, is sculpted by prolonged use; for example, a hammer is 'worlded' by use and changes to fit the fat or fast hand that uses it most frequently. A new pair of shoes are uncomfortable until they become 'worlded'. Nano allows objects to be specifically tailored to individual ergonomic criteria at the very beginning of their life. Products would be constructed inside domestic matter compilers, or vats, and grow from a series of molecular raw materials into an infinite array of forms. The scale of such machines would be about the size of a microwave oven. It would be just a matter of programming the machine.

Newly constructed objects would take their place immediately within the context of the domestic information ecology. The home would become not only a human habitat but also a habitat for multiple networked intelligences. Once linked together these individual smart objects will interact to create the meta-intelligence of the home. Such ecologies would live up to the old adage 'the whole is greater than the sum of the parts'. Consider a pen that never runs out of ink and when put down for a coffee break, turns the kettle on, or even better tells the matter compiler to make hot coffee or even better still, has hot coffee made based on a subtle evaluation of your caffeine levels and an understanding of your metabolism and psychology. In time the material products of matter compilers will not even have to comply with the tyranny of the periodic table. Artificial atoms have already been fleetingly created. Such atoms contain electrons 'shelling' around non-existent nuclei; new and never imagined materials are theoretically possible. Diamond structures become as cheap as any other structure because they are simply rearranged carbon atoms. What types of products would benefit from diamond being a viable material consideration?

HACKING THE HUSK

Nano will be augmented by genetic algorithms with varying criteria for fitness of survival. It is conceivable that products may be modified using the accumulated experience of many matter compilers and their users. The machines would be smart enough to learn from previous incarnations of products to create more effective designs. Not only the matter compilers of the future but their products would be equipped with evolutionary intelligence, one informing the other. A shoe, for example, may know how its owner walks since he got fatter and his propensity for walking unevenly, and calculate the extra load on the shoe's left heel, causing itself to activate nanoreplicators to build up its scraped off layers as the abrasion takes place.

Nano allows buildings and objects to expand and contract and change form either at a diurnal rate or even continually, to evolve dependent on a variety of stimuli. Objects, large and small, can become programmable – dependent on the software on the microscopic 'seed' computer placed in the vat at the initial stage of reconfiguration. Designs for buildings could self-replicate. A building might have generational ancestors and be the product of a formal genetic algorithm that determines a search for a 'fitness' of some sort, whether that is aesthetic or functional. A search for longer bookshelves, a thinner, warmer or colder skin or a currently fashionable facade could be some of the possible fitness criteria. Obviously in a nanobuilding the air would always be fresh and the structure thin, light and strong. Honeymoon couples could grow a new home whilst sunning themselves on a foreign shore, providing a neighbour made sure it did not dry up.

These examples are but a few of the infinite possibilities of a nanotechnological revolution. It is also clear that the power of the 'aesthetic control police' of architects, designers and planners will be eroded as everyone has the potential to create form. The liberation of an individual's creativity, whether repugnant or beautiful to the rest of us, would be fully realisable. Could it be that the future will see a software embargo on nano much like the provision of 'v-chips' in televisions? 'Come down to the basement and play cards on my new Barney Rubble card table, what, yeah that's real hair, hell what's real anymore, oh yeah he was a space shuttle wing last week.' Curiously, the concept of wetness on contemporary construction sites is anathema to 'fast track' building erection, but in the future wetness could be the major constituent of successful swift fabrication.

CRACKING THE CODE

Other types of seed computers exist in our biological cells. Once we can fully understand our genetic codes, gene manipulation becomes an everyday occurrence. The body could be re-engineered, becoming resilient to disease and old age. Numerous processes become possible; for example, cryogenic resurrection is made more likely

Neil Spiller

if nanomachines could stitch together ice cracked neural and other body tissue of previously frozen bodies. Nanotoothpaste, antiperspirant or even beautiful skin earrings for that special night out would be a reality. In *Wetware*, Rucker has characters concerned with the acquisition of addictive 'merge' that is a type of deconstructive nanotechnology that can be used for a more personal relationship, as it initiates a dissolution of body parts in a vat and causes a merge with a partner also dissolved in the vat, to achieve a new type of togetherness.[7] One of the most difficult issues that nano raises is that of conscious materials. Buildings and their components could become conscious-alive. Descartes' 'cognito ergo sum', translated by Spinoza as 'I am conscious, therefore I exist', becomes important in relation to the built fabric of our cities. It has recently been said that some apes have the intelligence of a two year old child and therefore apes should be given human rights. In time buildings will become more intelligent than this. Will buildings be given human rights? Would demolition without the building's permission be murder? Perhaps what is needed is a series of laws akin to Asimov's Laws of Robotics:

1   A robot may not injure a human being or through inaction, allow a human being to come to harm.

2   A robot must obey the orders given to it by human beings except where such orders would conflict with the First Law.

3   A robot must protect its own existence as long as such protection does not conflict with the First or Second Law.

This huge philosophical debate is one that is happening in the scientific community, particularly in reference to Artificial Intelligence, but not in architecture. Architects must research these avenues as it is architecture where the philosophical issues of the 'aliveness' of smart materials will become paramount.

One thing is sure, with the scope of this technology, our products are about to become more the products of our imagination than ever before. All that will hinder us is the quality of our imagination, and even that may not be for very long. Perhaps we could evolve a machine to have a better imagination than a human. Nanotechnology will be not only in your face, it might be on your face or even sulking because it does not like your taste in music.

7 R. Rucker, *Wetware*, London, Hodder and Stoughton, 1989. One of Rucker's merge trips is described as follows: 'Stahn slumped back. God this was fast dope. His left arm looked like candle wax, and he was having trouble staying in his chair. He let himself slide down onto the floor and stared up at the ceiling. Oh, this did feel good. His bone joints loosened, and his skeleton sagged beneath the puddle of his flesh . . .'

Neil Spiller

HOT DESKING IN NANOTOPIA

In his recent book *Being Digital*, Nicholas Negroponte extols the virtues of the inherent flexibility and speed of transmission of bits as opposed to atoms.[8] The virtue of the virtual against the substantial may be short lived. Could atoms, one day, be as equally manipulated and programmable thus gaining the advantages of 'bittiness'? Atoms could combine their ability to make real with the transmutability of information bits. Such an eventuality would allow the bit a ubiquitousness now unavailable outside the cathode ray conduit or the liquid crystal display. The bit's escape could be aided and abetted by the advent of nanotechnology. The impact of this idea could be to further shrink the mechanistic armature to unbelievable minuteness causing the machine, for all intents and purposes, to disappear. Whilst cyberspatial evolution has been hyped ever onward, nanotechnology, its chronological twin, has been ignored from most discourses of futurology.

As one does not normally write about cyberspace without crediting the word's creator, William Gibson, it does not seem right to evoke nanotechnology without crediting its main advocate and designer, Drexler. Since the late 1970s Drexler has postulated theories and designed a series of devices that operate at the scale of the nanometer, the scale of molecules.[9] Nanotechnology utilises devices the equivalent of solenoids, pipes and pumps, to create microscopic 'factories' of assemblers and disassemblers. These diminutive installations will have the ability to reconfigure all matter, atom by atom, creating a conceptual utopia of superabundance and so an architecture of cheap and infinitely malleable material.

THE NANOLITHIC AGE

We are on the cusp between what I shall call the Nanolithic Age and the Monolithic Age, at the beginning of Nanotime. We have at last sensed that we are nearly at the end of the tyranny of formal inertia. Some of our crucial nanotools are still dreams and operating at this scale is like trying to be a surgeon in boxing gloves, but as every day goes by, our microscopic tool shed is becoming stocked with implements that move us towards theoretically total molecular dexterity in our battle to make nature ours. We have started on a track that will ultimately encourage the husbandry of all atomic arrangements and their material results. Technology has become both magician and assistant; the agent of disappearance and the subject of that disappearance. The machine becomes 'prompt' at the side of the stage's molecular song and dance routine. I sense that there will be further nanological

8 N. Negroponte, *Being Digital*, London, Hodder and Stoughton, 1995.

9 K. E. Drexler, *Engines of Creation*, op. cit.

Neil Spiller

eras or ages, much like the geological ones that aid the classification of the geo-morphic layers of landscape. The Nanological Ages will, likewise, be used to chart the evolution of the mobility and erosion of certain forms. As already stated we are at the beginning of the Nanolithic Age. One supposes that the subsequent age will be classified as the Plasticine Age, where materials are gently morphed or trans-formed by, perhaps, only one quality such as flexibility, colour or tarnish. The next age might well be the Panacea Age, characterised by the widespread use of nano-technology as an internalised prosthetic. The Panacea Age would provide cures for all ills, including old age. Intelligent nanomachines will patrol the bloodstream, removing malignant or benign detritus that the body's white blood cells are unable to deal with. The medical applications of the nanotechnological machine, or nanites as they are starting to be called, are almost infinite. Another age could be the Pro-toplasmic Age, an era where the body's sensibility and its information processing abilities are so amplified that the whole material world becomes a series of nested arenas of computability – the evolution of the nanocyborg. This is where cyber-space becomes truly biological. When virtual reality becomes real the liberation of the bit is complete. The marvel of nanotechnology will be able to produce Spidey and the Hulk for real; the elasticity of the body, among other comic book attributes, will be assured.

FROM THE BOTTOM UP

Nanotechnology is a 'bottom up' science: starting from the interaction of the compo-nent parts of a system and through them generating a complexity. 'Top down' tech-nologies are also pushing the barriers of miniaturisation; small machines such as colon-crawlers and arterial plaque scrapers are already in prototype form. Concurrent with these diminutive machine experiments is the use of biotech gene splicing on, for example, *E. coli* bacteria to force them to produce human insulin. *E. coli* is the bacte-ria commonly responsible for the infection cystitis. Coincidentally, the same bacteria have been viewed by scientists as a lesson in how Drexler's nanites might either propel themselves or pump fluids. This theory is based on the bacteria's flagella, a hair-like propulsion system. This system can generate 6,000 revs per minute at body temperature to a maximum of 38,000 revs per minute at higher temperatures before burn out occurs. With the technology already provided by nature and its subsequent supercharging by humanity, biological computers become a distinct possibility. In a few years – and by a few I mean a few – bacteria will be made to fully compute. Some believe that the full synthesis between nanotechnology and the human body will

Neil Spiller

occur by 2014. If such computational power is realised, then a typical work surface might be inhabited by enough bacteria to provide more computing power than currently exists in all the world. If every surface becomes not only computational but, through nanotechnology, also a surface of formal reconfiguration, then the hermetic vessel of alchemy (the alembic – the site of transformation of material) becomes the thickness of the bio-nano-mono-layer whose dimension is one bacteria thick, or perhaps even less. The womb of nature would be set in the arena of surface tension. Crazy? Maybe: the successful printing of one molecule thick mono-layers for circuits has already been achieved. Any surface will have the potential to be the demiurge's clay or the anvil of the Gods.

DESKTOP THEATRES

In her seminal book *The Art of Memory* Frances Yates describes the evolution of various memory systems from the classical mnemonic recorded by Cicero and others, through the memory theatres of Robert Fludd, to the occult memory wheels of the Renaissance magi Guiordano Bruno and Ramon Lull.[10] The mnemonic device of the memory theatre depends on the formulation and the inhabitation of mental architectural places (loci); each specifically honed with images (imagines). The consequent inter-relationships between the images and the loci provide a strategy for the 'mind's eye' to 'see' and store many complex concepts. Such systems were used to memorise speeches, songs and religious cosmology. Yates was prophetic enough to recognise similarities between these mental structures, particularly Bruno's and the 'mind' machines of the day (*The Art of Memory* was first published in 1966). This strand of thought was picked up at MIT's Media Lab and the relationship between image and location used as a way to represent and store information on a computer-controlled screen. They developed the spatial data management system (SDMS); this included an electronic picture window and a 'wired' Eames chair. Negroponte describes it as follows: 'The user could zoom and pan freely in order to navigate through a fictitious two dimensional landscape called Dataland. The user could visit personnel files, correspondence, electronic books, satellite maps and a whole variety of new data types.'[11] The SDMS was populated with a series of icons, with this project the relationship between the imagine and the loci was established as an advanced user interface. The concept then evolved into the now familiar Apple desktop. With the aid of folders, files, archives and menus the user of the desktop can construct complex interactions of information. This system of connections has a specific yet flexible architecture. The desktop also provides a danger-spot, albeit covered with a

10 F. Yates, *The Art of Memory*, London, Routledge and Kegan Paul, 1966.

11 Negroponte, op. cit., p. 110.

Neil Spiller

detachable safety net, a single area of destructive power situated in this landscape of constructive opportunity – the trash can. The 'can' is a recycler of memory, the gaping mouth of the void, hungry for malformed or ancient bits and bytes. The current Apple desktop is an ascalar topology – a hi-tech palace of the mind situated in fields among fields.

THE MAKING OF THE NANOCYBORG

Biosmiths have been forging the future of mankind and as usual have started experimenting with woman-kind. There are many more prosthetics for women than there are for men. Meanwhile, as man remakes woman in the magazine image, the much trumpeted cyborg is about to be nanoed. As Charles Ostman has said in a recent interview in *Mondo 2000*, nano offers exciting 'modification(s) made directly to the human body'. He uses this example: 'A German electronics manufacturer has invented a seminal duct implant designed to electrocute sperm before they leave the body.' Tumours will be dismantled by smart nanites and even molecular-scaled super-computers inserted into the existing neural net, augmenting the brain's already awesome capabilities. Such neural enhancement, when possible, will probably create a two-tiered civilisation: those who do and those who don't have the advantage of neural upgrading. This is just one of the major and many ethical and philosophical problems of such technology. The prospect of us all being 'all Cray-Z now' seems remote in the context of the prevailing capitalist system. Even so, nanotechnology's effect on world capitalism remains to be quantified; in theory it could lead to its demise. One thing is sure, this technology opens up a world of surreal or hyper-real aesthetic experience. Could it conceivably allow the nanocyborg to grasp objects, ornaments or icons (they are all the same in nanotopia) and read information directly through the hands and fingertips? In the face of nanotechnology, unassisted evolution is dead; it was too slow and made too many mistakes. The psychologists' much debated bipolar discussion in relation to human physical and social development is about to go tripartite, as behaviour and genetic coding (nature or nurture) is joined by the machine code influence.

ANVIL OF THE GODS

What of the future, where the virtual becomes really real, oscillating in and out of solidness and where every surface is a neural network with the potential to create the Garden of Eden or Babylon, at any scale, and at the flick of millions of nanoscopic

Neil Spiller

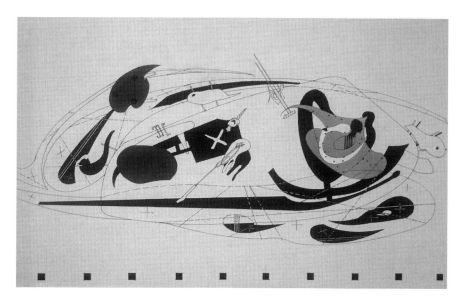

Figure 14.1 Neil Spiller, *Hot Desk: Turbulence Drawing*, 1995.

switches? If we achieve total control of nature, nature ceases to exist, a casualty in a collision with technology at speed. The landscape becomes purely artificial and arte-factual, its binary coded fictional narrative told millions of times a second. The nano-object will have to take its place in an environment where objects contain various scales of information: symbolic, functional, memorial and such like. So the design and

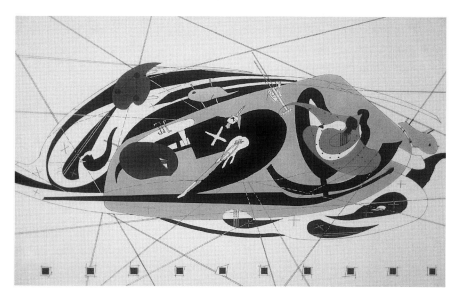

Figure 14.2 Neil Spiller, *Hot Desk: Turbulence Drawing*, 1995.

Neil Spiller

Figure 14.3 Neil Spiller, *Hot Desk: Turbulence Drawing*, 1995.

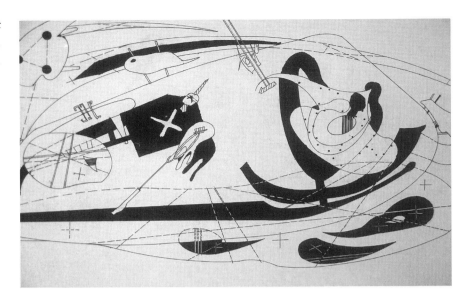

construction of objects and memory structures in the real reality engine as opposed to the virtual reality engine will be fundamentally different; the latter depending on atomless bits, the former on bits of atoms. The 'Anvil of the Gods' project seeks to try to chart the concepts that will help us quantify some of the opportunities of these impending technologies. The 'Anvil of the Gods' is the desktop (a nanodesktop) of the near future. Such devices are intrinsically difficult to describe as our description is always dependent on lexical and typological constructs, some of which are likely to disappear as a consequence of this technology, but we must try. Such a nanotechnological device might not choose to always inhabit the desktop scale, it could be palm sized or even smaller, or suddenly increase in scale, or exist simultaneously at a variety of scales, the board for a game of multi-dimensional complexity populated by a mixture of the mundane, the weird and the downright crazy. What would such a thing do? What would it be like? First, it is important to introduce a formal scenario. Creating three nanoicons can do this; each is an icon in the traditional computing sense. Each carries 'within' it a narrative concerning issues that may emerge as important in the future. These icons will act as the imagines and a table on which they are situated will act as the loci. The table top and its supporting structure becomes an active field. This field of multi-dimensional proactivity creates formal interventions that store information within. Nanotechnology at this level is perhaps understood as a series of currents or turbulences of formal potential between two fields – the desk and the air.

Neil Spiller

IT'S A REAL PEA-SOUPER, NO MISTAKE

How can the air around a nano-object be considered the macro field of interaction? With minor engineering and programming, air can be made into transparent and receptive Utility Fog. The conceptual framework for such a fog was laid down by JoSH Hall, as an idea to avoid the inevitable whip-lash caused in car accidents.[12] The dream essentially consists of the notion that nano-doctored air will be able, in a split second, to solidify and cushion us from dangerous impacts. Once this approach is achieved, and it seems that there are no particular insurmountable physical problems, then it will be possible to conjure objects or fluids from thin air; a final nanoage – the Magicio-kinetic Age. The Magician returns: technology and magic meet again at this point. Telekinesis and all manner of psycho-kinetic arts will be available to all-comers. So this infinitely thick but infinitely thin fog will be the large desktop, a global ether from which existence is conjured. All ornaments, icons or atomic substance, call them what you will, can be spliced together forming hybrids or even be susceptible to the constant nibbling of the nanoether. As one 'launches' icons on to other icons, allowing consummation of one by another, so nano-objects – and let's face it, all objects – are nanomorphable, able to create various information hierarchies.

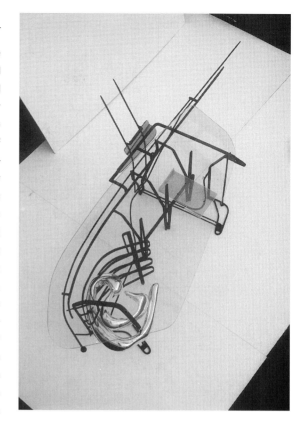

Figure 14.4 Neil Spiller, *Hot Desk*, 1995, fabricated by Sixteen*(Makers).

WHAT'S IN STORE: FROM THE MUNDANE TO THE DIVINE

At the usual scale of the family house, the desktop situated in the makeshift study, in the spare room, or just the makeshift spare room (we don't all study you know), might have a mundane yet highly liberating use. It could have the ability to deconstruct objects and act as a storage unit, an object shredder also capable of reassembly when necessary, thus solving the 'real' world problem of domestic storage space. Interestingly, such a technology might also solve the 'book/screen' problem. This problem concerns the known fact that people prefer to curl up in bed with a book, not a plastic laptop display and assorted manipulation devices such as

12 E. Regis, *Nano – Remaking the World Atom by Atom*, London, Transworld Publishers Ltd, 1995. JoSH Hall's Utility Fog is described on p. 218.

Neil Spiller

mice, trackballs or even finger-tickling erogenous pad zones. The book could now become fully digital, reconfiguring from thin air into the weighty leather bound tome or the dog-eared paperback to which we are all accustomed. Our own books, digital yet coffee stained, staining obviously a menu option, like the removal of hairs or dust caught in the spine, as well as other personalisation facilities. The library becomes the black hole trash can where molecules are torn asunder and thrown into an anti-matter (or anti-anthropomorphic-matter) universe awaiting the demiurge's summons of materiality.

Nano-Deskworld™ is also Nano-Dreamworld™, a world where the Burroughsian jump cut happens not just in text or in theories about the art of the real, but in the creation of actual synaesthetic formal articulations that will be mostly useless. Yet some will provoke profound and revealing previously unimagined ideas and hybrids of ideas. The ability of the Nanodesktop to have such a multi-dimensional screen saver, a type of 'hyper-Nirvana', will allow it to push machine thought into matter, the desktop dreaming of not only electric sheep but, perhaps, even edible duvets – patterned with the cuttlefish's pulsating colour morphing skin – tasting of cardboard with a slight hint of parmesan.[13] But this is a small-scale idea, what of the divine and cosmic? Baudrillard might well rejoice as this technology seems to be becoming one of the final names of God, that once uttered or recorded will bring about the disappearance of the universe.[14]

THE WEATHERING OF FORM

If such desks are but micro turbulences in a chaotic, turbulent macro Utility Fog (The Big Desktop in the Sky), then we could create a visionary geography, a hybrid of cybergraphy and nanography. The world will become a series of geographical icons, a dreaming landscape or a landscape of memory. It is here that our physics of space and matter bring us in full circle back to more arcane religious views of the world and its formation. Luckily, we have an odd parallel to help us unravel some of the potentials of our new world, and that is the Aboriginal Dreamtime. Aboriginal creation mythology bases itself on a mythic time during which the Aboriginal culture and landscape were formed. It was a time of Sky Heroes, one of the most fundamental being the Rainbow Snake, which it seems could be an ancestor of Utility Fog and the Nanodesktop. The Rainbow Snake seems to be the creator of the world, or at least its moulder, and this creative act is linked to its supposed journey across the landscape, from inland to the sea or from the sea to the mountains. For the Aboriginal, landscape features become memory icons of the journey and meaning of the Snake. Just

13 Nirvana™ is a recently issued screen saver that is different every time. It is characterised by its psychedelic and constantly mutating screen patterns. Acid for computers.

14 J. Baudrillard, 'The Perfect Crime', extract from his recent lecture at the ICA, transcribed in *Wired*, 1.02, p. 56. 'This is the same as Arthur C. Clarke's fable about the names of God. In that, the monks of Tibet devote themselves fastidiously to transcribing the 99 billion names of God, after which, they believe the world will be accomplished and the end will come. Exhausted by this everlasting spelling of the names of God, they call in some IBM types who install a computer to do the job. A perfect allegory of the achievement of the world in real time by the operation of the virtual. As the technicians of IBM leave the site, they see the stars in the skies fading and vanishing one by one.'

Neil Spiller

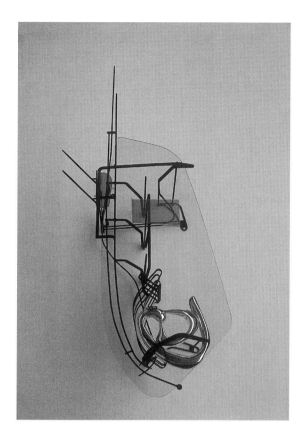

Figure 14.5 Neil Spiller, *Hot Desk*, 1995, fabricated by Sixteen*(Makers).

as Aboriginals believe that sacred images – such as those of their cave art – were not made by human hand, our future sacred forms and macro and micro landscape features will not be made by human hand but by Nano-Dreamtime, the inheritor of nature's tricks. In the Antipodean mythology, geographical landmass has made the transition to a story-mass. With nanotechnology it is conceivable that the Nano-Dreamtime will burst from its Southern Cross shackles and make a further transition from story-mass to info-mass, or perhaps even info-weather, a dream theatre of global proportions. The Aboriginals 'recognize that the natural object is capable of being imbued with supernatural power'.[15] This supernatural power concerns itself with the synthesis of the natural object and its symbolic shadow or double. For them every natural thing has totemic identity; this duality links the viewer into the Aboriginal grand narrative and provides both metaphoric and physical navigational signposts. It is clear that in the future it will be harder and harder to separate the augmented human form, or nanocyborg, from its utility ether; and further, that the concept of weather will have

15 J. G. Cowan, *The Elements of The Aborigine Tradition*, London, Element Books, 1992.

Neil Spiller

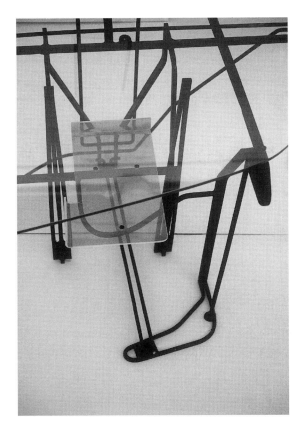

Figure 14.6 Neil Spiller, *Hot Desk*, 1995, fabricated by Sixteen*(Makers).

to be reassessed in the light of the Nano-Desktop-World and the Nano-Dreamtime. Strange weather indeed. Will the architect become a formal meteorologist?

An earlier version of Neil Spiller, 'Nanotechnology – The Liberation of Architecture' appeared as part of Neil Spiller, *Digital Dreams – Architecture and the New Alchemic Technologies*, London, Ellipsis, 1998.

Neil Spiller

biological (or 'wet') architecture

Scientists consider themselves able to understand the architecture of life and universal processes whilst architects are looking for new tools, new methods to manipulate and create harmonious environments. What more radical and intimate interface could there be to explore radical new forms of experience and design than the intersection of the environment with the human body?

The body is generally understood to be an organic machine. Scientific disciplines propose a model that, like a machine, can be understood in terms of its mechanics. Despite the fact that over 98% of our body is fluid, these contemporary models essentially treat the body in the same manner as mechanical systems: being repairable, upgradeable and ultimately fully replaceable. The implications of this are that once the whole of our anatomy, and the fundamental particles from which it is composed, are fully understood, we will have control over our lives and perhaps even reach immortality: a premise proposed by a group of radical pioneers calling themselves 'Extropians'.

Owing to the advances of technology, the territory of the body is no longer the sole property of medical researchers and scientists. Designers, artists and architects are already starting to use these advances to rethink and redesign the human body and its interfaces as an architectural project. By adopting this view of the body, and seeking to exert such a degree of control over our lives, the architectural approach to improving the relationship between the body and the environment embraces the principles of Extropianism. Architects, designers, engineers, medical practitioners and scientists with access to new technologies, and belief in their capabilities, are recognising the potential of the technologised body that is more easily linked to, and able to interface with, its environments. Ultimately radical new technologies will hybridise with external structures more freely and provide a positive evolutionary pressure that may result in a technologised change in our species known as posthumanism.

THE BODY MACHINE

René Descartes first proposed a model of the body that could be embraced by objective and scientific rationale. Descartes believed that humans are composed of two distinct parts: a physical body that moves about in the physical world, and a non-physical or spiritual mind that thinks. Although the atoms and molecules that ultimately form the human body may be considered indestructible, their arrangement is alterable, so the body is not eternal. The mind or soul, however, is intangible and Descartes argued that it is composed of an indestructible and unalterable substance.

Rachel Armstrong

In freeing the human body from the essential substance of the soul, Descartes set the scene for a fundamental change in physical interventions and anatomical studies.[1]

1 H. Robin, *The Scientific Image From Cave to Computer*, New York, Harry N. Abrams, 1992, p. 70.

By creating a model of the body as an extended unthinking thing, Descartes removed the ethical and religious objections from intervening in its design. Since humans could be thought of as spirits occupying a mechanical body, altering the body's structure did not change the essential attributes of the spirit, such as thinking, willing and conceiving. This province was left for religious guidance. By distancing the body from the person that it contained, Descartes essentially positioned it as an architectural structure ready for scientific analysis and structural redesigning.

As the scientific method became more sophisticated, the body was understood in increasing detail, but although the units became smaller, the fundamental mechanical way in which they interacted did not change. Models of the body reflect the trends in science and human biology and are still largely described according to the laws of Newtonian physics, although chaos theories are starting to be used to describe more intangible phenomena such as cardiac rhythms and brainwaves.

BIOMECHANICS

The current mechanical model of the working human body is based on biomechanical principles. The body machine is thought of as being a hugely complex system of interacting proteins, metabolites and minerals. Looking at the properties and interactions of the building blocks of life allows scientists to suggest and even design new ways of repairing, upgrading and interfacing with the body.

It is thought that complete understanding of the mechanics of the body-machine offers the opportunity to shape and build life itself. Taking an extreme view of the possibilities on offer, Extropians have proposed a series of principles upon which the body can be upgraded in this fashion. Selecting their own anatomy as the object for redesign and reinvention, they seek to improve its quality in their own lifetime through the use of new technologies.

Extropian is derived from the term 'extropy', the degree of positive energy in a system; the opposite being 'entropy', a destabilising energy. Extropians have adopted this terminology and use extropy as a measure of their success in their endeavour to perfect themselves, embarking on a trans-human journey that will ultimately bring intelligence, information, energy, vitality, experience, diversity, opportunity and growth. At the end of the Extropian rainbow lies an evolutionary leap to post-human status and possible immortality.

Rachel Armstrong

241

THE EXTROPIAN PRINCIPLES

1   Boundless Expansion
2   Self-Transformation
3   Dynamic Optimism
4   Intelligent Technology
5   Spontaneous Order

1 BOUNDLESS EXPANSION

Extropians do not perceive any technological limits to their quest. They believe that any obstacle in their self-transformation will eventually yield to new inventions and technologies. Ambitiously, they seek to understand the universe and to master reality up to and beyond any currently foreseeable limits. Extropians regard humans as occupying a unique place in the evolution of the ecosystem, having developed their understanding and control over nature to a point where they have secured the opportunity to advance nature's evolution to new peaks. Natural processes are regarded as being the haphazard configuration of mindless matter, following a painfully slow evolutionary ascendance. The controversial French performance artist Orlan illustrates this attitude of 'conquering nature' in her manifesto:

> My work is a fight against the innate, the inexorable, the programmed Nature, DNA
> (which is our direct rival as artists of representation) and God![2]

2 Orlan, Omnipresence Conference, 1993. Broadcast live from the Sandra Gehring Gallery, New York.

Orlan is a multi-media performance artist who has been working with performances using her body since the 1960s, making herself available as a projection screen for scrutiny of the current symbols of femininity, their social and political status. The artist studies the female body, its appearance, its manipulability and our idea of corporeality and beauty, challenging rather than endorsing the accepted values of our society. Orlan's 'operation-performances' question the status of the body in our society and the implications for future generations' expectations of the body-image.

Her demonstration of 'boundless expansion' originates from 30 May 1990 in Newcastle-upon-Tyne, England, when Orlan embarked upon a project, *Images/New Images or, The Reincarnation of Saint Orlan,* that would last ten years. Her methodology was to use Carnal Art, and by working with teams of doctors and designers made radical use of surgery in a series of operation-performances in the attempt to transform her body. Carnal Art is a highly architectural procedure. In true Extropian style its canvas is the artist's body, which doubles up as the object for redesign and

Rachel Armstrong

improvement. Orlan combined surgical procedures with new technology, demonstrating that she was using cosmetic surgery, for the first time, to achieve a completely different outcome. Her goal was not to achieve an idealised state of beauty but to contradict the culturally accepted standards of idealised beauty and replace them with her own designs. Medical advances made this project possible and new technologies in medicine and performance have featured as an important part of Orlan's work. She works with the limits of all the current possibilities in these fields that offer her body freedoms and restrictions. For example, she has used advanced techniques in local anaesthesia to remain in control of her operation-performance without pain. She has also used morphing techniques to combine photographs of her own face with her own designs, which were used to 'workshop' the live operations with each surgeon. For example, the final operation, the creation of a very large nose, was modelled in a virtual space using her own data. The natural co-ordinates were then manipulated to produce the desired result and the surgical feasibility of this performance was discussed with a panel of medical experts.

When de-robing her costume (when her skin is cut by the surgeon's knife) during the *Images/New Images or, The Reincarnation of Saint Orlan* performances, Orlan brings into play a language of the body that is staged under her direction as a carefully planned, choreographed spectacle. The pictures she produces from these operation-performances are shocking for non-medical viewers since the inside of a surgical theatre is a bizarre environment for performance and also because the act itself does not follow the protocol of a conventional medical operation. Her video images relay the live dissection of a female body which, at the same time, is actively directing, choreographing and acting in a medically sterile, operating theatre. To add to the audience's bewilderment, a company of actors accompanies this exhibitionist show of 'boundless expansion'. These performers add ceremony and action to the operation-performance with their carefully staged appearances to the cameras and the audience in the viewing gallery. Amongst all the action, Orlan reads aloud from chosen texts that relate to the specific theme of the operation-performance: 'Carnal Art'; 'Identity Change'; 'Initiation Ritual'; 'This Is My Body, This is My Software'; 'I Have Given My Body to Art'; 'Successful Operation(s)'; 'Body/Status' and 'Identity Alterity'. Famous fashion designers such as Jean Paul Gaultier, Issey Miyake, Franck Sorbier and Paco Rabanne design the costumes, including those of the medical team. The resulting performance is a carnivalesque extravaganza of comedy, tragedy, horror, humour, music, images, religious iconography, sexuality and visceral anatomy.

Orlan is looking for a new self-portrait. She is creating a new face that defies her natural looks and the ageing process, and exactly corresponds to her perceived identity. The resultant images of this fusion have so far generated anatomical features

Rachel Armstrong

that are not recognised as 'natural' parts of our anatomy but are woven into cultural mythology. For example, the 'bumps' on her temples which were inserted by a woman surgeon at the last and most radical operation performance *Omnipresence*, 1993, are in keeping with the notion of Gall's phrenological anatomy, according to which contours on the head are indicative of intelligence. Orlan's excess of bumps suggests her advanced intelligence like the alien Mia, from the TV series *Space 1999*, who could transform herself into any living creature in the galaxy.[3]

3 Gerry and Sylvia Anderson, *Space 1999*, UK (ITC/ITV), 1975–77.

In aspiring to post-humanity, the Extropians reject natural and traditional limitations on our future. They champion the rational use of science and technology to eradicate constraints on lifespan, intelligence, personal vitality, freedom and experience. Significantly, they also recognise the absurdity of meekly accepting 'natural' limits to the human lifespan. Indeed, Orlan plans to continue her artwork even when she is technically dead, possibly being frozen and exhibited in a gallery.

2 SELF-TRANSFORMATION

As neophiles, Extropians study advanced, emerging and future technologies for their self-transformative potential. They support biomedical research to understand and control the ageing process and examine new means of conquering death, including interim measures like biostasis, and long-term possibilities such as migration of personality from biological bodies into superior embodiments ('uploading').

Many Extropians subscribe to cryonics institutions with the intention that they will be awoken when technological understanding is sufficiently advanced to bring their bodies back to life. Although they admit that the restorative technologies may not exist now, they believe that in the near future it will be possible to restore and even upgrade their current anatomy. The first cryogenically suspended person was a doctor.

Dr James Bedford was frozen on 12 January 1967 at the age of 73 by the Cryonics Society of California and was joined by others in the belief that cryosuspension would offer a potential 'cure' to their death-related, biological system failure. According to the largest cryonics organisation, the Alcor Life Extension Foundation, approximately forty out of the sixty people who have already been suspended are still in suspension today. Those who have not 'survived' cryonic preservation have been thawed and buried as a result of financial failure of their cryonics organisation, rather than through any failed scientific attempt at revival.

Cryonisists believe that their practice redefines death in such a way that they are offering a 'curative' therapy. Currently, the process of freezing a newly dead body is presented as offering the potential to restore the bodies of terminally ill patients who are past all hope of cure with modern technology.

Rachel Armstrong

3 DYNAMIC OPTIMISM

Extropians espouse a positive, dynamic, empowering attitude and direct their energies to enthusiastically confronting today's challenges, their inventions and discoveries enhancing the quality of living, not degrading it.

Mariko Mori, an artist, designer and inventor who makes creative use of technology to create her optimistic visions of future living, challenges the conventions of separatism that exist between art, science and spirituality. She takes a directorial role in her projects and characteristically appears as a muse in all her images. *Enlightenment Capsule* is Mariko's most ambitious design to date. The transparent sculpture, in the form of a lotus flower, follows and collects the sun's energy, to produce rainbow patterns on the gallery floor. The sound light transmitter encapsulated in the sculpture uses pure visible light; computer software ensures that the pod always follows the sun. This is a prototype. In the future, Mariko intends that people will sit inside and levitate inside the capsule, energised by daylight.

4 INTELLIGENT TECHNOLOGY

Extropians affirm the necessity and desirability of science and technology. Not only do they use technologies to construct better environments but embrace interventions that improve their internal character, radically transforming both the internal and external conditions of existence. The Extropians regard technology as a natural extension and expression of human intellect, creativity, curiosity and imagination, encouraging the development of evermore flexible, smart, responsive technologies. They believe that they will co-evolve with the technological products of the human mind, integrating with them and finally merging with intelligent technology. The Extropians believe that this post-human synthesis will ultimately amplify their abilities and extend their freedom. This technological transformation will be accelerated by genetic engineering, life-extending biosciences, intelligence intensifiers, smarter interfaces to swifter computers, neural-computer integration, virtual reality, enormous interconnected databases, swift electronic communications, artificial intelligence, neuroscience, neural networks, artificial life, off-planet migration and nanotechnology.

The integration with intelligent technology is imminent, regardless of whether we aspire to Extropian principles or not. On Wednesday 15 December 1999, 9:46 am Eastern Time, a company press release was made by Applied Digital Solutions [http://www.adsx.com] which had just acquired the rights to the world's first digital device of its type, a tamper-proof miniature digital transceiver fully implantable in humans. The implant has a wide variety of potential applications ranging from e-com-

Rachel Armstrong

merce to business security, locating lost or missing individuals, tracking the location of valuable property, monitoring the medical conditions of at-risk patients and criminal justice. The implantable transceiver sends and receives data and can be continuously tracked by GPS (Global Positioning Satellite) technology. The transceiver's power supply and actuation system are unique. When implanted within a body, the device is powered electromechanically through the movement of muscles, and it can be activated either by the wearer or by the monitoring facility. A new sensation feedback feature even allows the wearer to control the device to some extent and is small enough to be hidden inconspicuously on or within valuable personal belongings, furniture and artworks. The transceiver, an intelligent chip referred to as Digital Angel(r), can remain implanted and functional for years without maintenance. The device also can monitor certain biological functions of the human body, such as heart rate and send a distress signal to a monitoring facility when it detects a medical emergency. A prototype for the device was expected to be available by the end of 2000. A huge uptake of the device is expected and the potential global market of all of its applications is even thought to exceed $100 billion.

5 SPONTANEOUS ORDER

Rather than centrally planned, imposed orders, Extropians emphasise self-generating, organic, spontaneous orders that they believe are crucial for our social interactions and more important to future communities than previously recognised. Spontaneous orders have properties that make them especially conducive to Extropian goals and values in many contexts, including biological evolution, the self-regulation of ecosystems, artificial life studies, memetics (the study of replicating information patterns), agoric open systems (market-like allocation of computational resources), brain function and neurocomputation.

The Extropian libertarian approach to community and identity is consistent with the 'cyborgisation' of individuals through the advances of new technologies. Donna Haraway, Professor of the History of Consciousness at the University of California, Santa Cruz, is an expert in the human-machine relationship. Haraway's most famous essay, 'A Cyborg Manifesto', first published in 1985, proposes that the relationship between people and technology is now so intimate that it is no longer possible to tell where humans end and machines begin:

> By the late twentieth century, our time, a mythic time, we are all chimeras, theorized and fabricated hybrids of machine and organism; in short we are cyborgs . . . a condensed image of both imagination and material reality.[4]

4 D. Haraway, 'A Cyborg Manifesto: Science, Technology and Socialist-Feminism in the Late Twentieth Century', in D. Haraway, *Simians, Cyborgs and Women: The Reinvention of Nature*, London, Free Association Books, 1995, p. 150.

Rachel Armstrong

Haraway's analysis of this relationship focuses not just on hybridised bodies but where we interface with and are incorporated by a host of intricate networks. Like a cyborg, we are continually reconstructing ourselves, not in isolation from one another but as integrated beings. Information systems document out vital statistics, banking networks hold details of our earnings and the telephone networks connect us with other humans. Our dependence on these networks is so integral to our everyday identity that we almost fail to notice them and often we are reminded of their significance only when they are absent such as when we go on holiday to a remote island or when our telephone does not work. In the absence of these technologised networks, it is usual to feel anxious and seek to restore the links to our 'virtual' communities as soon as possible.

PROSPECTS OF IMMORTALITY

Genetic advances are still the most realistic solution to building the post-human body sought by the Extropians. Despite our increasing knowledge of the structure and mechanisms of the biological building blocks of life, we are still unable to determine how these are assembled and coordinated to operate together. Without fully understanding the role played by the DNA, the body's blueprint, and its relationship to the messenger nucleotides, the RNA that transmit these commands into the cytoplasm, it is impossible to design replacement systems.

It is expected that 'cloning via nuclear transfer' will offer Extropians the possibility of creating identical copies of themselves. Cindy Jackson is a minor celebrity who came to notoriety by embarking upon a series of over twenty cosmetic procedures in order to manufacture a dominant image of power and beauty. Her views on taking control of her own destiny by improving her looks are in keeping with Extropian principles. She will use any procedure or technology to maintain the recognition and success that she has worked hard to achieve. Cindy aims to be the first woman to give birth to her own clone, avoiding the dilution of her own gene pool with that of a man.[5]

However, a great deal more research and development of the nuclear transfer techniques used to clone the now famous Dolly the sheep is needed. This landmark experiment established that it was possible to grow a new being from adult DNA, an event that was previously considered to be impossible. However, this procedure is still very new and it must be improved and perfected before use on human embryos. Sheep embryos have some special characteristics that make cloning them much easier than cloning human embryos. Cloning an adult sheep was extremely difficult to

5 C. Jackson, *Sci/Fi Aesthetics, Art & Design*, vol. 12, no. 9/10, September–October 1997, p. 35.

Rachel Armstrong

do; over 270 attempts were needed before Dolly was born. Many foetal lambs did not survive the early stages of development. Those lambs that were carried to term were born with health problems, including malformed kidneys, and all but Dolly subsequently died.

Although it may be still a long way to go before the Extropian is able to discover true immortality by continuously replacing broken body parts or even synthesise a new (post-) human being, the first steps in creating primitive synthetic life forms have begun. The University of Texas has already announced the first project that proposes the creation of organisms from artificial DNA. This breakthrough means that the first artificial organisms could be 'born' within two years. Researchers have mapped out the exact way they will create synthetic organism one (SO1), the microbe destined to be the world's first man-made creature. That SO1 will have no specific function is more in keeping with artistic philosophy than a traditionally scientific one, but once it is brought to life, the research team will be able to customise it and create other new life-forms on computer. The implications of their approach is radical; this is digital evolution whereby computer blueprints will be used as the selective pressures that shape the designer progeny.[6] The building blocks of life are now subject to architectural investigation.

6 'News', *The Sunday Times*, 23 January 2000, p. 30.

BEYOND CARBON

Ultimately, the Extropian search for an upgraded human biology may lead to challenges to the whole framework of carbon-based biology, which may even be superseded by silicone- or polymer-based biology, which is hardier and less susceptible to breakdown. These new substrates may form the architectural body-material from which we evolve in the future.

It was lucky for me that Old Dad had bequeathed me a tough, surgically altered body. My skull was sheathed with thin plates of ceramic reinforcement, and my teeth, all false, were white ceramic over a crystalline metal core. The leather body armor under my costume protected heart and kidneys, and my ribcage was reinforced.[7]

7 Bruce Sterling, *The Artificial Kid*, San Francisco, Wired, 1997, p. 50.

Rachel Armstrong

INDEX

Page references in *italics* refer to illustrations.

A

Aalto, Alvar 124
Abeles, Kim 134
abjection 111–12
Aboriginal Dreamtime
    236–7
affect animals 215
affect architecture 216,
    218
African–American culture
    181, 184–5, 187,
    189, 191–2
Age of Masters (Banham)
    58
Alcor Life Extension
    Foundation 244
Alexander, Christopher
    109–10
algorithms 219–20
    genetic algorithms
        226–7
Allsopp, Hermoine 147
aluminium 13
The Ambassadors
    (Holbein) *194*, 203–6
American Civil War 187–9
among 137, 148–9
An Original Copy (Hill) *59,
    60, 61, 64, 65, 68,
    68–71, 69*
anamorphic art 198–206
Anamorphic Ghost 206
*Anamorphic Portrait of
    Charles I 200*
angelology 136–7
Angels: A Modern Myth
    (Serres) 136
animal architecture
    208–21
*Animal Architecture and
    Building Behaviour*
    (Hansell) 217
Anvil of the Gods 232–4
apostasy 77
Appliance House
    (Nicholson) 78, 81,
    83, 84, *87*

Applied Digital Solutions
    245
Arcades Project
    (Benjamin) 2
architects, legal definition
    75–6
architectural photographs
    62
Architecture Foundation
    35, 39
Architecture Practice Act
    (1989) 75–6
Aristotle 209, 215
Armstrong, Rachel vii, 7,
    240–8
Art of Memory (Yates)
    231
Artificial Intelligence 228
Asimov, Isaac 228
assembly methods 13
atoms 229

B

*B-2 Spirit Stealth Bombers
    201*
B-52 Pickup (Nicholson)
    82, 82, 83, 86
Babycom *99*, 100
bacteria 230
bacterial symbiosis 213
Baltrušaitis, Jurgis 198,
    203–4
Banham, Reyner 58
Barcelona Pavilions 4, 24,
    59–71
    water lilies 67–8
Baroque 42
Barthes, Roland 205
Bauhaus 167–74
    entrance exam 168
    feminisation of
        architecture 172–3
    festivals 169
    theatre 170
Bauman, Zygmunt 115
Bayer, Herbert 168
beads 133

'becoming' theory 215
Bedford, Dr James 244
Being Digital (Negroponte)
    229
Benedikt, Michael 80, 81
Benjamin, Walter 2, 63,
    108
Bernstein, Basil 113–14
between 137, 152–3
beyond 137, 154–5
Bio-Centrum projects 208,
    210
biological architecture
    240–8
    biomechanics 241
    body machine 240–1
    Extropian principles
        242–7
    prospects of
        immortality 247–8
biological evolution
    208–10
biomechanics 241
bits 229
Black Matter(s) (Lokko)
    180, 181
blackness 176–7
    see also African–
        American culture
Blaser, Werner 66
blasphemy 77
Bloom (McLaughlin and
    Richman) *46, 47, 48,
    49, 50, 51, 52, 53,
    54, 55, 56*
Bluetooth technology
    106
body implants 245–6
body machine 240–1
body-image 162
Bon, Christoph 120, 122
Bonta, Juan Pablo 62, 66
Borden, Iain vii, 5,
    120–30
'both/and' 135–6
boundary consciousness
    108–30

boundless expansion 242–4
Bourdieu, Pierre 164, 165
Boyarsky, Alvin 81
Brachmann, Käthe 172
Braidotti, Rosi 152
Brion Cemetery 23–4
broadband radio scanners 98–100
Bruno, Guiordano 231
Brutalism 39, 41
Buildings of Europe (Woodward) 50

C
cabinet studies *96*
car radio *100*
Carnal Art 242
catoptric anamorphosis 198
Cellular City *103*, 103–6, *104*
Certeau, Michel de 198
Chamberlin, Joe 120, 122
Chapman, Tracy 37
Charles I 200
Chicago, Judy 134
Christchurch 39
Cirici, Christian 61, 65–7
Citroen, Paul 168–9, *171*
City of Tomorrow (Le Corbusier) 109
Cixous, Hélène 134, 136
cladding 24–6
Clarke, Katherine 37
Classical Foot (Lokko) *177*, *179*
Classical Mouth (Lokko) *176*
Classicism 42
cloches 50–2, 55
cloning 247–8
collages 84–8
Colomina, Beatriz 12, 179
Commercial Street 30
communication skills 219
computational communication 219
conceptual architecture 81
construction waste 20
contemplation of architecture 63–6

contemplation of art 63
Cosgrove, Dennis 191
creating space 36–7
critical dwelling space 140–1
Crowd 186
cryogenic resurrection 227–8, 244
cultural capital 164–6, 174
Cultural Weapons (Lokko) *188*, *190*
cyberspace 92, 229
cyborgs 232, 246–7

D
Dangerous Idea: Evolution and the Meaning of Life (Darwin) 209
Darwin, Charles 208–10
Dawkin, Richard 209, 218, 220
Daz 51, 53
de-materialisation 80, 83, 96
Dear, Michael 117
deconstruction 135–6
Deleuze, Gilles 215–17
Dennett, Daniel 209
Derrida, Jacques 83, 115
Descartes, René 240–1
Detail 19
detailing 12–28
    German pavilion columns 17
    windows 16
Digital Corporation 95
Dirt is Matter out of Place 30–43
DNA 208, 209–11, 213, 247–8
    see also nanotechnology
Dolly the sheep 247–8
Domestos 33
dominant fiction 163
Dorrian, Mark vii, 6, 194–206
Douglas, Mary 36, 38, 111, 113
Dr Gauss *101*
Drexler, K. Eric 225, 229, 230
Droste, Magdalena 167

dry nanotechnology 225
Dunne, Anthony vii–viii, 5, 92–106
dwelling space 140–1
dynamic optimism 245
Dzenus, Katrin 37

E
E. coli bacteria 230
économie feminine 148–9
Economist Building 37, 39, 41
écriture de la femme 138
education 164, 166
Eisenman, Peter 208, 210
Elan, Diane 135
electromagnetic radiation 101–2
Elevations of the Telemon Cupboard (Nicholson) *76*
Ellis, Tom 124, *125*
embodied cultural capital 164–6, 174
Enlightenment Capsule (Mori) 245
environmental considerations 27–8
Era of De-regulation 34
Era of Disuse 33, 39
Era of Inversion 32, 39
Era of Petrification 34, 39
Era of Regulation and the Division of Labour 32
evangelists of sanitation 32
Evans, Bob 17, 24
Evans, Robin 42, 66
exchange relationships 144–5
Extropianism 240–8
    boundless expansion 242–4
    dynamic optimism 245
    intelligent technology 245–6
    self-transformation 244
    spontaneous order 246–7

F
F-117 *Nighthawk 195*,

199–203, *201*, *202*, *203*, 205, *206*
fabric 24–6
Face Name Collage (Nicholson) *85*
Fairy Snow *34*
fantasy 163
Favored Circle (Stevens) 164
feathering *30*, 34, *40*, 41–3
Feeding Each Other (Wells) 150–1, *151*
Feininger, T. Lux 167
feminisation of architecture 172–3
feminism 134–5, 157–8
festivals 169
fetishisation 142
Finders Keepers (Wells) 148–9, *149*
Fludd, Robert 231
for 137, 146–7
Form and Matter 194–5, 198, 209–11
Foster, Norman 18
Foucault, Michel 114
Frampton, Kenneth 22–3
Frankl, Paul 124, 126
Frascari, Marco 22, 23
Freud, Sigmund 115, 162
Fused 46

G
gabions 20–2
Gablik, Suzi 134
Gage, Professor 16–17
Gaulke, Cheri 134
Gaultier, Jean Paul 243
Gehry, Frank 216, 220
genetic algorithms 226–7
genetics 208, 209–11, 213, 247–8
  see also nanotechnology
German pavilion columns 17
Gibson, William 229
  Neuromancer 81, 92
Giedion, Sigfried 129
gift giving 146–7, 148–9
Golden Lane stairway 120–30, *121*, *122*,

123, *125*, *127*, *128*
Gombrich, E.H. 195
Greene, David 37
Gropius, Walter 167, 171–3
Grünfeld, Thomas 211
  see also Misfits
Guardini, Romano 15
Guattari, Felix 215–17
Gunkel, David J. viii, 4–5, 74–88
Gurak, Laura 81
Gypsies 112, 117, 118

H
habitus 165–6, 174
Hansell, Michael 217
Haraway, Donna 246–7
Hawksmoor, Nicholas 30, 39
Hayden, Dolores 134
Healing Quilt (Wells) 152–3, *153*
Hegel, G.W.F. 198, 204
Heidegger, Martin 226
heimlich 115
Hermes (Serres) 136
hierarchy of architect and user 58–9
Hill, Jonathan viii, 58–71
Holbein, Hans 194, 203–6
home space 108–30
Hongkong and Shanghai Bank 18
Hot Desk (Spiller) *233*, *234*, *235*, *237*, *238*
Hottentot Venus 185
House of Straw 12–28, *14*, *16*, *18*, *21*, *25*
Hubbe House 66
Hunter, John 196

I
Illinois Architecture Practice Act (1989) 75–6
Images/New Images (Orlan) 242–3
immortality 247–8
in 137, 140–1
intelligent technology 245–6
Interbuild 13, 18

Irigaray, Luce 134, 136, 144, 146, 150–4, 157
Itten, Johannes 168
Iverson, Margaret 205
Izhar, Siraj 38

J
Jackson, Cindy 247
Jacobs, Jane 109–10
the Jago 38
Jay, Martin 115
Jenaer Realphilosophie (Hegel) 204

K
Kant, I. 196
Kardomah Coffee house 16
Kelly, Mary 134
keloids 178
Klee, Felix 169
Koolhaas, Rem 61
Krell, David Farrell 74
Kristeva, Julia 111–12, 113, 115

L
Lacan, Jacques 162, 203–5
Lacis, Asja 108
Lack 162–4
Lacy, Suzanne 134
Lair (Wells) 140–1, *141*
lavatories 30–4, 113–14
law-of-the-father 171–3
Laws of Robotics 228
Le Corbusier 109, 122, 124
legal definition of architects 75–6
Lem, Stanislaw 116
Leviticus 36
light 46–56
Lingis, Alphonso 196
Lippard, Lucy 134
Loaf House (Nicholson) *78*, 79–80, *80*, 82–3
Lokko, Lesley Naa Norle viii, 6, 176–92
Loos, Adolf 19, 196
Lords Media Centre 13
Lovetectonics 105

Lubetkin, Berthold 126
Lull, Ramon 231

M
McLaughlin, Niall viii–ix, 4,
    46–56
Magicio-kinetic Age 235
*Male Subjectivity at the
    Margins* (Silverman)
    162–3
Manhattan Transcripts
    (Tschumi) 2
Margulis, Lynn 213
Mayne, Roger 108
Mazdaznan 168
memes 218–20
Memories of a Molecule
    216
memory 180–1, 187, 231
micro-spaces 114
microbiology 213
Minuchin, Salvador 116
mirror anamorphosis 198
Misfits 211, 213
    Nandu 214
    St Bernhard 212
Miyake, Issey 243
mobile telephones *103*,
    103–6
modernism 58
molecules
    Memories of a Molecule
        216
    molecular
        nanotechnology 224
moral authority 58
Morales, Ignacio Solà 15
Mori, Mariko 245
Morrison, Toni 191
Mudd Mask 31
Muf Architects ix, 4,
    35–43
mullions 17
Murray, Freeman 188

N
Nano-Deskworld™ 236
Nano-Dreamtime 237
Nano-Dreamworld™ 236
nanocyborg 232
nanodesktop 234, 235–6
Nanolithic Age 229–30
nanotechnology 224–38

Anvil of the Gods
    232–4
genetic algorithms
    226–7
gestation period 225
nanodesktop 234,
    235–6
Utility Fog 235, 236
see also genetics
Naples 108, 109
natal alienation 189
National Radiological
    Protection Board
    (NRPB) 101
natural selection 208–10
Negroponte, Nicholas
    229, 231
neighbourhoods 116–17
Netherlands Design
    Institute 96
Neuromancer (Gibson) 81,
    92
Nicholson, Ben ix, 4–5,
    74–87
    Appliance House 78,
        81, 83, 84, *87*
    B-52 Pickup 82, 82,
        83, *86*
    collages 84–8
    *Elevations of the
        Telemon Cupboard
        76*
    Face Name Collage 85
    Loaf House 78, 79–80,
        80, 82–3
    *Thinking the
        Unthinkable House
        74*, *75*
Nighthawk stealth fighter
    195, 199–203, *201*,
    202, *203*, 205, *206*
Noiseman *94*, 94
Nonconsumables (Wells
    and Allsopp) 146–7,
    147
Noval, Marcos 218
NOX Project 218

O
Occupying Architecture
    (Borden) 5
oedipal animals 215
Oliver, K. 111

OMA 19–20
Omnipresence (Orlan) 244
on 137, 142–3
On Monsters and Marvels
    (Paré) 197
Origin of Species (Darwin)
    209
Orlan
    Images/New Images
        242–3
    Omnipresence 244
Ornament and Crime
    (Loos) 196
Ostman, Charles 232
O'Sullivan, Frank ix, 4, 30,
    31
*Outline of a Theory of
    Practice and
    Distinction* (Bourdieu)
    164, 165

P
Pallasmaa, Juhani 63
Pallazzo Farnese 50
Panacea Age 230
panelled buildings 35
Paré, Ambroise 197
patriarchal values 171
Paulsgrove estate 117
pavilion columns 17
Perin, Constance 116
petrification through
    conservation 34, 39
Phillips, Adam 110, 111
Phobic Thing 202, *203*
photographs 62
Pixel Kissing 104–5, *105*
placebo furniture *101*
plastic 132
Plasticine Age 230
Plato 209
Plug Bug 4000 *99*,
    99–100
Portsmouth 117
positionality 140–1
potentiality 154–5
Powell, Geoffrey 120,
    122
prepositions 136–56
    among 137, 148–9
    between 137, 152–3
    beyond 137, 154–5
    for 137, 146–7

in 137, 140–1; on 137, 142–3
through 137, 150–1
to 137, 144–5
with 137, 138–9
Pretty (Wells) 142–3, *143*
private/public boundary 108
Protoplasmic Age 230
public lavatories *see* lavatories
purifiers 108–10
Purity and Tolerance 30, 35–43

Q
Quantrill, Malcolm 65
Quetglas, Jose 66

R
Rabanne, Paco 243
Raby, Fiona ix, 5, 92–106
race 176–7
race *see* African–American culture; blackness
Radiant City 109
radio scanners *98*, 98–100
Rainbow Snake 236
Ramos, Fernando 61, 65–7
Raven, Arlene 134
Rawes, Peg ix, 6, 208–21
re-materialisation 96, 104
re-memory 189
recycled concrete 20
Rendell, Jane x, 6, 132–58
RIBA Architecture Centre 46
Richman, Martin x, 4, 46–56
Robotics 228
Rogers, Richard 220
Rucker, Rudy 225, 228
Rüedi, Katerina x, 6, 162–74
Ruskin, John 24, 196–8

S
sandbags 26
sanitary towels 37

Sargisson, Lucy 135
Savage, Kirk 187–8
scanners *98*, 98–100
Scarpa, Carlo 22, 23
scars 178, 196
Schlemmer, Tut 168, 170, 171
Schreyer, Lothar 168
Scruton, Roger 17
self-dematerialisation 80, 83
self-transformation 244
Sennett, Richard 109, 117
sensels 218
Serres, Michael 136
Seven Lamps of Architecture (Ruskin) 24, 196
Shapiro, Miriam 134
Shepheard, Paul 74
Shonfield, Katherine x, 4, 30–43
Sibley, David x, 5, 108–18
Silverman, Kaja 162–3
skateboarding 5
skin 110–11
skulls 206
Smithson, Alison 39
Smithson, Peter 39
SO1 (synthetic organism one) 248
social order 108–30
Soja, Ed 110
Solà Morales, Ignasi de 61, 65–7
Sorbier, Franck 243
The South (Lokko) *182*
Space 1999 244
Spaeth, David 15
spatial data management system (SDMS) 231–2
spatial purification 109
Speculum (Irigaray) 154
Spiller, Neil x–xi, 6–7, 224–38
spontaneous order 246–7
Sqezy Sqezy *33*
stairway architecture 120–30, *121*, *122*, *123*, *125*, *127*, *128*

Standing at the Martin Luther King Jr. Memorial (Lokko) *184*
state animals 215
stealth fighter *195*, 199–203, *201*, *202*, *203*, 205, *206*
Stevens, Gary 164–5, 166
stitching 133
straw house 12–28, *14*, *16*, *18*, *21*, *25*
Stretchy, Shiny Ceiling Filled with Water 35
symbiosis 213
symbolic capital 164
synthetic organism one (SO1) 248

T
tattoos 196–7, 198
Taut, Bruno 167
Tea for 2000 (Wells) 144–5, *145*
technical development 17
technical standards 12
technology transfer 26
tectonics 22
telekinesis 235
telephones
    mobile telephones *103*, 103–6
    touch tone telephone systems 95–7
text on street level windows 37–9, *38*
theatre 170
Thinking the Unthinkable House (Nicholson) 74, *75*
through 137, 150–1
Tigerman, Stanley 76, 78
Till, Jeremy xi, 4, 12–28
to 137, 144–5
Tomy Babycom 100
torso studies *97*
touch tone telephone systems 95–7
Towards a New Architecture (Le Corbusier) 109

*Treatise on Venereal
  Disease* (Hunter) 196
Triadic Ballet 170
Troubadour of Knowledge
  (Serres) 136
Tschumi, Bernard 2, 192
Tuskegee University 181

U
U R What U Eat (Wells)
  154–5, *155*
ultraviolet light 51
under-stair cupboards
  120
unheimlich 115
Utility Fog 235, 236

V
van der Rohe, Mies 12,
  15, 17, 19, 22
  Hubbe House 66
  see also Barcelona
  Pavilions

vanish *31*
*View of a Feathered
  Interior 30*
Virilio, Paul 199
visionary architecture 81

W
Walkman *93*, 93–4
war 163–4, 166, 167–71
water lilies 67–8
Water (Lokko) *183*
weather architecture
  69–71
Weimar Republic 172,
  173
Wells, Pamela xi, 6,
  132–58
West, Cornel 189
wet nanotechnology 225
Wetware (Rucker) 228
Where Have You Been?
  (Wells) 138–9, *139*
Whiteman, John 84

whitens softens all in one
  32
Wigglesworth, Sarah xi, 4,
  12–28
Wilson, Mabel 109
windows 16
wireless landscape *106*
with 137, 138–9
women on the market 146
Woodward, Christopher
  50
workshops 170

Y
Yates, Frances 231

Z
Žižek, Slavoj 204, 205